D0208211

Texts and Dialogues

Contemporary Studies in Philosophy and the Human Sciences

Series Editors:
Hugh J. Silverman and Graeme Nicholson

Published

* Also available in paperback

Texts and Dialogues

—◆—

Maurice Merleau-Ponty

Edited and with an Introduction by
Hugh J. Silverman and James Barry Jr.

Translated by
Michael B. Smith et al.

Humanities Press
New Jersey ▼ London

First published in 1992 by Humanities Press International, Inc.,
Atlantic Highlands, New Jersey 07716, and 3 Henrietta Street,
London WC2E 8LU

© Hugh J. Silverman and James Barry Jr., 1992

Library of Congress Cataloging-in-Publication Data

Merleau-Ponty, Maurice, 1908–1961.
   Texts and dialogues / Maurice Merleau-Ponty ; edited and with an
introduction by Hugh J. Silverman and James Barry, Jr. ; translated
by Michael B. Smith, et al.
     p. cm. — (Contemporary studies in philosophy and the human
sciences)
   Includes bibliographical references and index.
   ISBN 0-391-03702-1
   1. Merleau-Ponty, Maurice, 1908–1961. 2. Philosophy.
3. Philosophy, Modern—20th century. 4. Philosophers—France—
Interviews. 5. Phenomenology. I. Silverman, Hugh J.
II. Barry, James, 1955– . III. Title. IV. Series.
B2430.M3763T49   1992
194—dc20   90–46082
                                          CIP

A catalog record is available for this book from the British Library.

Printed in the United States of America

Contents

Acknowledgments

———◆———

This volume was originally conceived nearly twenty years ago. Since that time when one of the editors was living in Paris, the project has undergone various additions, deletions, and other refinements. Many people have contributed in one way or another to its final form. We wish to express here our gratitude for their generosity, their efforts, and their patience.

We are particularly indebted to Professor Michael B. Smith, who not only contributed his own translations of a number of pieces, but who also gave the whole manuscript his careful examination and review. His knowledge of the French language and of Merleau-Ponty's interest in the problem of expression have been invaluable in helping us complete this project. We have listed him as principal translator in recognition of his gracious and helpful contribution to the translated portions of the volume.

In addition to the translations of specific essays provided by the editors and by Michael Smith, we are most grateful to Jeffrey Gaines (who has provided excellent translator's notes to the East-West Conference), to James Hatley (who has worked with us in so many ways), to Allen S. Weiss, Stephen Michelman, and Drew Leder (who each produced the first version of their translation while also completing their doctorates in philosophy at Stony Brook), to Gerald Wening (whom we never met), and to Forrest Williams (veteran translator and commentator of the French scene) for the many hours, weeks and months of translation and retranslation that have helped to make these texts accessible to the English reader. Naturally, we the editors remain responsible for the final shape that the volume has come to assume.

The editors appreciate the considerable contribution of Elizabeth Mac-Nabb, who compiled the final draft of the bibliography and who read over the manuscript. Also Professor Camille Garnier reviewed the Chapsal interview and offered many valuable suggestions.

The Indiana University Southeast Office of Academic Affairs offered financial support toward final preparation of the manuscript. The assistance of numerous members of the Indiana University Southeast faculty and staff was invaluable to the production of the final manuscript, most notably the work of Julie Crecelius. The interest, encouragement, and support of philosophical colleagues such as Curtis Peters and William Rumsey reminded us of the importance of this project, even when the blockades seemed almost insurmountable.

Reanimated as a collaborative editorial project at Stony Brook in the early 1980s, it has been finally brought to fruition through many long-distance (continental and intercontinental) phone and modem calls, and even airplane flights. We are grateful to the airlines, the phone lines, and the computer lines for their facilitations.

There are many colleagues from the Merleau-Ponty Circle (and others outside the imaginary circle) who have been awaiting the publication of these materials. Since its formation in 1976, the Circle, whose membership is open to anyone interested in the work of Merleau-Ponty, has encouraged work of this kind. Through its annual September conference, it has fostered discussions that not only comment upon the philosopher's texts but also advance his thinking beyond his time. In the context of the Circle and its wider range of collaborators, these writings, dialogues, and interviews will be able to take on the value and significance that is surely their due. With these texts, new insights into Merleau-Ponty's philosophical, political, and aesthetic thinking will surely become possible. Research on Merleau-Ponty can now enter a new stage of development in the English-speaking world. While it would be excessive to name all those who have contributed and continue to contribute to the growth of the Circle and its meetings, some— such as Martin Dillon, Alphonso Lingis, Stephen Watson, Dennis O'Connor, Anne Ashbaugh, Galen Johnson, Véronique Fotí and many others— have actively encouraged work of this sort and the dialogical exchange that animates the Merleau-Ponty Circle.

To our European colleagues, such as Claude Lefort, Marc Richir, Mikel Dufrenne, and Jacques Taminiaux, who have participated in meetings of the Circle and who have enhanced the meaning of Merleau-Ponty studies, we are most grateful.

We are also glad to acknowledge our special debt to Madame Merleau-Ponty for her willingness to support the project in its present form and for granting translation rights to the pieces included in the volume. The assistance of Claude Lefort was invaluable in working out final arrangements for the publication of these texts and dialogues in English translation, especially during his semester at SUNY/Stony Brook as Distinguished Visiting Professor of Philosophy in the fall of 1986. Over the years, since one of the editor's first meetings with him in 1972 and again at various junctures in Paris and in the United States, his generosity and philosophical acuity have been much appreciated.

And lastly, we wish to express our gratitude to Keith Ashfield, President of Humanities Press, for publishing this project. While it began under an earlier aegis, we are pleased that this volume is now appearing in the context of the new Contemporary Studies in Philosophy and the Human Sciences.

Notes on Translations

◆

"Merleau-Ponty in Person" originally appeared as "Merleau-Ponty en Personne" in *Les Ecrivains en personne* (Paris: Julliard, 1960). Translated by James Barry Jr.

"Crisis in European Consciousness" originally appeared as "Crise de conscience européenne" in *La Nef*, 3, no. 24 (1946). Translated by Michael B. Smith.

"L'Express *Forum*" represents four articles taken from Merleau-Ponty's short-lived column (1954–55) in *L'Express*. Translated by Michael B. Smith.

"East-West Encounter" originally appeared as the second section of "Rencontre Est-Ouest à Venice," the transcript of a major conference in Venice in 1956. The transcript was published in *Comprendre*, 16 (September 1956). Translated by Jeffrey Gaines.

"Phenomenology and Analytic Philosophy" originally appeared as "Phénoménologie contre *The Concept of Mind*" in *La Philosophie analytique* (Paris: Minuit, 1960). Translated by James Hatley.

"The Nature of Perception: Two Proposals" first appeared in English translation in *Research in Phenomenology*, 7 (1977). The piece originally appeared as an appendix to T. Geraets' *Vers Une Nouvelle Philosophie transcendentale: la genèse de la philosophie de Maurice Merleau-Ponty jusqua'à la Phénoménologie de la perception* (The Hague: M. Nijhoff, 1971). Translated by Forrest W. Williams.

"Christianity and *Ressentiment*" first appeared in English translation in *Review of Existential Psychology and Psychiatry*, 9 (1968–69). The review originally appeared as "Christianisme et ressentiment" in *La Vie intellectuelle*, 36 (1935). Translated by Gerald G. Wening.

"Being and Having" originally appeared as "Être et avoir" in *La Vie intellectuelle*, 45 (1936). Translated by Michael B. Smith.

"On Sartre's *Imagination*" originally appeared as "L'Imagination" in *Journal de psychologie normale et pathologique*, 33, nos. 9–10 (1936). Translated by Michael B. Smith.

"On Sartre's *The Flies*" originally appeared as "*Les Mouches* par Sartre" in *Confluences*, 3, no. 25 (1943). Translated by Michael B. Smith.

"Apology for International Conferences" originally appeared as "Pour les rencontres internationales" in *Les Temps modernes*, 2, no. 22 (1947). Translated by Michael B. Smith.

"The Founders of Philosophy" and "The Discovery of History" originally appeared as "Les Fondateurs de la philosophie" and "La Découverte de l'histoire," respectively. They appeared as part of *Les Philosophes célèbres* (Paris: Mazenod, 1956). Translated by Michael B. Smith.

"The Philosophy of Existence" originally appeared as "La Philosophie de l'existence" in *Dialogue*, 5, no. 3 (1959). Translated by Allen S. Weiss.

"Five Notes on Claude Simon" originally appeared as "Cinq notes sur Claude Simon" in *Méditations*, 4 (1961–62). Translated by Hugh J. Silverman.

Forrest Williams' "Merleau-Ponty's Early Project Concerning Perception" originally appeared in *Research in Phenomenology*, 10 (1980).

H. L. Van Breda's "Merleau-Ponty at the Husserl Archives" originally appeared as "Maurice Merleau-Ponty et les Archives-Husserl à Louvain" in *Revue de métaphysique et de morale*, 67 (October–December 1962). Translated by Stephen Michelman.

Xavier Tilliette's "Husserl's Concept of Nature (Merleau-Ponty's 1957–58 Lectures)" originally appeared as "Husserl et la notion de Nature (Notes prises au cours de Maurice Merleau-Ponty)" in *Revue de métaphysique et de morale*, 70 (1965). Translated by Drew Leder.

Bibliography compiled by Elizabeth L. MacNabb.

Introduction:
Philosopher at Work!

◆

Maurice Merleau-Ponty was perhaps the most important French philosopher of the twentieth century. His publications span the period from just before the Second World War until the time of his death in 1961. When he died he was preparing an untitled manuscript which was to be his account of ontology and more specifically the problem of philosophical questioning. In that work, which has come to be known as *The Visible and the Invisible*,[1] Merleau-Ponty develops his own notion of "interrogation" and sets it off against the projects of "reflection" (Husserl), "intuition" (Bergson), and "dialectic" (Sartre). He elaborates, in terms of his new concept of "flesh," his account of the "chiasm," or "the intertwining," as the ontological reformulation of his earlier phenomenological description of the body. "Flesh" is intimately linked to what he called "visibility"—the intertwining of the visible and the invisible, a theme which he discussed in specifically aesthetic terms in "Eye and Mind" (1960), the last publication during his lifetime.[2]

Also in this last year (1960–61), Merleau-Ponty offered two sets of lectures at the Collège de France: one entitled "Cartesian and Contemporary Ontology" and the second "Philosophy and Non-Philosophy since Hegel." The former has not been published in any substantial way, except to the extent that its content is also the basis for *The Visible and the Invisible*. The latter has been translated into English and is now readily available.[3] In this course, Merleau-Ponty sought to reread Hegel's Introduction to the *Phenomenology of Spirit* through and against Heidegger's interpretation of it.[4] The second half of the course, which coincides with his untimely death in May 1961, was devoted to Marx's understanding of philosophy in the 1843–44 writings. In "Philosophy and Non-Philosophy since Hegel," Merleau-Ponty's concerns range from issues of fundamental philosophy to those of political thought—a trajectory which also characterizes his whole philosophical career.

Merleau-Ponty's career goes back to the early 1930s, when he offered two research proposals on the nature of perception. These proposals, included in this volume, indicate his budding interest in the philosophy of perception and its links with the dominant trends in psychology at the time. Like most French academic philosophers of note, he studied at the École Normale Supérieure and passed the Agrégation exams in his early twenties. The two proposals (concerned with the question of perception) were submitted to the Caisse Nationale des Sciences in 1933 when he was twenty-five years old and teaching at a *lycée* in Beauvais.[5] Prior to the completion in 1938 of his first major philosophical work *The Structure of Behavior* (which he submitted as his *"thèse complémentaire"* for the *doctorat d'état*, but did not actually publish until 1942), Merleau-Ponty wrote review articles of important pre-war philosophical books. These included accounts of Max Scheler's *Ressentiment* (in *La Vie intellectuelle*, 1935), Gabriel Marcel's *Being and Having* (in the same journal a year later), and Sartre's *Imagination* (in the *Journal de psychologie normale et pathologique*, also in 1936—the same year that his friend Jacques Lacan produced his famous account of the mirror stage). We have included translations of these early reviews—along with a fourth devoted to Sartre's play *The Flies* (1943)—as evidence of Merleau-Ponty's early philosophical thinking.

During this wartime period, Merleau-Ponty travelled to the Husserl Archives in Leuven (Belgium) where he not only consulted Husserl's writings (which Father Van Breda had brought out of Germany) but also negotiated with Van Breda concerning the possibility of establishing another archive location in Paris. Van Breda's account of these multiple visits to the archives is included as Appendix 2 in this volume.

This was also the time when Merleau-Ponty completed his major philosophical achievement, the *Phenomenology of Perception* (published in 1945). With this, presented as his *thèse d'état*, he made his mark on the philosophical scene at the age of thirty-seven. As the Second World War came to an end, it was a crucial time not only for Europe but also for young French intellectuals. The enduring publishing project which brought Merleau-Ponty together with Sartre, de Beauvoir, Leiris, Aron, and Pontalis came under the name of *Les Temps modernes*. It set the tone for the avant-garde thinking that linked philosophical, literary, aesthetic, and political activity in a bold new way. This exciting, pathbreaking movement which combined the phenomenology of Husserl with the existential writings of Kierkegaard, Heidegger, Jaspers, and Marcel came under the aegis of "existential phenomenology." For Merleau-Ponty, this also meant the adoption of *Gestaltpsychologie*, or "Psychology of Form" (as it was characterized in the French context). And particularly the writings of Gestaltists such as Köhler, Koffka, Gelb, and Goldstein—all of whom he cites in his 1933 project—signalled for him the groundwork for a budding phenomenology. With respect to the relationship between phenomenology and other directions in psychology, he was not as negatively disposed toward Freudian psychoanalysis as Sartre. He saw Gestalt psychology as moving beyond both psychoanalysis and the behaviorism that had come to attract many English-speaking psychologists.

With the completion of *Phenomenology of Perception*, Merleau-Ponty added another dimension to his thinking. He began to teach the structural linguistics of de Saussure at the École Normale Supérieure (where he had been a student), while at the same time lecturing as a new philosophy professor at the University of Lyon on topics such as child psychology, aesthetics, philosophy of language, and the body-soul relation.[6] The "discovery" of de Saussure was a breakthrough for Merleau-Ponty. He was now able to link up the semiological theory of language with his by then well-developed phenomenological account of perception as a bodily experience of being-in-the-world. This new hybrid philosophy was the bag of tools that he brought with him to the Sorbonne in 1949 when he was appointed Professor of Child Psychology and Pedagogy at the Institut de Psychologie.

Two years earlier Merleau-Ponty had gathered some of his disparate reflections in aesthetics, metaphysics, psychology, and politics into two books: *Sense and Non-Sense* and *Humanism and Terror*. From this same period we have included two related items: (1) his 1947 editorial for *Les Temps modernes* in which he discusses the idea of "international conferences" as a means of maintaining dialogue between American-oriented and Soviet-oriented intellectuals and (2) an example of his participation in a 1946 congress, which took place in Paris on the "Crisis in European Consciousness."

The period following this crucial year (specifically from 1949 to 1952) was a time of transition for Merleau-Ponty. He left aside his position at Lyon, his supplementary teaching at the École Normale, and his broader philosophical writing. In their place, he devoted concentrated effort to his new post as Professor of Child Psychology and Pedagogy at the Sorbonne. In these three years, he focused specifically on theoretical questions related to developmental psychology. The three lecture courses which he taught each year were full of detailed information and research data drawn from current experiments by psychologists such as Piaget, Wallon, Köhler, Horney, Klein, and Guillaume. Merleau-Ponty would incorporate their findings into his own phenomenological position and offer an understanding of their research that would lead significantly beyond them. While we do not offer any texts from this period, we will be publishing a separate two-volume translation of the aforementioned courses.[7]

In 1952, Merleau-Ponty was appointed to the Chair of Philosophy at the Collège de France. This was the chair that had been held by Bergson for many years and which was similar to the one which Lévi-Strauss, Foucault, and Barthes would hold in subsequent years. Holding the most prestigious academic post in philosophy for all of France carried enormous responsibility. These next eight to nine years were very intense for Merleau-Ponty. He developed his thought in the philosophy of language, history, and politics. He had to abandon his project on "indirect language" and "the prose of the world" in order to devote more time to matters of dialectic and political thought.

The dispute with Sartre became critical. They disagreed over the role and efficacy of the Communist Party: Sartre moving more toward political activism, Merleau-Ponty developing a skeptical position concerning marxism as a guideline for political practice. In 1955, Merleau-Ponty published *The Adventures of the Dialectic*. This text marks the break that had already occurred. Disagreements about the role of dialectic carried into their common editorial work for *Les Temps modernes*, and finally, in 1953, Merleau-Ponty resigned definitively from the editorial board. The first volume of Sartre's *Critique of Dialectical Reason* was published in 1960. However, it was clearly in production from at least 1956. It was a kind of response to Merleau-Ponty, but one that in many ways incorporated his former friend's insights concerning dialectic. After Merleau-Ponty left *Les Temps modernes*, he began to write editorial responses to questions posed by readers of the socialist weekly *L'Express* (which is still a leading publication in the popular French press today). We have included four such editorial responses (with their questions) in this volume. They deal with a range of topics, from the role of intellectuals in contemporary society to issues at the origins of the feminist movement and finally to the limits of liberal "objectivity." These attempts to address current topics in social and cultural theory brought him into the broad public debate. And the 1956 East-West Conference, which took place in Venice, reiterated concerns he had already articulated in his "International Conferences" editorial nine years earlier, most particularly the need to establish dialogue across differences. In the Venice conference, which included participants as diverse as Silone, Spender, Sartre, Ungaretti, Bernal, and Vercors, the theme of Merleau-Ponty's contribution addressed matters of culture, engagement, and dialogue as well as the role of intellectuals in East and West relations.

In the latter half of the 1950s, Merleau-Ponty began to devote more time to his professional obligations as a philosopher. He edited an enormous project, entitled *Les Philosophes célèbres* (1956). Merleau-Ponty gathered together contributions from many of the most important academic philosophers of his time, including Beaufret, de Gandillac, Lalande, Polin, Alquié, Caillois, Belval, Starobinski, Gusdorf, Jessop, Ryle, Vuillemin, E. Weil, Löwith, Deleuze, Duméry, Bobbio, Quinton, de Waelhens, Schütz, and

Damisch. This cavalcade of philosophical stars was an extraordinary accomplishment and one that only someone of the stature of Merleau-Ponty could realize. It provided an encyclopedia-like account of the major philosophers, from the ancient Greeks and oriental philosophers to contemporary figures such as Bergson, Blondel, Croce, Alain, Russell, Husserl, Scheler, Heidegger, and Sartre. Merleau-Ponty's own introductions to the sections of the book were notable—many were republished in *Signs* (1960).[8] Two such introductions, however, did not find their way into *Signs*—one on the "founders of philosophy," that is, the early Greek and Roman philosophers, and the other on the "discovery of history," emphasizing the writings of Schelling, Hegel, Comte, Marx, and Nietzsche. Merleau-Ponty's evaluations of these two periods of Western philosophical tradition are included here.

During his nine years as Professor of Philosophy at the Collège de France, Merleau-Ponty lectured on a wide variety of topics. The summaries from these courses are published in *Themes from the Lectures at the Collège de France, 1952–60*.[9] Among them was a two-year study of Husserl's concept of Nature, for which Xavier Tilliette provides a detailed summary in Appendix 3. This summary and assessment is valuable because it gives a good sense of the orientation that Merleau-Ponty's metaphysical thinking had begun to take in his last few years. Correspondingly, in his 1959 radio broadcast for the Maison Canadienne, he attempts to give a personal assessment of the status of existential philosophy at the time. In these last years, Merleau-Ponty sought to give an account of the philosophies of his own time in relation to the dominant political, social, and cultural issues that plagued the European intellectual.

In his lectures and writings, Merleau-Ponty was moving toward a fundamental ontology—inspired by a rereading of Heidegger. He also sought to open a space for his new theory of visibility—his account of a philosophy oriented toward the fabric of contemporary experience. He called this orientation "non-philosophy."

The volume we offer here portrays the texture of Merleau-Ponty's whole philosophical enterprise from its earliest phases to its final moments of development. We make no attempt at an overview, for, as Merleau-Ponty continually pointed out, a *"pensée de survol"* will not accomplish the philosophical task; rather one must turn to experience itself and give a description (or "interrogation") of its manifold dimensionality. In this spirit, *Texts and Dialogues* provides the details of the philosopher's diverse and yet highly penetrating thinking on a wide range of topics in political theory, cultural understanding, aesthetic practice, and metaphysical investigation. As a testimony to this diversity, we have included at the very beginning of this book the extraordinary 1960 interview with Madeleine Chapsal in which Merleau-Ponty assesses his whole philosophical enterprise.

The reader will also find detailed notes, which we as editors and our translators have provided as supplements to the interviews, dialogues, and texts included here. They are complemented by a complete Bibliography of Merleau-Ponty's own writings (in both French and English) as well as a comprehensive listing of books, chapters, and articles written in English on Merleau-Ponty. While we make no claims to completeness in this second part of the bibliography, it is nevertheless substantial and should be a helpful aid to readers.

This book is a chronicle of a philosopher at work. It is also a portrait of a philosopher alive with ideas, thoughts, and explorations into the meaning of art, literature, intellectuals, philosophy, science, and politics. Past readers of Merleau-Ponty will be led into unfamiliar areas, and the newcomer to Merleau-Ponty will gain insight into the range of his views, his metaphysics, his politics, and his personality. *Texts and Dialogues* is an indispensable guide to those seeking a window into this exceptionally important twentieth-century philosopher's professional life and thought.

II

As a companion to the contents of this volume, we provide a brief summary of each of the pieces included as well as an account of its overall structure and significance. This should help the reader to select aspects of the collection that will be pertinent to any particular research investigation. It will also serve as a plan for the reader seeking a general sense of the contents.

Part I of this volume, entitled "Interviews and Dialogues," brings together the transcripts from interviews and conferences in which Merleau-Ponty figured centrally. In the lead interview, "Merleau-Ponty in Person" (1960), he discusses questions such as the role of the philosopher in contemporary society, the relation between philosophy and the sciences, and the crisis concerning the relevance of philosophy and politics in a scientific and technical world. Descartes, Husserl, Heidegger, Sartre, and Eugen Fink are among the many intellectual figures discussed in this interview. While out of chronological order, this presentation of his position gives the reader a good general introduction to Merleau-Ponty's thought as a whole.

In "Crisis in European Consciousness" (1946), he takes up the question of what it means to be European in the middle of the twentieth century. The discussion revolves around the nature of historical awareness, particularly in the alternative views of Lukács and Jaspers. Merleau-Ponty uses this difference to stress the need for a recognition of the ambiguity of our relationship with the future, a relationship which is neither absolutely consistent nor fatalistically secure.

"*L'Express* 'Forum'" (1954–55), four pieces from Merleau-Ponty's newspaper column, offers examples of his direct interchanges with the public.

Through responses to questions raised by readers, Merleau-Ponty demonstrates his ability to deal clearly and thoughtfully with the common social and cultural problems of his day. These include: "Where Are the New Masters?" (on new intellectual leadership), "Is the Philosopher a Civil Servant?" (on the role of the philosopher), "Are Women Men?" (on the problem of gender conflict), and "What Is the Use of Objectivity?" (on the limitations of liberal politics).

Merleau-Ponty's contribution to one of the major intellectual gatherings of the 1950s is presented in "East-West Encounter" (1956). The central topic of this conference involved the nature of the intellectual's engagement in society, East and West. Intellectuals, including many of the leading writers of the day and representing England, France, Italy, Yugoslavia, the Soviet Union, and Poland, were among the participants. The Merleau-Ponty session deals directly with the question of the role the intellectual should play in contemporary political movements and developments. Given the Marxist orientation of a number of participants, as well as Merleau-Ponty's own departure from this orientation, the discussion tends to gravitate toward the issue of ideology.

"Phenomenology and Analytic Philosophy" (1960) represents one of the few meetings of major figures in two frequently opposed philosophical movements. Ostensibly the conference focuses on Husserl's phenomenology, but the discussion concerns more directly specific questions within the philosophy of language. In the midst of this debate, Merleau-Ponty raises certain questions which emphasize the difference between his approach to the question of language and that of the other participants, whether continental or analytic in orientation.

Part II—"Texts"—begins again chronologically with "The Nature of Perception: Two Proposals." These were official projects to study the phenomenon of perception, which he submitted in 1933, and represent one of his earliest statements on what was to become his major philosophical concern. One finds the beginnings of the work that reaches fruition in the *Phenomenology of Perception* (1945), as well as the important role played by the Gestalt thinkers on his thought at the time.

Merleau-Ponty's review of Max Scheler's book entitled *Ressentiment* (1935) is an early demonstration of his philosophical talents. It reveals the extent of Merleau-Ponty's reading of Nietzsche and Freud and offers a detailed discussion of issues cutting across psychology, religion, and history. Merleau-Ponty makes it clear that his own philosophical sentiments and those of Scheler are largely sympathetic.

Merleau-Ponty's 1936 review of Gabriel Marcel's *Being and Having* illustrates recurrent themes in his later work. In particular, it raises the question of how our possession of our bodies differs from our grasp of ordinary objects. Also in evidence here is a hint of what will later become Merleau-Ponty's own position in relation to the still developing movement of existentialism.[10]

The two reviews of Sartre—"On Sartre's *Imagination*" (1936) and "On Sartre's *The Flies*" (1943)—are concerned with philosophical psychology on the one hand and the theater on the other. These studies reveal the dynamic intimacy which Merleau-Ponty shared with his friend and philosophical antagonist. Both reviews demonstrate his enormous respect for Sartre's work, as well as the subtlety of Merleau-Ponty's critical stance.

"Apology for International Conferences" (1947) shows Merleau-Ponty maintaining the importance of dialogue between the West and the Soviet Union at a time when political divisiveness was at a high point. One sees in this piece his unwillingness either to offer an apologia for Marxist political philosophy or to support those who oppose the Soviet point of view.

"The Founders of Philosophy" and "The Discovery of History" (1956) are short pieces comprising part of Merleau-Ponty's introductory material to *Les Philosophes célèbres*. These pieces show Merleau-Ponty's increasingly radical reading of history, as well as his substantial commitment to the history of philosophy.

In "The Philosophy of Existence" (1959), he evaluates the importance of existentialism. The essay represents a lengthy reflection on Sartre's conception of "nothingness." Merleau-Ponty indicates that questions of existence have greater relevance to issues such as history and thought than existentialism *per se* been able to show.

"Five Notes on Claude Simon" (1960) consists of five short notes in which Merleau-Ponty muses on certain passages from Simon's *La Route des Flandres*. These pieces resemble the "Working Notes" to the posthumously published *The Visible and the Invisible* in their suggestiveness and provocation. As in his earlier scattered comments on Proust, Valéry, Stendhal, and others, Merleau-Ponty provides his insights into the effects of the literary enterprise.

The essays which form the Appendices offer accounts of three periods of Merleau-Ponty's work: the early 1930s, the early 1940s, and the late 1950s. They trace the development of his thought, particularly in relation to the writings of Husserl. Here one sees the growing independence of Merleau-Ponty's philosophical project as well as the valued esteem of his contemporaries.

This volume brings together materials that are practically inaccessible even in French. It is offered as a resource for and supplement to the in-depth study of Merleau-Ponty's work as a whole. At the same time, it offers many insights into the development of phenomenology, existentialism, marxism, and recent French thought. The principal themes of contemporary continental philosophy, such as the nature of the text and of writing, the limits of rational discourse, and the institution as a fundamental entity, emerge out of a philosophical atmosphere "seeded" in large part by Merleau-Ponty's interrogations and considerations.

On the American scene, Merleau-Ponty's work has been acquiring a continually growing audience. As the Bibliography demonstrates, a large and expanding group of books and essays has been appearing in relation to his work as a whole. These run the gamut from perception to ontology, from politics to ethics, offering further evidence of the significance of his philosophical enterprise. Finally, the annual Merleau-Ponty Circle, which has met for more than fifteen years, is a major context for debate and discussion in the wake of Merleau-Ponty's contribution. It attracts many members from a wide range of "non-philosophical" disciplines as well as the more philosophically trained. The project for this volume began even before the formation of the Merleau-Ponty Circle, as a result of considerable research into the archives of the Parisian academy. Its preparation and accomplishment has been realized in the context of work fostered by the Circle. Hence, this volume is dedicated to its members and their commitment both to the study of Merleau-Ponty and to the persistence of his thought in their own philosophical activities.

HUGH J. SILVERMAN AND JAMES BARRY JR.

PART I

◆

Interviews and Dialogues

1

◆

Merleau-Ponty in Person (An Interview with Madeleine Chapsal, 1960)

CHAPSAL: Finding oneself face to face with a philosopher is a rather unsettling privilege. What is the status of the philosopher? Is the philosopher in fact a member of the same species as other people? In your inaugural lecture at the Collège de France, didn't you yourself speak of what you called the "philosophical life"?

MERLEAU-PONTY: I never said, nor meant to say, that the philosophical life was another life and the philosopher another species. Nietzsche considered the married philosopher a vaudeville character. He thought it was impossible to be a philosopher and also participate in secular life. This is certainly not what I meant.

Let's consider an example. What I said in 1952 is that political commitment never consists for the philosopher in simply accepting the dilemmas of the time; nor in taking them up does the philosopher thereby embrace them without any reservations. Obviously, from the moment one voices such reservations, there is no question of acting as directly or as immediately as the political individual does. The action of the philosopher is much more long-term, but it is action all the same.

Hegel said that truth could not express itself by a single proposition, and this phrase could serve as a motto for all philosophers. There are moments for affirmation and moments for negation: these are moments of crisis. Beyond these moments, "yes" and "no" are the politics of an amateur. Let me emphasize this point: by refusing to abide by the *yes* and the *no* the philosopher does not stand outside politics, but is confined to doing what everyone, and especially the professional politician, *does*. For I do not believe that great politicians are ever as Manichean as is purported. Marx, who had his philosophical side, was not Manichean. He thought that capitalism was decadent *but* that it had been a great thing, that it is necessary to destroy philosophy *but* that it is also necessary to realize it, that the revolution is a rupture with the past *but* that it is also its accomplishment. Lenin may have been Manichean or, more precisely, forced himself to be so. It is said that after listening to a Beethoven sonata, he declared that one should not listen to this kind of music since it tended to promote forgiveness, and that on the contrary one must continue to be ruthless.

But precisely the great lesson of these last years is perhaps that, in being Manichean and ruthless, communism has become distorted. This means that, even when you have chosen, you must say why and under what conditions. You continue to think beyond what you do. Or rather, political action is not the confounding thunderbolt Hitler believed it to be. It is an action upon humans, which therefore seeks to persuade or seduce. The "yes" and the "no" are interesting only in punctuating a cycle of action. For my part, I wanted to react against a sort of purism of action which would oblige us to choose between action and truth, but that is ultimately a caricature of action.

CHAPSAL: Do you mean that philosophers are not only responsible to themselves and their truth, but that their function makes them responsible to other people as well?

MERLEAU-PONTY: These are inseparable, and this is the difficulty of being a philosopher, and even a writer in general. . . . One does not write solely for oneself, or solely for truth, but not simply for others either. One writes. That is all, and in doing so all of these concerns are in play simultaneously. Those who write imply that all of this can somehow be reconciled.

The peculiarity of the philosopher here is only to practice the same principle even more strictly, because, unlike the writer, the philosopher does not have the right to enclose himself in an inner life. The philosopher strives to think the world of everyone. Very few philosophers have been anarchists. Nearly all of them admit that there must be some kind of state and power. They do not wash their hands of it, and yet they do not consent to the myth. Or, when they do, they nonetheless give warning that it is a myth. This is the source of their uneasiness. It is not an anomaly nor an aristocratic malady.

CHAPSAL: Accepting the existence of a state power, isn't this something of a novelty for the philosopher, a submission imposed by the modern shape of society?

MERLEAU-PONTY: The case of Socrates is a good example.

CHAPSAL: With the difference that Socrates could rise against the powers that be, which he did openly and publicly whenever he judged it appropriate to do so.

MERLEAU-PONTY: He did so only by risking his life.

CHAPSAL: In a modern society, if you find yourself in disagreement with a tax-collector or the justice of the peace, philosopher though you might be, you find yourself compelled to comply. . . .

MERLEAU-PONTY: Socrates complied when he saw fit. He had been a soldier and behaved honorably. He thought that where it is necessary for there to be an army, the soldier must obey when the general commands. He also thought that the soldier could question the generals either before battle or once back home. This raises a further issue: How far must one obey and how far should one question? The Communists simplified it. They thought that one should obey certain generals and disobey certain others. Things are not so simple. Should a Russian revolutionary in Budapest (if there are any) obey the general or not? It is not so easy to know where the revolution is, and Socrates' question remains crucial: When must one obey and when must one criticize?

CHAPSAL: If, in every case where individuals find themselves in conflict with society, you, as philosopher, decide to abide by your principles and comply only with that which points toward liberty, you will come quickly and directly to martyrdom.

MERLEAU-PONTY: No more than the non-philosopher. People would be very unhappy if they were to look closely at what lies beneath the words they use so readily. This is why they prefer, for the most part, not to do so. But sooner or later, events put them in a state of philosophical uneasiness.

CHAPSAL: How did you enter the philosophical life? Suddenly? For intellectual reasons?

MERLEAU-PONTY: To the biographical question, I would say that the day that I entered a philosophy class, I knew that it was philosophy that I wanted to practice. Neither then, nor since, have I ever had the slightest doubt about this.

CHAPSAL: Does being a philosopher imply separating oneself from the society in which one lives? Have you experienced a crisis comparable to the one of which Lévi-Strauss speaks? He claims that the ethnologist who studies other societies comes to feel like a stranger in his or her own society.

MERLEAU-PONTY: When Lévi-Strauss left Europe for South America in search of societies which he appreciated, he sought immediate beauty, innocence, and nature; he proceeded like a poet or a rebel. With this adventure, as with all things, one can produce philosophy. Someone different from Lévi-Strauss would not have extracted a philosophy from it. Poet and philosopher are, in this case, united in the same individual. This is not to say that the philosophical rupture is always as sensational as the poetic one. The ethnologist, having returned from South America, sees the West with new eyes, like those of the primitive. But Husserl, who hardly ever left

Germany, became interested at the end of his life in primitives.

The philosopher's break with society may be silent and may not even involve travel. This is not a matter of uncertainty rather than certainty, emptiness rather than fullness. Instead, it is a question of distancing the world, but only in order to see it and understand it.

CHAPSAL: Philosophers, then, are always freeing themselves from their surroundings. Do they break with their own ideas in order to serve them better?

MERLEAU-PONTY: The philosopher does not have ideas in the way that one has a table and a chair; other people talk about the philosopher's ideas. The philosopher, like the writer or the scholar, has an attentive yet very simple gaze.

CHAPSAL: But isn't there a contradiction in what you say? How can one feel like a gaze over all things, free and detached, and at the same time feel that one is in the service of others?

MERLEAU-PONTY: I see that I still haven't succeeded in making you see what it is to be a philosopher! When a philosopher works, there is no thought of serving others, and even less of his or her work. Philosophical work, like any other work, has its own self-evidence. The philosopher has no more devotion or ambition than the peasant who tills the soil or the worker who produces things. Is it inconceivable that one could both be involved and be distant at the same time? And yet this is the very definition of the philosopher and perhaps even of human existence.

CHAPSAL: The philosopher may very well be a person just like the farmer and the worker. However, isn't the philosopher's work elevated above that of the farmer and the worker? Hasn't philosophy been accused precisely of being a gaze which scans all fields of work or investigation without having one of its own?

MERLEAU-PONTY: Philosophy does not have a field as in the sciences. But this is because in another way it is concerned with all fields. Scientific thought seeks to *anchor* itself in the reality that it *manipulates*. It allows itself to be guided initially by a foundation of prescientific ideas which help to formulate hypotheses and to study facts. Later, scientific thought realizes that the conceptions it has developed by successive corrections are hardly compatible with its original philosophy: it therefore seeks to find another philosophy to replace it. Thus, scientists come to question space, time, causality, the object, being, etc. Their science does not entirely shape the philosophy which is needed nor is this philosophy to be obtained by calculation or experimentation. Were this the case scientists would agree sooner or later. They are, however, divided over their philosophy of science as philosophers are over philosophy in general. This is our contemporary situation.

Laplace's famous phrase is often quoted in which he defines his ideal for knowledge of the physical world as a single great fact in which its state at any given instant strictly determines its state at any future instant. Today most physicists no longer accept this image of the world. Some say that physical being is comprised of "behaviors" and others say "operational groups," even when they cannot identify the subject of this behavior or of these operations. Often, they do not even sense the need to assume the existence of a subject. Others still remain Cartesians. You say that philosophy is expelled from physics, when in fact it is physics that is overrun by philosophy.

CHAPSAL: But aren't you talking about the philosophy of physicists and not the philosophy of philosophers?

MERLEAU-PONTY: When physicists depart from their own language, mathematics, and offer an interpretation of their science in meaningful language, they are no longer the sole judges of what they propose, because their science does not hold the key to the notions which they invoke ("observer," "object," "existence," "truth," etc.). Philosophers cannot ignore the critique of common-sense ideas to which science devotes itself. They also cannot find in science the complete elucidation of the notions of which I just spoke and which stem from total human experience and not simply from scientific experience. What is true of the natural sciences is even truer of the so-called "human sciences," which you mentioned earlier.

CHAPSAL: You mean that psychoanalysis and ethnology require a philosophical elaboration to take them farther than they can take themselves? Fine. But is this also the case with respect to marxism?

MERLEAU-PONTY: I find that the situation is the same everywhere. Does psychoanalysis render the human individual transparent? Does it allow us to dispense with philosophy? On the contrary, the questions that psychoanalysis now asks, even more energetically than ever before, are questions that one cannot begin to answer without philosophy: How can the human being be at once wholly spiritual and wholly corporeal? The psychoanalyst's techniques contribute in conjunction with many other investigations in resolving this question, and philosophy is again at their crossroads. The ethnology of which you spoke cannot decipher culture without wondering what a culture is, what a symbol is, how it is that we are able to comprehend cultures, and whether it is possible for us to compare and classify them. The ethnologist is then at home with the philosophical problem of our knowledge of others [*connaissance d'autrui*], and there is indeed something of the philosopher in every ethnologist.

As for marxism, to say whether it is ultimately philosophy or not is an enormous problem. The classical Marxists thought that philosophy was an indirect manner of expressing the contradictions of class society and that in a society where an equilibrium of people with people and humans with nature had been realized, there would be no place for philosophy. Without arguing over the fundamental issues and without being polemical, let us say that today the Soviets emphasize that even a society which has experienced the Marxist revolution must live with contradiction. They add only that contradictions are not antagonisms. In terms of the question with which we are concerned, it suffices to say that existing society is not transparent even for Marxists, and, to that extent, philosophical expression remains necessary. Precisely from their point of view, the "suppression" of philosophy would be historically false. Philosophy would be overcome only if the individual had become, as they say, the total human being [*homme total*], without enigma and free of problems. But this total human being does not exist: to act as if it did is to throw away the arms of critical thought. To affirm that it *will be* is, precisely in the Marxist sense of the word, utopian. Thus, philosophy has never had more to do than today.

CHAPSAL: Then how do you explain the impression that philosophy is in a state of crisis?

MERLEAU-PONTY: I do not share this impression at all.

CHAPSAL: In a small book called *Why Philosophers?* [*Pourquoi des philosophes?*] J.-F. Revel echoes a common attitude.[1]

MERLEAU-PONTY: On the contrary, I believe that it is an opinion peculiar to him. One gets the feeling in reading the book that the author does not like anything at all. He tips his hat to the so-called human sciences, but one is not sure which ones he supports, since he derides their best practitioners. He tips his hat to grand philosophy, but which one does he mean? He does not acknowledge its renewed existence in contemporary work. Whether or not one likes Husserl or Heidegger, it must be admitted that with all the shortcomings of contemporary philosophy (which is the price of their radicalism), they ponder the same issues as Descartes and classical philosophy, namely, being, time, the object, the body, etc. This book is the work of a jaded consumer, one who is quick to ridicule with anecdotes those whose only sin lies in attempting to act, without proposing anything definite of his own.

This book brings to mind the exposés written at the height of Stalinism, which, in the name of some non-existent philosophy, were used to smash all human effort. At least the Communists had their hidden god and believed that they were serving a great cause. Anyone fair-minded would take this into account. In Revel's book, this sort of attitude is nowhere to be found. It offers nothing. Moreover, when I see Jean Paulhan crowning Revel with his right hand and slipping a rather difficult Heidegger text into the *N. R. F.* with his left,[2] I tell myself that there really is some love beneath this hatred, and that philosophers might be wrong to be so concerned.

CHAPSAL: Does one not find in the public spirit, as well as in academe, a distinct preference for scientific culture, a kind of priority of the sciences over philosophy?

MERLEAU-PONTY: I do not believe that what one gives to the sciences is taken from philosophy. There are not enough engineers or statisticians in France; we will need many more. I do not object to efforts to attract young people to these fields. What I regret is the often implied polemic against philosophy. There is a bad humor toward philosophy, because in the period following the war, students often mused nostalgically about communism, and, as you know, the wind does not blow in that direction anymore. But in fact, if we need more statisticians and engineers, we also need (and will need more than ever) sociologists, psychoanalysts, psychiatrists, ethnologists, and even psychologists and economists to think about the "artificial mechanisms" necessary for regulating capitalism.

However, I do not believe that these questions can actually be considered without philosophical preparation. If our problems did not concern the principles of our thought and our societal system, officials and business leaders would not need philosophy. But if, on the contrary, as I believe, our problems call into question contemporary mental, political, and economic systems, then we will need many people who can see beyond the surface into the depth of such things. We will not be able to rely solely on common sense in matters of social and political philosophy. We will need, as Balzac said, "profound people," and not merely those who calculate; radical minds and not merely technicians. Thus, we will need people trained through doubt and questioning. The havoc caused by routine thinking and political improvisation is clear enough today.

The emerging scientific practice has to come to terms with these profound concerns. Moreover, the emerging scientific practice is not the science taught in the schools, and such an education leaves young people without any critical resources to confront the present crises.

CHAPSAL: But is the philosophy on which you count so heavily alive today? Is there a philosophical life—encounters, debates, and exchanges?

MERLEAU-PONTY: There are congresses, conferences, and journals. There is a philosophical life just as there is a medical or scientific one, and it suffers from the same perpetual malaise: one never sees Heidegger or Sartre at a conference.

There are some informal meetings: Heidegger came to Cerisy, the English to Royaumont.[3] Yet Western philosophy is not only divided, which would be natural, but even worse partitioned. Logical positivism reigns in Anglo-American countries and Scandinavia, the Heidegger Circle thrives in Freiburg, and philosophers inspired by phenomenology and marxism are writing in France and Italy today. Clearly, these tendencies shrink from mutual engagement, each proceeding with its own monologue.

Why is this the case? One might wonder whether it has not always been so in philosophy, as in any other discipline. The rifts were profound between Einstein and the microphysicists. It is an American idea—and an extreme one—to believe that clarity comes from a conference. One might wonder if truly productive and creative work can take place in the midst of such impromptu personal exchanges. However, having said that, perhaps philosophical society has never been as dispersed as at present. Properly understood, the disease is not only a Western one. In July 1957, the *Institut international de philosophie* organized an East-West meeting at Warsaw.[4] Judging from all accounts, no active philosophizing took place and no real problems were addressed. The East also has its formalisms, which are even more imperious than our own.

On the whole, philosophical life remains provincial, almost clandestine, the sacred fire passing from individual to individual. One could say that an occultation of philosophy is now occurring. However, this does not mean that philosophy has nothing more to say or that it is destined to disappear.[5] On the contrary, what paralyzes or renders philosophy mute is that it cannot, by traditional means, express what the world is now living through. Anglo-American analytic philosophy is a deliberate retreat into a universe of thought where contingency, ambiguity, and the concrete have no place.

Marxism should have been a philosophy of the concrete, but it assumed all too quickly that it had discovered the key—the proletarian philosophy of history. It turned away from all the problems to which this key could not give immediate access, whether it be the sophisticated literature of the moderns, the study of painting, the analysis of sexuality, the neocapitalist experience, or social demography. Official marxism did not inspire progress in economic and social knowledge; it may in fact have paralyzed these developments. This is where we stand and will remain as long as both [analytic philosophy and marxism] refuse to desist or to recognize the weaknesses of their position.

CHAPSAL: What you have just said, why do you not write about it?

MERLEAU-PONTY: Refutations are not very interesting. It is better to attempt to produce what one reproaches others for not bringing forth.

CHAPSAL: For instance?

MERLEAU-PONTY: A philosophy. Far from being already finished, everything remains to be done or redone. We can catch only a glimpse of what is on the horizon by studying Husserl, Heidegger, and Sartre, and in some intuitions of biologists, ethnologists, and psychoanalysts.

CHAPSAL: Do you think, then, that Heidegger and Sartre prefigure the philosophy of tomorrow? And what place would you give to marxism in this philosophy of the future?

MERLEAU-PONTY: Both Heidegger and Sartre have long maintained, and quite rightly, that philosophy must redefine being. In particular, it must redefine the connections between what is a thing and what is not a thing, between being and nothingness, and between the positive and the negative. It must reformulate what the traditional correlation between the object and the subject, preponderant even in Hegel, does not adequately express.

Whatever the accomplishments of marxism, it suffers because it has not raised this issue. In principle, it has relied on the Hegelian categories of subject and object, and limited itself to reversing the relation. This inverted, and yet conserved, Hegelianism was profoundly obscure. One could show that the origins of all the surprises that marxism has left for those who follow it through history can be found in this initial obscurity. The ontological problem posed by Heidegger and Sartre is now more than ever the order of the day.

Nature, animals, bodies, humans, discourses [les paroles], thought, social bodies, institutions, events—knowledge of the properties of all of them are divided up among the sciences. After all, this extremely rich landscape is drawn like an etching in black and white. Ontology is preoccupied with this black and white. It investigates the plenitudes and the voids as well as the brushstrokes; thus, it maintains contact with all the sciences, with all human endeavor, and yet remains something different.

Ontology is everywhere—in the painter's articulation of the world, in the scientist's flashes of insight drawn from things, in the passions, in the modes of labor and sociality, and so forth. There is an ontological history, a deployment of our relation with being, or a modulation of the relation of being to nothingness. This ontological history is not outside "history"; it might even be, in its most rigorous rendition, the truth of dialectical materialism.

Marx's error was not that he attempted a philosophical reading of history, but rather that he believed (or did not discourage the belief) that the philosophy of philosophers was a lie. His error was not that he understood history to be both matter and spirit, but rather that he believed (or did not discourage the belief) that this combination was headed toward non-contradiction or identity. His error was not that he believed that civilization is an ontological complex, but that a civilization was emerging that would take the place of ontology. There is no "destruction" of philosophy which could be its "realization." To posit such a state of history is precisely to produce bad philosophy, to produce an ontology without depth or dimension, as Hegel had said.

CHAPSAL: Could you offer an idea of ontological investigation as you understand it?

MERLEAU-PONTY: One of the important ontologies of the West treats the visible world as the only possible manifestation of an infinite productivity. If something had to be, it could not be other than this world. Being is thus conceived as full being [être plein]. There is not a trace of wavering, it manifestly could not be otherwise. It has the solidity of the object.

This ontology is not the only one the West has known. In any one of its philosophers, for instance in Descartes, one could find along with this ontology a sketch of many others. But this suffices by way of example. Consider the idea of an absolutely transparent world where all visible properties result from a fundamental, sustaining infinity, a world in which clear reasons are developed for what appears initially to be a simple fact. An ontology of this sort has been very favorable to the development of science as well as to that of "enlightenment" politics. In short, we owe much of what has engendered Western historical progress to it. But it is also clear that this ontology is no longer justified in either our understanding or in our life. By continuing to preserve it forcibly one cannot preserve what it once protected. It no longer encourages research as it has in the past, but rather obstructs it. It no longer inspires us; it persists only on the margins of our life.

Science itself has often been forced to surrender its conception of being as a pure object. The crisis running through the politics and the wisdom which accompany this ontology need not be emphasized. It has outlived itself for a long time. Even scientists such as Laplace, who proclaimed that it is useless to hypothesize an infinity at the origin of the world, reintroduced it under other guises. The mind of the scientist, supposed to be all-powerful in principle, or simply the world itself, taken as a single fact, coherent and homogenous in all its parts, preserved the ontology of the object. Yet today, even science has stopped looking for inspiration in this secularized god, namely, Laplace's ideal physicist.

CHAPSAL: Do you mean the new ontology is atheistic?

MERLEAU-PONTY: I would prefer not to *define* it that way, not out of a false spirit of reconciliation or in order to equivocate, but because it is unworthy of philosophy to begin with a negation. Yet, having said this, it is nonetheless true that Catholicism, for example, is closely tied to the ontology of the object. Frankly, I do not believe that another ontology could be compatible with traditional forms of theology. But what good is it to defend these [forms] when one knows that all that is alive in Christian philosophy is in fact rather alien to an ontology of *ens realissimum*? Sooner or later, formal relations between Catholicism and non-Catholicism—like those between communism and non-communism—must begin to reflect their real relations, as in the minds of our best students. Catholic or not, atheist or not, they know all too well that neither the philosophy of the Enlightenment, nor marxism, nor the philosophy of *ens realissimum* is *the truth*. Their intimate certainty about this matter betrays itself in conversation. But this is still only willingness and intelligence on their part. If they succeed in moving beyond the limits of these philosophies, it is only at the risk of an inner rending. Philosophy must reunite what remains for them disjointed, held together only by the strength of their courage. For the time being, all of this is lost when they enter "the real world," that is, the adult world where each pursues his or her own whims.

Eugen Fink, a contemporary German philosopher, writes that we live in the "ruins of thought." In these ruins (or because of them) one finds an immediate possibility of a great and healthy skepticism which is indispensable for the recovery of what is most basic. The very idea that in France today some people are divided as to whether Thomas Aquinas and Friedrich Engels held the same view of Nature astounds me when one considers all there is to know and understand.

A philosophy cannot be sketched out in a few words. Let us only say that it must necessarily be a philosophy of *brute being* and not one of docile being which would have us believe the world can be fully explained. It must also be an attentive study of *meaning*, a meaning wholly other than the meaning of ideas, a volatile and allusive meaning which lacks any direct power over things—even though it may appear and proliferate in things, once certain obstacles have been cleared away.

CHAPSAL: And politics?

MERLEAU-PONTY: Like all philosophy, the one to seek is the one that will inspire a politics. Negatively, it would have to reveal the illusions of classical politics. We do not possess the grounds to support the belief that the human world is a cluster of rational wills, that it could, like a learned society, be governed by rules of order based on laws derived from timeless principles, or make its decisions through academic debates in which the most rational end up convincing all the others.

As both life and animality have invented and scattered forms, mechanisms, organisms, and even some kinds of institutions across the surface of the earth, the human world must also create cultural forms and structures (except for fortunate periods during which it lives off its former accomplishments). The superior values in which it takes such great pride are sustained within these historical matrices.

Marx was not wrong in having said something like this, but in believing that there is a matrix for *true human society*, that this class already existed, and that when it seized power a true society would be born. This was all too geometrical.

The chaos of our politics may be derived from the disappearance of a ruling class. The bourgeoisie still exists, but it no longer leads and no longer has a body of ideas which empowers it to administer the State. The proletariat exists, but the party which is its principle representative no longer has a class politics and is tripped up by its own machinations.

Interests, rivalries, pressure groups, and antagonisms do exist, but lines of action and lines of history are now gone. This situation is undoubtedly tied to France's position in the world, that is, to its involvement in a game in which it does not hold the high cards, even though its stakes are nonetheless considerable.

Even taking the two superpowers into consideration, I do not think that the historical direction of their rivalry is clear: neither American capitalism nor Russian "socialism" can be defined by an essence. Everywhere, the struggle is confused, unaware of its proper goals (should there be any). The remedy? The question is precisely whether a single unambiguous force remains. Perhaps the exhaustion of the classes will bind us to a pure politics, founded above all on the propagation of information and knowledge. I do not have such a high opinion of our capacities for abstraction, but given the classes' current state of decadence I do not see what will make us *wise and profound in spite of ourselves* as the classes once did. There is no "Poujadist"[6] or military civilization. Unfortunately, the same causes which urgently require the renewal of inquiry and knowledge also render it unlikely.

CHAPSAL: You have written several books on politics. Will you write more?

MERLEAU-PONTY: Political philosophy will come with all the rest. As for practical conclusions, I have already indicated them. What good is it to begin again? The war in Algeria has revived passions that had just begun to die out, setting France back many years. We had begun to understand that the question of questions was not whether one was Communist or not. The war in Algeria has dimmed the dawn of this understanding. It has installed in France a feeble, torn, and hesitant regime which is no more capable of governing than the one preceding it. This regime has thus far been able to restrain a southern insurrection only by continuing the war. Everything will have to begin from scratch, in politics as well as in philosophy. This will become clearer as soon as the French hypnosis or (depending on the case) euphoria comes to an end along with the Algerian War. Under the pressure of an increase in population, the problems of modern society—from those of urbanism (including the question of traffic), employment, the new peasantry, and planning, to those of the motives, movement, and vitality of the nation—will have to be confronted. Suddenly it will become obvious that "national ambition," "counter-subversion," and the financing of private schools do not make a nation live and breathe. This *abyss* of modern society—one that certain writers and philosophers have sensed or suspected on the horizon for the past fifty or a hundred years—will become evident in everyday life. Our time is now experiencing this abyss as its misery and its greatness.

—Trans. by James Barry Jr.

2

◆

Crisis in European Consciousness (1946)

MERLEAU-PONTY: Mr. Benda has claimed that there is no European consciousness.[1] He seemed to mean that there has never been a consciousness of Europe, and by *consciousness* of Europe he meant a kind of intentional, explicit awareness—as if each and every European were supposed to say to him or herself: "I am a European." This led me to wonder what is meant by the unity of Europe, and whether European unity necessarily had to take that form. Is the sort of consciousness Mr. Benda has in mind—which philosophers call "representation," namely, the representation of Europe—the only possible, or even desirable, one? I believe that were all Europeans to say to themselves, "We are Europeans," they would be conceiving of Europe and themselves in opposition to something else. This is the kind of image one forms of Europe when wishing to oppose Europe to the United States or the U.S.S.R., for example, and I wonder whether, on the contrary, there is not a completely different type of European unity—a sort of Europe in act and not in representation.

Now, what would that Europe in fact be? What might it have been? That is what we now need to explore. I don't have time to do it here. I would simply like to indicate in what direction one might look. It seems to me that a European spirit should be defined less by an idea or a representation, as Mr. Benda does, than by a certain kind of relation between humans and nature or between an individual and others. For example, it seems to me that if we consider efforts as diverse as Hegel's lectures on the philosophy of history, certain writings on Chinese civilization, or even Malraux's first novels, we might find something typically European.

First, we might find a relation between humanity and nature that is not con-fusion: a distinction between myself and the world; and correlatively, the idea of objectivity and truth. Both of the authors I just mentioned

14

pointed out that in certain civilizations there is no idea of truth. The world is rather a kind of envelope, a kind of husk that we must get back into, enclosing ourselves within it—a meaningful whole rather than an object whose truth is to be assessed. Therefore, on the level of the mind proper (i.e., the intelligence), I believe there is a certain idea of truth at the origin of what is called Western science, and consequently, since that science ended up becoming technology, European forms of work.

Second, I believe work is precisely what constitutes one element, one of the inventions, of Europe. This is work taken in its Hegelian sense and not in Mr. Benda's limited sense. Mr. Benda sets up an opposition between economic and intellectual questions. Naturally, if you take economic questions in the narrow sense, the opposition can be justified. But should they be taken so narrowly? When Hegel said that the human is a being who works, I think he meant work in a deeper sense—the idea of productivity, or transformation of the world. Such an attitude toward the world, which consists not in enduring it but rather in transforming it, is an attitude which probably originated with Europe. This is, then, a second element in that European behavior we were discussing.

Third and lastly (and this would require much more elucidation), the State—considered as the realization of freedom as in Hegel—is perhaps an invention of Europe. Such a State is not like the Chinese quasi-State Hegel describes in his lessons on the philosophy of history (i.e., a massive reality), but rather a State he was to consider the human milieu proper, one in which human freedom can be realized.

These three elements of European behavior, or these three aspects of Europe, seem to me rather striking when one compares, for example, Europe with the Far East. One must consider that these three forms of reason—of behavior based on the rational faculty—are now in a state of crisis. Mr. Benda has taken note of it. But then, from the very fact that a crisis exists concerning the idea of truth and objectivity, respect for freedom, or the status of work, Mr. Benda appears inclined to conclude simply that, all in all, this crisis need not be understood. We should not try to understand the history of these past forty years, but simply condemn them. That is, we should revert to those thinkers who preceded this crisis, thereby recovering through them the secret of that rationality we now see slowly but surely dissipating. At which point I find myself wondering whether this is a sound way to proceed, and if what Mr. Benda is proposing is not a restoration. Mr. Benda would like to restore a type of rationality that has, in any case, been discredited by what we have lived through during the last fifty . . . even the last hundred years. Is not all restoration of this type artificial, and should rationality not be thought of in a manner entirely different from Mr. Benda's? Any attempt to confront reason with the concrete seems to

Mr. Benda an overly indulgent attitude toward the concrete, and a form of romanticism. But in reality, if we look more closely, we see that even a philosopher like Plato did nothing but confront the one with the many, studying their relations and the mediation through which they interrelate. Thus, it seems that the crises in the various orders I have mentioned should be analyzed; it should be considered a crisis of consciousness. . . .[2]

MERLEAU-PONTY: I am delighted with the turn our discussion took this morning. It seems to me that this exchange of views between Mr. Jaspers and Mr. Lukács has been conducted in such a way as to specify their respective opinions, so that now it is possible to compare their positions. Here is what I mean. Mr. Jaspers seems to oppose the idea posed by Mr. Lukács, the entity known as historical totality. Mr. Jaspers' objection to it is not just theoretical. He states, "In fact, I, a man, do not embrace the totality of history, and there is always, beyond what I can see, an encompassing horizon."

I think Mr. Lukács could reply, even from the Marxist point of view, that this is obviously the case. Neither Marx nor Hegel claimed to offer us a total view of universal history. (Some might say Hegel did in fact do so, but surely not Marx.) Mr. Jaspers even used a word from the Marxist vocabulary, "perspective"; he seemed to be saying, in short, that we can only perceive the future of humanity in perspective. The practitioners of marxism, such as Lenin, have always thought it impossible to foresee the future in any scientific manner. We can only know the general direction of life. Even the historical process in its details, the ways in which that future would eventually be realized, would remain mere objects of speculation. They might be sketched out on the basis of probability, but they do not appear as scientific certitudes. That is why Lenin had that famous theory of Marxist compromise, for example, in which he explained very clearly that whatever the direct path seemed to be, it was not in reality the true revolutionary path.

So it seems to me that even from Mr. Lukács' point of view, the notion of a horizon can be accepted on one condition: that the horizon does not remain inaccessible to us in principle. Mr. Jaspers seems to want to convince us that we cannot think for one moment of unravelling the secret of history, but rather that we must resign ourselves to it. But my response is that the will to foresee what is going to happen, the human will to master our own history, is not folly, because it is a necessity. If we do not understand this, events will befall us without our comprehending them; we will be broken, cut off from history, which will unfold at a pace we failed to predict. A certain degree of rationalism, a certain postulation of rationality in history, is something we cannot avoid, because it merges with the necessities of our lives. The moment individuals take a political stance, they have a certain overall conception of historical life, and although they may not put it into words they nevertheless express it in their actions.

I see, for example, a theoretician like Raymond Aron, who has maintained the idea that history is not subject to objective interpretation, nevertheless be led to imply a whole conception of the future when he takes up a personal position. Thus it is not up to us to accept or reject that idea; it is thrust upon us. In my opinion the word "existence," in the sense I have in mind, contains the following inextricably bound ideas: we are in a circumscribed environment and cannot know the whole, but at the same time are connected to this whole, and if we refuse to take this whole into consideration, we mutilate ourselves.

I would like to add something else, not in reference to the present discussion but to Mr. Lukács' lecture the other day. I agree with Mr. Lukács' method, and I don't think Mr. Jaspers disagrees with it in the final analysis either. That method, which consists in taking events not on the simple ideological plane, but on all levels, could be called the concept of totality, or even of incarnation. On the problem of liberalism, I also think everyone is in agreement. The negative side of the Marxist critique of formal democracy, portrayed extremely accurately by Mr. Lukács, seems to me to be extant in the public domain. I wonder who could deny that a crisis in democratic concepts now exists and that these concepts do not play the same role in actual history that they do officially. Therefore, I expected Mr. Lukács, having carried out this critique of formal democracy in the name of real democracy, to be an exposition of the Marxist solution, that solution being to move liberalism from the formal to the real. In Marx, that is presented in a very clear and precise way. Marx thinks that as liberalism empties itself, so to speak, of its contents, there is, by the very movement of history, simulta- neously prepared within the society itself, a category of people who are the carriers of the future. These people are what Marx calls the proletariat, and he qualifies them with a very interesting term, stating that they are the people of universal history. The proletariat is, for Marx, invaluable in history, because they are cut off from local or national particularities, so reduced to nothingness by economic conditions that they find themselves in a position to realize, by their agreements with the proletariat of all other countries, a concrete universality and a new humanity. This is the classical Marxist solution.

However, I did not see this solution offered in Mr. Lukács' exposition. After giving a critique of formal democracy, he concluded that those formal democracies that subsist should simply ally themselves . . . remain allied as they were during the war . . . with the U.S.S.R., the latter being at least a rough draft of real democracy. I wish to ask him a question, and it really is a question, for I'd like to elicit explanations and not simply start a debate. I wish to know how the solution is possible, if the first part of his presentation was accurate. That is, if it is true that formal democracy has been declining over the last century and has now sunk to its lowest ebb, and it now must be transformed into a real democracy, a proletarian one, how then can it be instructed to outlive its time historically, when it had been condemned to history? Categories like freedom and equality—categories that have become devoid of content by the historical process—are supposed to take on a new sparkle. Is this task, which consists in boosting the family fortunes by marrying a rich commoner or in refurbishing worn-out ideas, something we can accomplish? And how is it possible?

An analysis of the political situation in France would reveal a significant attrition of ideas, as well as the artificiality which stems from attempts to rejuvenate such ideas simply by literary or philosophical talent. If Mr. Lukács thinks that this prolongation of formal democracy is possible, if he ascribes to the turning point of 1941 (the alliance of the U.S.S.R. with formal democracies) the value of an event that ushers in a whole new phase of history, if in a word we take seriously what he tells us at the very end of his talk, then are we not abandoning the classical Marxist perspective I summarized a moment ago? This perspective presents history as the progressive advent of the proletariat. In other words, Mr. Lukács' suggestion, with regard to the case of France (to which I would prefer to restrict my comments), demonstrates the meaning of Stalin's formula concerning the importance of establishing socialism in at least one country. Socialism is prepared in only one nation, and in the others there is simply the maintaining of formal democracy, which makes the ideas of the first shine more brightly. Is this what Mr. Lukács wants to say?

We can now return to our recent discussion when Mr. Lukács said: "I am not in favor of a state religion." Of course, anyone who has read Marx will acknowledge that there is nothing like one in Marx. One even finds in the writings of Marx a theory of the withering away of the State. In other words, in the highest stages of communism, according to Marx, the State, as an instrument of control with no further reason for existence, fades away into the reality of existing society. This may be true, but if (as I suggested a moment ago) we abandon the final perspective of a proletarian society in which humanity truly ceases to be dependent upon humanity, then we must also abandon the theory of the withering away of the State. At that point we find ourselves close to the Hegel of the *Philosophy of Right*, mentioned earlier—the Hegel who, for his part, did not believe everyone could really participate in history, namely, the Hegel who held that the Prussian civil servant was charged with the responsibility of seeing the future, while everyone else had to carry out a history of which they knew nothing and which, in the final analysis, they could not fully *live*. We are very close to a transcendent *Wertkeim* like the one Hegel points to in his late philosophy.

I do not believe that this is what Mr. Lukács meant, which is one of the reasons I would like to hear him respond. Mr. Lukács has condemned irrationalism. We cannot be irrational; we are condemned to reason. The conditions of our existence, and the meaning of that existence, are such that we are open to universality which we search for in reflection as well as action. It is not enough to condemn irrationalism verbally. In brief, faced with the situation of the world and with Mr. Lukács' talk, the question I am asking is the following:

Are we witnessing simply a phase, albeit a surprising phase, in the evolution of history as described by Hegel and Karl Marx? Do we have here simply a bend in the road, or is it the meaning itself, the final meaning of that history as it has been decreed? Is this very meaning being abandoned? Are we dealing here with a turn of the dialectic or with the end of the dialectic, with that dimension of history Marx was sure was possible when he said that perhaps when the proletarian society has been realized we will reach chaos? Is that possibility becoming a reality? That is the question I ask myself. And I admit for my part I would very much hope Mr. Lukács might answer these questions, either in the theoretical form in which I framed them or in a very concrete form. After all, we are fortunate to find in Mr. Lukács, a professor of philosophy, a philosopher, and a Marxist theoretician of the first order, as everyone knows, a man with political experience, a man who lived in the U.S.S.R. throughout the war. It is an opportunity we do not often have. We in the West have all complained that the curtain was closed and that it was not possible for us to enter into discussion with the U.S.S.R. I am happy to seize the opportunity of Mr. Lukács' presence and ask him to tell us in passing how, in his opinion, the war was understood by the different social levels (civil servants, teachers, and so forth) found in the U.S.S.R., as well as tell us what is left of Marxist humanism in the teaching at the Soviet universities. Are there noticeable changes, or do they keep to the classical perspective I mentioned earlier? If Mr. Lukács could tell us what the Russians think of the West, of America, all that would be important and would be a more picturesque way, as it were, of answering the rather abstract questions I have asked.[3]

—Trans. by Michael B. Smith.

3

◆

L'Express "Forum" (1954–55)

WHERE ARE THE NEW MASTERS?

In the past, men like Alain, Barrès, even Bernanos, had a profound influence on their generation.[1] Groups of young intellectuals would rally around them. Nothing like that is taking place today. How do you explain the fact that there are no new masters? Is today's youth rejecting them, or do they not exist?

Bernard C. Mauville (Paris)

Merleau-Ponty answers:

Did the young "rally around" Alain, Bernanos, Péguy, or Gide? Even Alain, who almost always had an admiring class of students, was challenged everywhere else. Perhaps there are never any masters except after the fact and from afar. The influence they have, when it is a profound one, comes through their books and over a period of years. On a day-to-day basis, the fanatics who wear out their doorbells often bring with them more vague fervor (sometimes more envy and secret hatred) than docile attentiveness to their thoughts. Looking at both the plus and the minus side, is Malraux's or Sartre's position very different from Gide's or Alain's at their age?

Still, there may be a slight change in the feelings of young readers. They become attached to certain authors, but almost never reach the same conclusions they did: they keep their distance. I have, in fact, heard lots of students talk about Sartre, but I have scarcely heard one say simply that Sartre was right, not the way people used to say that Barrès or Gide "is right." And I don't see them imitating Malraux the way they used to ape Proust. Might that be because Sartre and Malraux are themselves more reserved than Gide or Péguy? (The former rarely say "I." They express themselves through

20

objective art forms, not in intimate journals. They wish to define themselves in relation to political facts, and do not talk of themselves openly.) That discretion inspires respect, not fanaticism. Might this not be for the better?

IS THE PHILOSOPHER A CIVIL SERVANT?

In the inaugural lecture of your courses at the Collège de France, you remarked that the philosopher of today tends to become a civil servant. Do you think there is any way to revive philosophy, any way it might again become a constituent of life?

Jules Dastarac (Agen)

Merleau-Ponty answers:
A "constituent of life"? No. When philosophers have taken up such themes as peace and war, the Republic, poverty, money, the passions, morals, or marriage, they have always done so with an alarming freedom, even if they ended up siding with tradition. There is a kind of decorum of satisfaction that the established norms of life cannot expect of them.

In yet another way, philosophy rebels against the positivism of life: it never merges with any of the philosophical sciences (economics, history, or sociology) which deal with human life in a systematic way. Philosophy reserves for itself what remains when those sciences have said everything, when the question comes up: What about us living human beings to whom all that is directed? What have we to do with that world and that history?

Philosophers must take their position in life, speak of the things of life, down to their most minute consequences, but in order to struggle against habit, revive demands, seek out and draw attention to the sublime, those almost impossible moments when contradictions are resolved. . . .

Socrates did this, but with a difference. For there is in Socrates a bit of disdain and provocation, a bias in favor of eliciting surprise or even shock— and that is doubtless one of the reasons why he didn't write anything. But Plato wrote for him, and as for us, in the voluminous societies in which we live, it is in writing that dialogues are carried on today.

ARE WOMEN MEN?

Are women men? You might end up thinking so. Their field of activity is expanding daily, though in a society that all the sociologists agree was created by men and for men. Why, then, do women succeed in assuming so great a role in it? I would like to know whether you think this is normal, and whether women really have the same nature, the same possibilities as men.

Paul Boyer (Annecy)

Merleau-Ponty answers:

With regard to the facts of the case involving the invasion of society by women, I don't know of any overall statistics. Responding to one personal impression with another, I haven't noticed any change. Has my vigilance been wanting, or has Mr. Boyer's been excessive? Consider the following, in making your determination.

Mr. Boyer continues: "The sociologists say that our society is made by men, for men." He does not question this thesis, which normally serves to show that, masculinity being the norm, as is the white and the adult in other domains, the woman, like the child and the person "of color," becomes a being both other and secondary. Many of her character traits, whether real or the creation of popular mythology, are in this view the result of that situation. Even the nun's life is seen as a loving form of imprisonment. No one in the world can know what women might be if they were not living in this peculiar state. In short, the *woman* we speak of is the woman we have created.

That is not the way Mr. Boyer understands the thesis. Society is made by men, for men: this he does not contest. But neither does he see anything wrong with it, anything that might distort woman's character. The anomaly for him is that women should advance in such a well-made society. And before suspending hostilities, he wants to be convinced that women are men. Perhaps one should first ask whether it is not as a result of a long history that men and women have become absolute others.

Thus, despite two thick volumes, the duel that Simone de Beauvoir wished to cut short continues. She was not saying women are men, and therefore did not have to prove they were. It was not a question of doing away with differences, but of seeing that they do not extend to the heart itself nor to the intelligence, and that women, overlooking whatever talents or vices may be due to their marginal condition, can be human beings. . . . The arguments from probability Simone de Beauvoir assembles do not seriously erode the position of the eternal masculine, which takes them as exceptions and holds on to its norm. The facts can be made to fit either scenario, more or less; here, as elsewhere, they fail to furnish decisive proof. They only give evidence against man if you decide to put your faith in the future.

Thus, it all comes down to the choice of a norm: the one that has held until now, or the one that may do so in the future? But how to convince, and is it a question of force? Will women in turn have to use violence to prove what they can do? But it will be a faulty proof, and the last men, surviving in slavery, might in turn mutter softly, dreaming of revolution: "You can never tell what men could do if they were not oppressed."

There can be no solution unless men and women stop sizing one another up warily, thinking of one another *en masse*, imitating one another, competing with one another, defining themselves once and for all, and *proving themselves*. In short, they must begin to think in a new way. Then, different as they are, they will suddenly begin to feel that they are living the same life. But, you may say, surely the oppressed must unite? Let them unite, but not as women, but mixed with other oppressed people . . . at least if they really want Mr. Boyer to change his mind.

WHAT IS THE USE OF OBJECTIVITY?

The most partisan politicians and newspapers are boasting every minute of their objectivity. I must admit I do not understand what continues to lend objectivity prestige in an era in which every event makes man commit himself and take sides. Doesn't being objective mean being a bit cowardly, shirking one's responsibilities and in the final analysis lying by omission?

François Ledoyen (Pau)

Merleau-Ponty answers:

An interesting question, which may be interpreted as an indication that the philosophies of "decision" or of "engagement" are today firmly established in France—and perhaps also that there is a misunderstanding between those who teach them and those who read them.

Thirty years ago, the average view was doubtless that to judge by will or feeling amounted to "blowing out one's lantern in order to see better," as Goblot's *Traité de Logique* put it. Since *Esprit* with its *"pensée engagée"* [committed, or partisan thought] section, especially since Raymond Aron's thesis (the subtitle of which was: "Essay on the Limits of Objectivity in History"), and since Sartre's works, the favorable prejudice has been reversed. Objectivity, distancing oneself from the situation, attention given to the facts—these appear as a turning aside from one's duty to decide for oneself, or else as a tacit stance, a mendacious manner of "letting the facts speak."

It is certain, however, that neither Max Weber, who is the source of these thoughts, nor Aron, nor Sartre ever thought of devaluating knowledge and critical examination.

They said that such examination never could nor should be impersonal, that facts never bring their meaning with them. Even with respect to the past—the way in which we carve events out of the historical continuum, put them in perspective and understand them—is a transposition of our present choices and ultimately of our choice of a future. The claim to be absolutely objective would limit us to tabulating brute facts. Even then we would be giving an interpretation and a general view of history as a chaos of events in which nothing is secondary and therefore nothing essential. . . .

However, granted that a decision can never be deduced from the situation itself, it does not follow that all decisions are of equal value, nor that a decision reached after an examination of the facts is the same as one arrived at without a knowledge of them, nor that there is not a personal *working over* of the facts and motivations that enriches the decision and changes it, as this process itself sheds light upon the facts and motivations. Thus there may be said to be pre-rational decisions and super-rational ones, the latter being those that are made after having done one's utmost to see the situation clearly.

If the only concern were really to be committed, to bear witness, to put oneself on the line, we would not see Aron and Sartre establishing at such length the motivation for their political decisions. A "yes" or a "no" would suffice. Neither they nor Max Weber ever taught irrationalism. They teach that, in the final analysis, the meaning taken on by the whole configuration will depend upon a decision that nothing can exempt us from having to make. But perhaps this goes little further than that famous reflection of Descartes, that even if the will cannot go against what is patently obvious or if the patently obvious predisposes the will, we always have the power to suspend our assent, which therefore remains an act.

This is already a lot to bear. For, once having granted that there is a moment of pure decision, how will we know when this moment has come, and that the decision is, if not well founded, at least "ripe"? How will we be able to tell the difference between ignorance and the super-rational? The question exists for everyone, even Marxists, who one minute are criticizing "bourgeois objectivity" in the name of "class truth" and the next are demanding proof and talking "science," without there being any criteria indicating in which case the "class" should be allowed to speak and in which we should be submissive to the facts.

The fact is, the *absolute* difference between a hasty judgment and a true one does not exist. The only difference is in the wide range of perspectives they give us on the situation, the amount of facts they elucidate, the degree of insight they offer into the decisions of others, the firmness of action they dictate. And none of this is immediately apparent; no strict assessment can be made before all the consequences of these judgments have appeared, that is, before the end of the world. This does not prevent there being, both for us and in truth, huge differences of fullness, value, and interest between decisions: some judgments being justly termed "narcissistic" and others that must consequently be called "objective."

Considerations of the limits of objectivity are, moreover, foreign to classical liberalism on which parliamentary institutions are, in theory, founded. In practice, our political life does not observe "objectivity," but that does not mean it no longer has any significance in that domain. Max Weber's thought heralds an epoch in which liberalism is conscious of its own limitations, recognizing that action, even in its liberal forms, contains an element of force. But Weber was never willing to abandon action to violence. He thought contestation could be maintained at a level above aggression, pure violence, or manipulations. A head of government does not necessarily govern solely for himself or his party; the opposition's sole purpose is not necessarily to topple him. Although Weber's heroic liberalism is pessimistic, within it "objectivity" still has meaning.

—Trans. by Michael B. Smith.

4

◆

East-West Encounter
(1956)

[Monday afternoon, March 26, 1956: The chair is given to Antonin Babel, who opens the session, then turns it over to the invited speaker for the afternoon, Maurice Merleau-Ponty].

MERLEAU-PONTY: Since you've so kindly given me the floor, I would like to take this opportunity to return briefly to what was said this morning, and which is not irrelevant to our debate for this afternoon.[1] I was rather surprised to see and hear Mr. Silone,[2] to begin with, objecting to the idea of an abstract discussion on culture, engagement, and dialogue. One of the reasons he gave for opposing this project was that we had all taken our respective positions and expressed them in our books, and consequently would only express them less well here. Such a discussion would thus be of no interest. What surprised me was not so much what Mr. Silone was saying, but the parallel between that and what one of our Soviet guests said, who, for his part, seemed to wish that our meeting would restrict itself on the whole to rather vague observations. We must, he said, speak of what unites us, and not of what separates us. And what I see as striking within the comparison of these two opinions is that they both spoke as if nothing had happened these past years or months. Silone said: "We have positions, we have themes, we've expressed them." Yet he did not seem to think for one minute that the famous thaw that brings us together here poses any problems for the intellectual, or that the task of intellectuals in particular is to understand what this thaw signifies. Not that the thaw cancels or nullifies our prior theses, but it obliges us to give them a coherent interpretation. For his part, the Soviet interlocutor seemed to speak a language that is, in a sense, a language out of season, an intemperate language. To speak of what unites us and not of what separates us—we have always been able to do this, we already did it here, when we came to a rather vague agreement on the defense

26

of culture. These terms disturb me, because I'm afraid that if we remain within them we'll be lured into vacuity. We have to state how we understand the fact of this thaw. And this already brings me within range of my subject, which is engagement.

What can we, as intellectuals, have to say about the thaw? How can we contribute to making it understood? There is naturally a political interpretation of the thaw, and there is also, I would argue, a philosophical interpretation of it. And these two interpretations are at once distinct yet convergent. I will say a word, if you like, on the political interpretation, about which I hasten to emphasize that it is not within our domain, nor is it the subject of our meeting. Yet, it seems to me indispensable to say a few words about it, precisely because the philosophical interpretation, the one that concerns us, runs parallel to it.

On the political level, what questions do we ask in light of the thaw? I think we ask ourselves, for example, the following question: Given that the Soviet Union has taken the initiative for the thaw, is the new course of Soviet politics a return to Lenin and Marx? Should we consider that the period 1934–53 was a kind of parenthesis, and that the new course of events is a direct resumption of the period prior to it? Or, on the other hand, is this apparent renaissance not a new phenomenon in the history of the Soviet Union?

Let's be even more specific. There was often talk, during the period 1934–53, of using the parliamentary route, the one spoken of by Soviet officials and the important political men of the Western countries, such as Mr. Togliatti. This was also an issue in Lenin's time. Yet what is perhaps new is the idea that the parliamentary route is not simply an auxiliary means of expression, destined to bring to power the class considered by every good Marxist to be the foundation of the new society: a method destined to prepare the dictatorship of this class. If, on the contrary, it is considered the route to be followed right to the end, the means for the realization of socialism, are we not then in the presence of something completely new, even as concerns the Lenin texts cited in this regard? You know that in the official statements, the texts are vague on this subject. After one spokesman has presented the parliamentary route as a novel and independent one, another spokesman reintegrates it within a revolutionary action, for which it would only be an auxiliary means. Not long ago, on the other hand, others—like Mr. Togliatti, for instance—presented the parliamentary route as a self-sufficient one, and one destined to allow for the coming of a new regime. The question we ask in light of these interpretations is the following: What difference is there between this attitude and reformism? As I see it, equivocation currently reigns over this question. It is not our task to discuss these alternatives, nor to judge them. If I have mentioned some problems posed by the political interpretation of the thaw, it is only in order to arrive at our subject, which is its philosophical interpretation. These two issues are profoundly related, and yet entirely distinct.

What is the philosophical problem presented by these events? Current events call into question what I would call the intellectual formula for the Cold War, according to which intellectual life is not a dialogue, but a battle. Universalism, which is always implied in the will to dialogue, was considered during the period just past as one of the attributes of bourgeois thought. Genuine action—which is always, let us say, Manichean, which always forces us to choose between two givens—this action, if it is taken seriously, forces the thinker to make the same choices. If one's thinking is to be complete, it must choose within the same conditions; and it cannot hope to justify itself in everyone's eyes. It follows from this way of seeing things that, as concerns art, painting, culture, and philosophy, there is no internal criterion. The discussion of a philosophy or a work of art can never consist in the act of understanding it first and discussing it from within; it consists more or less in the act of confronting the work with an external discipline, according to which this work, by virtue of its practical consequences, its supposed influences, and its propaganda value, either functions or does not function as an auxiliary discipline. In the final analysis, it is only geographical, or social, or economic criteria which intervene in all domains of culture. In the final analysis, the regime considered most economically progressive necessarily has the best literature.

The question today's events pose is the following: Has this concept been abandoned or not? This is not a strictly political question, in the sense that there is, in my opinion, something in marxism that allows for a relative autonomy of culture. I do not need to cite the famous Engels text, with which you are familiar, on "the graph of cultural evolution and the graph of economic evolution," according to which the two graphs are not parallel, and there can be in one certain anticipations and recoils that do not exist in the other. You are familiar with the Marx texts on the eternal value of Greek art, which show that a society that, economically speaking, is not an advanced one can nevertheless have anticipated—and that by centuries— what other, more advanced societies were incapable of formulating. One could find a number of other texts besides these; I cite only the most familiar. There is thus the means, within marxism, of restoring a certain autonomy to culture. In truth, if we push things to the limit, we transcend the boundaries of marxism; because if there really is no parallelism between the graph of culture and the other socioeconomic graphs, then in the face of a specific cultural given, we will ask ourselves whether the moment is right to apply the socioeconomic criterion, or if we should still remain within an internal, cultural discourse. And we are never certain whether it is permissible and possible to apply the socioeconomic criterion. It's my sense that, ultimately, we transcend the boundaries of marxism. But after all, since there are both Marxists and non-Marxists here, I believe it useful to state that within marxism one can very well restore an autonomy to culture. This does not mean, of course, that there is no relation between the two orders.

Does the thaw then signify, philosophically speaking, that we foresee the possibility that a non-Communist country can achieve, not only in physics and astronomy, but also in the domain of the human sciences, truths not attained or even formulated in Communist countries? I submit this as a possibility; and there is obviously no question here of justifying, for example, the whole of American sociology or psychology. Yet in principle, do we admit the possibility of such a cultural development, and upon foundations that up until now have been considered corrupt? If we admit this, we are dealing with a new kind of universalism. This is no longer the universalism criticized under the name of "bourgeois philosophy," that is to say, an abstract reason that imagined one could, on the basis of principles truly common to all human beings and independent of all situations, pronounce truths and discover values. This is no longer that kind of universalism, but there will be within it the seed of a new universalism; that is, a universalism encompassing the idea that if we place ourselves on the level of what men *live*, it is possible, in a non-Communist country, that living men will freely express what they live, and that they will find themselves going beyond the boundaries of their class or society. It would be the case for someone who was more than his or her class, given that we place ourselves on the level of what we live, and not on the level of abstract principles by which we are largely depersonalized and through which we are in much less contact with the social totality we live in.

If the events actually signify what I am suggesting, this would mean that the Marxists can reappropriate Hegel's famous dictum, with which you are familiar, and which seems to have been quite forgotten: truth is not a fully coined currency, and is recognizable from the outside only by the marks it carries.

This obviously brings me to the notion of engagement. Actually, this concept—as someone noted this morning—is perhaps not such a good discriminant between Marxists and non-Marxists. I say Marxists and non-Marxists, because I would like for our Soviet interlocutors to realize that there are certainly as many differences between us Westerners as there are between them and us. There are Marxists and non-Marxists among us, such that when I speak as I am now, it is not only of them but also of some of us that I have questions to ask.

Theoretically, the notion of engagement is not a good discriminant here, because this notion is not a Marxist one. Marxists in general looked askance at the notion in the period just after the war, even in France. It would take too long to say why, but I believe it is fairly obvious that a Marxist does not view a writer's engagement with much enthusiasm: the Marxist has both more and less respect for the writer. According to the concept of engagement, the writer must hold himself responsible not only for his books, but for everything he does in life, for his participation in injustices, in events; and in all this he must do something proper, in what he says as well as in what he writes. Consequently, this idea of engagement is completely different from that of the Marxists who place the writer within a framework, and within this framework consider him someone respectable. There are passages in Lenin insisting on the fact that literature is the thing one can least domesticate, something somewhat suspicious. There are also passages in Lenin stating that literature must be firmly controlled by the party—such that between the idea of engagement and the views of Marxists, there is a great difference in inspiration. It is not only in the eyes of the theoreticians of engagement that the writer is also a man, as Mr. Campagnolo[3] was saying. I noted this statement this morning. Mr. Campagnolo seemed to think that there is the writer who writes, and that, in addition, the latter is also a man who has responsibilities as a man. This would simply mean that the writer has, in addition, the duties of a citizen, and that he fulfills them as any other citizen could. According to the principle of engagement, the link is much more direct. The writer's own way of writing is tied to his human *being* and to his way of being. One can say that the writer is also a citizen, that's fine with me. In any case, let's leave that aside for the moment. Whatever the value given the term "engagement," it seems to me this term can be considered in two very different ways. One of these ways seems to me tied to the period I call the Cold War period, a period over for two or three years now; and the other, on the contrary, is very different, and would be on the verge of gaining ascendency. The question is precisely to know whether it *will* gain ascendency.

The conception of engagement I would call "pessimistic," to reduce it to a rather simple, crude formula, would be that according to which writers must keep silent, or even lie, rather than be disloyal to the institution, to the apparatus that, in their eyes, holds the promise of the future. Accordingly, writers must accept the dilemmas of an action that is Manichean and that they choose, even if this should lead them to lie or, what amounts to the same thing, not to say what they know or not to express themselves fully. This is thus a pessimistic conception, which seems to me tied to the period that is happily over. Ultimately, it would oblige us to consider the act of writing as an action like any other, neither more or less, which is not enacted according to rules other than those of action in the political sense of the word.

I believe there is another conception of engagement, an optimistic one, which consists in believing that there can be no alternative of the kind just mentioned; that if such an alternative presents itself, there is no reasonable choice for writers: they simply have nothing more to write. Nothing would justify a choice that would oblige the writer to lie. There is, in an immanent manner, a convergence between the values of culture and those of action. The writer does not have to choose between them, to put the one set of values before the other, to subordinate one set to the other. Thus what is written can have a very particular value, a value quite distinct from that of action, in the temporal and political sense of the word; and what is written can have this value even when it speaks neither of action nor of politics, even when it speaks about bees. This does not at all mean that everything written should allow for a political content, but rather that everything written has a political *bearing*, even in the case of a study on bees—there is no paradox here!—*vis-à-vis* the way one describes them or exhibits their relations with the world, nature, and other animals. All of this has a political bearing, all of this has the potential to teach those who read a certain way of situating themselves within the world, and consequently a certain political way of being.

I quite appreciated what Mr. Ponti[4] was saying this morning, when he spoke of culture considered not as an instrument of action but as an aid to action. I think he envisaged something like what I myself have in mind. You see, then, all the resonances that might result from this other conception of engagement.

My questions will be the following: Does the thaw unite us? Is an accord in the process of being built on this sole basis, that of a new universalism? To my mind, this is not possible except at the price of a very profound and substantial change in the Soviet regime. But this is not our subject. Our concern being the definition of truth, the definition of culture, the practice of truth and of culture, are *we* on the way to such a change? Are we leaving this period behind during which it sufficed, in order to qualify a work, to call it bourgeois or communist? And now, will we rather ask ourselves when faced with a work what its value is? And will we find books from both sides worthwhile?

CAMPAGNOLO: I have followed Mr. Merleau-Ponty's exposé very closely. It provides a useful opening for this discussion.

For my part, I would like to make a few remarks about what I said this morning on the distinction between the man and the writer. I probably expressed myself poorly, only believing to have indicated that the status of "writer" implied a specific responsibility; that by virtue of this status as a writer the cultured man[5] had a political responsibility. I would like to draw attention to this distinction—which I think could only facilitate our discussion—between the two conceptions of engagement I was alluding to: the engagement Mr. Spender[6] rejects and pessimistic engagement. I had not spoken of optimistic engagement, which is the kind we have already had occasion to speak of here within the context of our society. It is in the latter spirit that we have organized this meeting, and I think it helpful to clarify that.

SPENDER: If you want to say every writer is engaged whether he knows it or not, then I agree with you. To say, for example, that composing a poem on bees also has an extra-poetical signification, that's fine with me. But there is a difference between saying such a thing and declaring that one must be consciously engaged. I am thinking of all the conferences and congresses one would oblige writers to participate in. That is the principle I wanted to object to.

CAMPAGNOLO: We all admit that the written work always has a political import. Yet, because it is an inevitable consequence, this political import cannot constitute engagement. Such a conception, in my opinion, is rather to be identified with the very refusal of engagement.

I would like to propose here a third way of considering engagement. The artist and the writer have the duty to defend the very conditions of their work and of their creative activity. At certain historical moments, it is not necessary to defend these conditions. But it is necessary in other epochs, when the creative activity is thwarted for political, economic, or other reasons. It is then that the cultured man becomes engaged in a particular way, otherwise than through the bare political resonances of the work itself. These resonances are mere accessories and cannot constitute the object of a genuine engagement.

The specific duty of the cultured man makes his engagement different than the political engagement of the ordinary person. Of course, men of culture, like all other human beings, must fulfill their duties as citizens—voting, for example—but it is not in this that we see the cultured man's engagement. For even though everyone has a political duty, men of culture and common men have different objectives: ordinary politics, in effect, projects a definite goal, while the politics of culture seeks to create the conditions that make creativity, the overcoming of any situation, and the transcendence of any ordinary political objective possible. Ordinary politics only transcends itself logically through recourse to violence or by chance. The specific engagement of the cultured man only begins when he defends the rights of culture, such as, for example, the rights to dialogue and to the autonomy of culture, which are the very object of this engagement.

Engagement is a problem which does not have a philosophical but only an historical origin. It appeared as a polemical issue the day it was proclaimed, due to social conditions, that the cultured man had the right, and even the duty, to withdraw from political conflicts.

SILONE: I would like to clarify the meaning of what I said this morning, which in my opinion was not very well understood by Mr. Merleau-Ponty. I was saying that in a transitional phase, a certain empiricism and a certain intellectual prudence are called for. I do not claim that everything we've said up until yesterday is still viable; but a conference is not the place to try to revise it all. I quite understand, on the other hand, an invitation to anticipate reflections on events which have just taken place. I must say then that I found Mr. Merleau-Ponty very interesting; but I was already familiar with what he said, through his books. His comments did nothing but remind me of the spirit of certain of his ideas that I already knew.

Allow me a few observations. Your evaluation of the political thaw seemed to me not quite exact; in any case, it is premature. I do not believe that the only alternatives to the thaw are terrorist dictatorship or bourgeois parliamentarianism.

MERLEAU-PONTY: I did not say that.

SILONE: I'm sorry, but that could follow from what you were saying. I do not believe, in any case, that political revision, which is certainly the order of the day in the U.S.S.R., is situated within the dilemma of parliamentarianism or dictatorship. I believe, moreover, that there are possible forms of socialist democracy, very radical and at the same time very open, that could not be characterized as embodying a counter-revolutionary perspective. We will be able to say that the end of Stalinism marks the end of dictatorship only on the day there is a political and public debate in the U.S.S.R. that does not end in executions. The problem now, for cultured men, is: What are the consequences of the political thaw for cultural life and for the relations between our Soviet colleagues and ourselves?

We all know that a certain tyranny of politics over culture is a tendency much older than the Cold War and communism. Its most extreme intellectual expression is found in Charles Maurras' formula, "politics first," which claims the priority of politics over all other human faculties: politics as the primary source of all values. Now, what is essential to the revindication of the freedom of culture is the rejection of the priority of a *raison d'Etat*, of national interest, or of class interest: the refusal to submit the whole person to a particular interest.

The fact that the central committee of a political party can declare a resolution condemning a certain form of music is not only monstrous but stupid. Whether a painting is beautiful or ugly is not a problem that concerns the State. The basis for any judgment on this problem should be a realistic conception of the relations between State and society: the writer is a person who is part of society. Culture is an activity of society. A political crisis such as the Russian thaw concerns us because, in the final analysis, it expresses a contrast between Russian society and state. Russian society, in all its forms, in all its sectors, has grown and developed; the State has remained fixed. Now, the duty of writers is not to write according to State directives but to be interpreters of themselves and society. For me, engagement is the consciousness of belonging to the world of the oppressed; it is the loyalty to this world, even when my friends come to power and become oppressors in their turn. I cannot conceive of any other idea of engagement for a revolutionary writer, besides this loyalty to the persecuted. This is perhaps a limitation on my part. Yet once it is incarnated in a powerful institution, no idea, not even the most noble or universal, can escape historical determinism, servility to established interests, and decadence. The Pope[7] recently asserted that we should not "identify Christianity with a culture." Of course not. Yet scholastic philosophy, the Aristotelian philosophy of St. Thomas, which is obligatory in seminaries, belongs not to divine revelation but to history. On my way to Venice, I was reading a biography of Charles de Foucauld: there you have a Christianity that retains something of its original purity. However, one swallow does not necessarily signal the beginning of spring. I am thinking now of our Soviet colleagues' tragic situation, caught between the revolutionary State and the people. I have felt the attractive power of revolutionary discipline too strongly myself not to understand their tragedy. With what satisfaction we come to sacrifice our own individual freedom on the altar of the common cause! But what if the State betrays the revolutionary cause? What if the State turns away from society and tyrannizes it? Has there ever been a State that ceased being a State, in order to remain nothing but a revolutionary party? The sacrifice of individual freedom, in this case, misses its true goal, if that goal is in the interest of a new society. You are familiar with the story of the hermit who, continually persecuted by temptations of the flesh and wanting to concentrate on the love of God, castrated himself. Alas, with the loss of his virility came the loss of his love for the good Lord. In the same way, the writer who renounces critical spirit for love of the revolution ends by losing all love for the revolution.

SARTRE: I would like to respond to a point raised by Merleau-Ponty concerning the thaw and the conditions it lands us in. It seems to me Merleau-Ponty has forgotten to ask one question, because he obviously considers the thaw—he said so himself—as the thawing-out of that half of humanity which is Communist. Yet when it is so cold that half of humanity is frozen, we must assume the other half is also. Consequently, the question I would like to have heard asked is not only what we should do in light of the Soviet thaw, but also how we are going to thaw ourselves out, as regards the Soviets? It seems to me that in the way Merleau-Ponty posed the problem no progress was being made, since, as Silone noted, it had already been posed in the same way. I noticed a shift in his commentary. I was in complete agreement with him up to the point where, using the texts of Engels and Marx, he demonstrated that the masterpieces of humanity were not in immediately decipherable relations with socioeconomic conditions, and that consequently we could ask the Soviets and the popular democracies to appreciate works created within other conditions, without immediately referring to socioeconomic criteria. And right after that, he said he was putting the question to the Soviets in this way: Do you admit that, not only in the domain of American works of art, but also in American sociology and psychology, there may be truths that surpass the current state of research in the Eastern countries? Now, it seems to me this way of putting the question constitutes a leap. Because in such a case it is certainly a matter of realizing that a sociology has ends, belongs to an ideology, has methods—which are not dialectical methods—and that it has goals, even social goals; and even if truths can be discovered by these methods, a Marxist can never consider them in isolation.

MERLEAU-PONTY: In fact, I clearly stated that American sociology cannot be justified by this method. I asked whether, within the new perspectives, truths can be acquired by a regime that is socially inferior.

SARTRE: Fine. Only we would have to add: on condition that the recognition of these truths be made from within the Marxist perspective, and that the Marxists want to incorporate them into their system. Thaw or no thaw, I do not believe we can ask people in possession of a cultural ideology such as marxism to accept a truth belonging to another ideological system, without trying to see under what conditions it can be incorporated into marxism. I ask the question because, as a matter of fact, in the many discussions I had with communist intellectuals today, I noticed that this is the position they adopt.

We thus come to the very root of the cultural problematic: that cultures are also ideologies. This is what we in the West do not take into account, and in this respect I see proof that we Westerners have not thawed out. We are not aware that we live in a period of bourgeois ideology, that our ideas, in one way or another, are conditioned by bourgeois ideology, in exactly the same way the Soviets' ideas are conditioned by Soviet ideology. This occurs directly, in a systematic fashion. In the West, "diversity" is the hallmark of bourgeois ideology. Yet it would not be difficult, within most of what I have heard this morning, to reveal just what bourgeois ideology consists of, to show what standards it holds, and to prove that the difficulty between us is not quite clear. Because we have not only to discover the universal by trying to genuinely pose the question concerning it, we are dealing with two types of ideology that have come into contact. So to me, the real difficulty lies not in seeking a universal, in the sense of ideas that would be viable in one system or the other, but rather in calling for Communists to discuss some ideas within the Marxist perspective, in asking them to look for what they can receive from these ideas just as we would have to look for what we can find in these ideas from our own ideological point of view, from our own grounds. It would not then be the case of a universality without opposition, but rather of a universality *through* opposition, of a progressive universality. I believe we should initiate a *rapprochement* on the basis of discussions, but not hope to find a common content in some particular idea or other.

We Westerners should also try, within these discussions, to revise our own point of view. It seems to me that up to this point, we were the ones, for the most part, who were asking the Soviets questions, and I find it quite natural that we asked them: "What do you want to do? What do you find acceptable? What cultural changes are being produced by the current events in the U.S.S.R.?" These questions must be asked, and the Soviets would be right, in my opinion, to ask us similar questions.

MERLEAU-PONTY: I did not seek to elaborate a common content, resulting in the suppression of what separates us and for which the Marxists reproach us. I have no objection to the idea that we should make an effort to understand the socioeconomic origin of our prejudices or ideologies, while the Soviets would make an effort to incorporate into their thinking ideas found elsewhere. I do not believe I have said anything to the contrary.

SARTRE: There was still this question of universality, wasn't there?

MERLEAU-PONTY: I used the word "universality" because, after all, it is a matter of universality. And Sartre is within universalism when he speaks this way because if he reasons from the notion of ideology, what does our meeting here represent, then, from the ideological point of view? It is obviously a superstructure of Western bourgeoisie. Yet is all that can be done here to be condemned by this fact?

SARTRE: No, because we also have among us some representatives from the other side.

MERLEAU-PONTY: But they haven't spoken up to this point. And even if they don't speak, I do not count the time as lost because from the moment we begin discussing as we are now, we necessarily transcend the concept of ideologies. The latter, if I employ it while speaking to others, consists in telling them that I cannot intrinsically consider anything they utter, because it belongs to a specific social formation, and that everything I utter has no truth value, because I myself am also only the expression of another social class. From the moment we engage in discussion as we are doing right now, we transcend the concept of ideologies.

SARTRE: Not in my opinion because ideology is then considered from an extremist position, as in the case of the preface to Hervé's book.[8] Ideas can have value, even great value, within an ideology, but they depend on two simultaneous critiques. I reject the choice between internal critique and socioeconomic critique. In my opinion, both critiques are necessary, and each is tied to the other.

For some time now I have been calling for what I term, with an unfortunate word, a "totalitarian" critique, that is, an internal critique *and* a socioeconomic critique, but where each is tied to the other. It does not seem to me that we abandon the ideological point of view in this way. We simply abandon that sectarian ideology that consists in saying: everything that comes from there is false, because it is ideologically false; everything that comes from here is good, because it is ideologically good.

MERLEAU-PONTY: I have tried to put myself in a Marxist's place, by repeatedly stressing that what I was proposing goes beyond a Marxist framework, but that ultimately it could be incorporated into marxism, on condition that it be viewed in a specific way. Sartre was saying we cannot ask a Marxist to accept a truth that comes from without unless it is integrated into the Marxist way of thinking. But the question remains: what is marxism? . . .

SARTRE: Such a position cannot accept an ensemble of American investigations and inductions if they are not reappropriated within a Marxist context, that is, if at bottom there is still no study of the economic structure, etc., permitting the discovery of a superstructure. I am so convinced of this that I was saying to a Communist recently that the whole of psychoanalysis can be incorporated into marxism, but I will never ask Marxists to accept psychoanalysis as an isolated discipline. I will ask them to reintegrate it, while pointing out that, for example, the individual history of a poorly raised individual does nothing, after all, but repeat the history of that family, which is to say the history of society; and that consequently, one can very well, to a certain extent and even quite legitimately, recuperate psychoanalysis as an auxiliary discipline into socioeconomic analysis. But I will never ask Marxists to take psychoanalysis for the truth by claiming that it goes beyond the status of an auxiliary discipline.

MERLEAU-PONTY: In order to incorporate psychoanalysis within marxism, the Marxist would have to begin by taking it seriously, and not devalue it by calling it bourgeois ideology.

SARTRE: It is true that it is bourgeois ideology, but it will no longer be such if it is liberated from the other side. It is bourgeois in its limits and its negations. It can cease to be so, if taken up into a totality.

MERLEAU-PONTY: That's a transubstantiation. We must still begin by recognizing that this bourgeois problematic has touched on something, and that consequently, to the extent that it refuses to recognize the value of some bourgeois endeavors, this theory of ideologies is flawed.

SARTRE: We may always assume that a particular truth can be found in any ideology whatsoever; but if we import it into another ideology, it must be grasped, reappropriated, and integrated. I believe that on this point you would encounter no opposition, at least not among the French intellectual Marxists I've spoken with. We can accept the possibility of reappropriating any particular truth, if it is situated within marxism.

MERLEAU-PONTY: My point is precisely that all this is possible in conversation. We have been doing it for years in our conversations with our Communist countrymen, who are intelligent and agreeable in conversation; but in practice, it's another matter entirely.

SARTRE: All I ask is that instead of striving for the kind of coexistence Merleau-Ponty seems to be calling for, with a common idea here and there, we admit that coexistence can only be a dynamic movement of integration.

CAMPAGNOLO: I must say that a debate is no longer easy after such a closed exchange. You'll excuse me if I'm concerned with bringing us back to certain notions basically familiar to us all.

We should not lose sight, it seems to me, of the immediate object of our research—engagement—and therefore we cannot stop with the examination of political situations which are often susceptible to very different judgments: French politics, Italian Communist Party politics, French Communist Party politics. . . . Independently of what we may think of these political phenomena, we can, I believe, resolve our particular problematic.

I would like to venture a very precise remark concerning the idea that dodecaphony—which is only an example—is not an issue for the five-year plan. Now, through sound reasoning, I could discover—and not only in contemporary thought—that dodecaphony *can* be an issue for the five-year plan. For example, the great constitutions of antiquity accorded high importance to music, from the perspective of political action. But I will not belabor the point. I only wanted to say that it is possible to reach the latter conclusion through sound reasoning.

SILONE: Take military music!

CAMPAGNOLO: Of course, there are all kinds of music. If we entertain a certain system of ideas, it is possible to see the relationships—I do not want to defend them, but they exist—between art and politics; and for my part, I recognize these relationships. We do not need, at least for now, to explore this question further, which is leading us to the criticism of a particular regime. Yet if this question has been raised, it is in order for us to focus our attention on certain problems.

SILONE: It's the problem of the autonomy of art.

CAMPAGNOLO: Yet I will consider this problem of art's autonomy from an entirely different perspective. In my opinion, under no regime—be it liberal or totalitarian—can we propose the radical suppression of censorship. I even believe it is possible, all things considered, to identify censorship with a given juridical order; every juridical order is a form of censorship, and we cannot reject juridical order. It is on this point that I find myself in disagreement with you.

You have quite rightly created a sort of classical opposition between State and society, but by taking these two terms, it seems to me, in a way that is a bit too static.

SILONE: On the contrary, for me it's a matter of a dialectical relationship.

CAMPAGNOLO: This means, therefore, that the State changes in a way different from the way you think, but that it does change, just as society does, and because of society. But we could also say the opposite: that the State makes society change. I am not defending either one of these two conceptions; I only want to avoid our falling into pessimism, because in the end you concluded there was nothing to be done about it, that we would always be the enemies of the State, since the State, by definition, is always the conqueror, and that consequently we will always be on the side of the oppressed. Engagement, according to you, would therefore consist in always being on the side of the defeated.

SILONE: That definition is not the only one, and definitions are always given with reservations.

CAMPAGNOLO: That, by the way, is a constraint quite common to us all. Yet you would not have me spend my life engaging myself with the defeated because it is not necessary to be beaten in order to be in the right. For the moment, if you think this situation will not last, you are perhaps more in the right than I am.

I consider engagement, before all else, to be a positive attitude with regard to the State, an attitude whose goal is to fight against the tendency toward inertia that is the natural tendency of any State. I would like for us to develop a clearer and less pessimistic notion of its function than what you offer, because culture needs the State, just as the State needs culture.

I do not think it useful to conceive engagement solely as loyalty to the exploited and persecuted. Moreover, the identification of the latter with the defeated seems to me unjustified. In the word "exploited" there is already the notion of injustice, as there is in the word "persecuted"; but not necessarily the notion of defeat.

To say that the State is egotistical means nothing, if not that it is of its very nature to be so.

You spoke of sacrifices of the critical spirit. This is a point that, for us, is very important. Do we sacrifice our critical spirit when we adhere to an ideology, to a faith? I don't think so. On the other hand, there is a kind of freedom that is nothing but the will to remain exterior to events, nothing but the rejection of faith. We should pursue this question a bit further, which has more to do with individual experience than with a general law.

I am quite aware of all we have in common. I would simply like to point out again that pessimism is, in a certain sense, the logic of the moment; yet we cannot accentuate or privilege the interpretation Mr. Sartre gives of the link between ideologies and cultures. If we were obliged to conceive cultures simply as the expression of ideologies, it would be very difficult, at least for me, to understand what their integration might mean. To integrate a culture which is logically tied to an ideology would mean to integrate one ideology with another, which, hypothetically, must be excluded. Ideology is never exhaustive, it is never capable of exhausting a culture nor of exhausting human experience; there is always something that escapes it, in spite of all the ideologues' pretentions. This is why, in reality, you can speak of integration. You integrate culture within the human element of ideology, within that which transcends ideology.

To come to the example Mr. Sartre cited, if psychoanalysis expresses a human truth, a universal—I mean a culture that is always in the process of creating itself dynamically—in a sense it depends on an ideology; yet in another sense it transcends it. It is therefore possible that certain elements within this bourgeois doctrine of psychoanalysis coincide perfectly well with a psychological science born of a non-bourgeois ideology, because their meeting takes place not on ideological, but on scientific ground. I believe we can agree on this point.

SARTRE: There is still the question of perspective: from the point of view of Marxist ideology, psychoanalysis will be considered false and abstract, as long as it has not been placed within a Marxist perspective; that is, as long as it has not been subsumed and surpassed. To put it another way, as the Marxists see it, psychoanalysis taken on its own terms can only be considered false, yet they are aware that if taken from another perspective it could prove fruitful. That, in general, is how a Marxist can approach an idea situated on the side of bourgeois ideology and culture.

CAMPAGNOLO: Our perspective here is not necessarily bourgeois. You said this was a bourgeois meeting.

SARTRE: It was Merleau-Ponty who said that.

CAMPAGNOLO: But you insisted you shared his opinion. I must say that this meeting, which we all agreed should take place, does not include only participants of bourgeois origin. In reality, our meeting is neither bourgeois, nor proletarian, nor Marxist, nor anti-Marxist; and I am convinced that it offers the possibility of a continual transcendence of Marxist or non-Marxist ideologies. If we can meet today, it is because we are not tied absolutely to any ideology. This should have been, at the very least, the significance of this meeting. If we were obliged to accept the logic of ideological systems, I am convinced that the feelings of pessimism you demonstrated would be insuperable.

SARTRE: We must be lucid about this. We cannot hope to transcend the two ideologies we're talking about.

CAMPAGNOLO: In fact, we *are* transcending them.

SARTRE: We are not transcending them. There are a certain number of us here who adhere to Marxist ideology and who are open about it. They come here not because they are transcending it, but because they believe it possible to do useful work with men who are not ideologists. But this meeting is not as you described it. In fact, there are non-Marxists, pseudo-Marxists, and Marxists gathered here; and the Marxists have no intention of transcending marxism.

CAMPAGNOLO: It is enough that it be transcended in fact.

SARTRE: There is a crude and insuperable contradiction here, but one which can lead, as I said, to certain kinds of reciprocal integrations. That is all we can ask for, and it is already a lot. That is all I mean to say. I am not advocating pessimism; I only want to set limits to what, in my opinion, we can hope for. We certainly cannot hope that a third ideology, a synthesis, will result from our encounter. We *can* hope, on certain points, for possible integrations.

CAMPAGNOLO: As far as our work here is concerned, we may consider ourselves agreed.

SILONE: Allow me two remarks concerning Sartre's statements. I believe Marx would never have accepted that his method be called ideological. Marx always rejected and was suspicious of the word "ideology." I find a lot of "Trotskyist" abstractions in the way Sartre conceives marxism. His rigid view of a world divided in two baffles me, and now above all, after the thaw. The strength of socialism lies outside of ideologies; it lies in the effective solidarity of workers against the capitalist system, and for a new society. The greatest wrong one can do socialism is to posit it as an ideology. The scientific view of reality changes now with every generation; for example, in the face of psychoanalysis. . . .

SARTRE: In fact, psychoanalysis is condemned by Marxists.

SILONE: I do not see that as being in the interest of socialism. What Sartre has told us is like a foreign language to me. After some forty years' activity in the workers' movement, this is the first time I'm hearing marxism spoken of in a way that's incomprehensible to me. I want two things unequivocally understood. I am and I remain a democratic socialist. As concerns my personal conception of the writer's role, it is so non-exclusive that in the fight against censorship it often happens that I demand freedom for artistic forms quite distinct from my own preferences. I find that even those artistic expressions farthest removed from social reality have the right to express themselves. I am happy to see that, among the Italians present here, we have, for example, the poet Ungaretti,[9] who is certainly very far removed from our political and social preoccupations. I think it would be a sign of impoverishment to want to impose a determinate conception on literary activity. A German poet has said, apropos of the silkworm, that a day may come when human beings have become so brutish they will only love very crude clothing of wool or hemp, but the silkworm will continue to spin silk. I would like to see respect for the artist who continues to create beautiful things even if, for the moment, we insist we don't need them.

CAMPAGNOLO: I would like to take up the image of the silkworm and of the cocoon. I do not believe the artist or the writer is like the silkworm. The latter encloses itself within its cocoon because it is not sociable. As for ourselves, we are the bearers of a social responsibility, and we cannot isolate ourselves if we would accomplish our task. Fables may be pretty, but they can also be dangerous.

It may be that we're here to defend the individual who refuses to assume his social responsibility; we would then be doing him a free service. Normal people can walk, and yet we don't do away with those who no longer have use of their legs. In the moral sphere, there exists a certain responsibility, and this moral responsibility can, at certain historical moments, become a juridical responsibility.

You are right to lean as far as you can toward this social magnanimity, which you so strongly desire, and in that I am wholly with you. I understand your position; but in order to clarify our situation, and above all to understand situations different from our own, where engagement has perhaps become habitual, we must necessarily push our analysis further.

SILONE: Well, in pushing it further, I said that the republic where poets commit suicide is to be condemned.

CAMPAGNOLO: Of course, that must not be allowed to happen, but in order to stop it, we must also assume *our* responsibility. You can dream of the republic of your choice, or of an empire—that of Augustus, for example. But since there were some great poets under Augustus, it is indisputable that the conditions for them existed. What is important for us, in our particular historical conditions, is to know how we can engage ourselves. For you, perhaps, the ideal is a republic where artists live like silkworms. But the silkworm is a luxury in society, as Virgil and Horace were. Is this silkworm-existence possible at present? That is the question. Your behavior, your adherence to our society, seem to me proof that you believe in the responsibility of the cultured man.

SILONE: I have only been doing literary criticism.

CAMPAGNOLO: But you're an engaged writer, in the sense that our society understands this term. You spoke of your forty years of political activity. In my view you represent the very model of the engaged writer, and not because you've sought to highlight your ideas through your books to make them effective; you could have written very different novels, and you would have been just as engaged, through your behavior. Within certain conditions, it is possible to write hermetic poems and still be engaged. I am not speaking of the engagement produced through a work, but of the engagement of the cultured artist: a conscious, voluntary political engagement. Perhaps there remains a certain distance between our positions on this question. Yet it would still be useful to clarify this distance so as to pursue our discussion.

SARTRE: I believe the distance between ourselves and our friend Silone is that between feelings and ideas. He spoke mostly of feelings. It's fine that there's a sentimental representative among us. But it's confusing us somewhat, and I would like to return to some very precise issues. I would like, for example, to ask that we revive the ensemble of questions that have been asked since the beginning of this session, and that we ask our Soviet friends for their observations. Otherwise we'll just be conversing among ourselves.

[Mr. Ponti suggests the Soviet participants open the discussion at the next session, once they have familiarized themselves with the typed translations of previous statements].

* * *

FEDIN[10] *(translated from Russian)*: Can we accept the idea that within any given social structure, the rupture between State and society is always the same? What should artists do when they see that the interests of the State and those of society approach each other, and even sometimes coincide? It's a very interesting question Mr. Silone has asked. I am not quite ready to discuss it at the moment, but I will do so tomorrow. I would like to reiterate two things. First, that writers, like all cultured men, must before all else be honest with themselves as concerns their ideas on the human condition. Writers are, if you will, responsible to the society to which they dedicate their work. They are responsible for the development of the society in which they live. Consequently, they must create forms that are accessible to the society and the social milieu that surrounds them and sustains their work. The necessary combination of these two responsibilities—the responsibility to oneself and the responsibility to society, for which and within which they create—is the fundamental directive for all writers' activities. This bond with reality is a concrete fact for each writer. There is an abstract form of art, which we spoke of today, but it belongs to a more or less exceptional domain. A writer cannot live without being tied to the concrete, just as a fish cannot live without water. I am always ready to condemn those republics where poets commit suicide, but I believe these suicides take place in all republics. We would have to see what the structural conditions are that precipitate suicide, and it *is* a question of determinate social structures. In any case, we must seek to create conditions such that a poet is *not* constrained to commit suicide.

POLEVOI[11] *(translated from Russian)*: I would like to make just one small point. Being invited guests, we do not want to establish our own rules here, but we would like it to be noted that once we abandon the domain of culture in order to enter into political discussion, we run the risk of indefinitely prolonging the discussion without attaining any result. There have been discussions between East and West, on other topics, which have led nowhere, and I would not like for this to be the fate of the present meeting. I was recently in the United States, where there were a great number of discussions, even on television, in front of five million viewers; but we carefully avoided all political discussion. Political discussions, as lively as they are, do not force people to change their ideas. But if we remain within the domain of culture, I believe we can genuinely encounter each other. Discussions on culture offer many opportunities for the enrichment of culture and for finding common ground.

LEVI:[12] I would like to respond to Mr. Polevoi by saying I am certain we will encounter each other, and not only as concerns cultural views, since we are already gathered around this table. In my opinion, we should not even search for common ground; we have this already, and it is thanks to it that we have come from very different countries, with very different ideologies; but we are already starting from common ground, and we will have no difficulty encountering each other, on condition that we do not limit our discussion to ideological or political problems, at least not chronically. I do not believe that our meeting-point has to be an ideological accord, or the idea of engagement or of ideology within culture, or anything of the sort, although these are admittedly interesting issues and we have rightly opened this discussion with them. Nor do I believe it serves our purpose to know whether our culture, from the sentimental point of view, is the culture of the oppressed and defeated. I would even say, to the contrary, that our culture is a culture of victors, because it is the poor person's culture, that is, the culture of those who are coming into existence for the first time, who are entering history for the first time. It is true, I believe, that culture can be defined as the invention of truth. This is the point that affects us, that creates an initial unity between us, and which even creates new historical conditions. Because in all the countries of the world, the new historical fact according to which we as cultured men must orient ourselves is the coming into being of great masses of new men. That is what is constantly creating new forms of culture. That is what creates great historical movements, such as the European Resistance, the awakening of the peasantry, etc. For us, becoming aware of this new reality is the mission of culture, which should allow us to recognize the unity of all cultured men. This is a new stage we must strive to attain.

PIOVENE:[13] I would like to ask just one question: I would like to know what difference there is between a discussion on ideology and a discussion on culture. I haven't quite grasped the difference.

IWASZKIEWICZ:[14] I have hesitated to speak on the subject of engagement, due to the fairly unique position I'm in. Yet I do not think we can make an issue of my particular case. I am a writer with a thoroughly bourgeois background, living and working in a socialist State. I am not a Marxist. You have no doubt read an anecdote, which was repeated in all the Western papers, on the supposed conversation—which never took place—between Queen Elizabeth and me in a Warsaw church, where incidentally I did not happen to be on this day of the Ascension (I will not kneel at this point), and where the Queen asks me: "Are you Catholic?" And I answer: "I believe, but I don't practice." "In that case, you're a Marxist?" "No, I do not believe in it, but I practice it."

I meant to say by this that my idea of engagement corresponds perfectly with the definition Merleau-Ponty proposed. I regard every work of art written for humanity—which also allows us to better understand life and the meaning of life—to be already an engagement. I know that my works, which do not reflect any philosophy or ideology, are read by millions and millions of new men—I am thinking here of those Carlo Levi spoke of—and that they make my life easier . . . perhaps not in terms of comprehension but in terms of the example I cited yesterday to my friend Sartre. A Polish Communist recounts in his memoirs that, in the prisons, when there were very sick men who could not be comforted, they were read Goethe's poems because all forms of beauty make life easier and help human beings attain a goal common to us all. To tell the truth, the difference that exists between us comes from the different paths we choose. We are always thinking of humanity, of the reader. And the writer who does not think about the reader is no writer at all. You cited the example of Mr. Ungaretti, but he is no "silkworm." His verses are read; he is a great poet, and a great poet is obviously engaged for the betterment of the human lot. That is what is important and what is common to us all. When I write, when I work in my country, when I edit an article for a review, I am always thinking of building a better life; that is my engagement. All writers should feel that their engagement in life, in the construction of life, in the amelioration of life, is their most important task. In the present historical conditions, it has become easier to express ourselves—through fine books, beautiful forms, good thoughts, and aesthetics—concerning this engagement.

SARTRE: In distinguishing between ideology and culture I wanted to draw attention to a facile optimism which would consist in believing that culture is simply a sum of beautiful books, scientific truths, and attempts at understanding. I believe that, whether Marxist or not, we would all agree in supposing that in reality there is a unity within the ensemble of phenomena, that they mutually condition each other and are conditioned in one way or another by the social ensemble—that is, by the socioeconomic regime. Consequently, as autonomous as they may be, we can discover within these phenomena traces of the society in which they exist. I have not the least intention of condemning a book or an idea by denouncing its bourgeois traits, for example, or by stressing its adherence to a world where the bourgeoisie represents the ruling element; no more, by the way, than I will condemn or approve an idea *a priori* on the pretext that it belongs to the Soviet world. I only mean to say that cultures are also ideological and that our problem is more complicated than it seems. It is not a matter of bringing people of good will together around two great masses of works in order to look for what may be considered common to them. In reality, it is a matter of seeing how, by way of these two ideologies—which, generally speaking, are mutually exclusive, even though the Marxist ideology is systematic and well-defined and the other is much more diffuse—we can come to understand each other, we who are more or less pulled about between these two ideologies. That is a slightly different problem.

In my opinion, we must not so much seek a genuine accord as see to what extent we can understand and accept each other's positions. For example, I like very much what our friend Spender writes. I do not agree with the position he expresses, but it doesn't bother me; I accept it just as he can perhaps accept mine. It seems to me that if we and our Soviet colleagues achieve analogous results, we will have made real progress. But we cannot hope to achieve actual unity.

BERNAL:[15] I would like to ask Mr. Polevoi a question. I understood him to be asking that we not discuss politics and that we separate ideologies from culture. But is he referring to politics or ideologies? Does he object to our discussing ideologies?

POLEVOI (*translated from Russian*): Ideology is naturally a part of culture, and I would like to avoid a political discussion concerning our conceptions of the world.

BERNAL: For us, a conception of the world *is* ideology. But discussing the actual state of the world and its conflicts is doing politics. Isn't that so? And is that what you want to avoid?

POLEVOI *(translated from Russian)*: It is the application of ideology to politics that I would like to see avoided in this discussion.

BERNAL: I asked for this explanation because Mr. Sartre's statement is surely going to greatly complicate our task, at least as concerns the first part of what I would like to say. Most of us seem to accept the idea of a solidarity between culture and the social milieu. This solidarity is therefore a very powerful idea, which involves the concept of engagement and the responsibility of culture. We can either be aware of this connection or not. But we have to recognize that in the past, and even now, a great number of artists, writers, and men of culture, as well as those of science, have too much ignored it. This is a point about which Marx has taught us more than anyone: as soon as the awareness of this situation manifests itself, a new responsibility is born—not the responsibility to accept such and such an explication of this relation, but to realize that this relation exists and to investigate what its nature is and how it affects our own works. If we believe there are still writers and other cultured men who are not yet conscious, we also admit that, for ourselves and for the future, this consciousness must become much more widespread. I also want to explain the danger I see in raising this lack of consciousness to the status of a law, the law of the artist's freedom, as Mr. Silone did. This freedom is an evasion. Theology speaks of absolute ignorance: something may warrant your attention, but you don't know of it and don't have the means for knowing of it; your ignorance therefore carries no responsibility with it. Yet there is a partial ignorance, according to which one says: I have no knowledge of this particular thing, and I will make no effort to know about it. One of the world's greatest intellectuals said to me one day: "I don't know anything about political issues; I don't want to know anything about them; and if I don't know anything about them, I don't see what effect they can have on me." This is a fairly common attitude. This sort of wilful rejection of engagement is partially responsible for this provisional state, for this state of transition we're in.

In the past, this ignorance was absolute. Perhaps in a somewhat distant future, it will no longer exist. For the moment, certain societies view this consciousness of the relations between culture and society in one way, and others view it differently. But we all have the duty to investigate it, because we do not stay enclosed within an absolute freedom; we associate ourselves with all the social forces that exist in dependence on established orders. Wanting to know only what one wants to know is to refuse this responsibility.

I come now to the point that seems to me most important, which was raised by Carlo Levi. There is something in his attitude that seems to me in need of clarification. The question arises about the duty of associating oneself with what is being created that is both new and good. Because culture is not limited to art; it is society as a whole that should be a work of art. This work in all its aspects, even its material ones, must be elaborated further. Those who grow wheat also accomplish a cultural work on the material level. We live in a more absurd world than the one prior to 1914, because to tell the truth, we are suffering today from completely avoidable evils, and we have at our disposal much greater potentialities than at the time of our youth. The difficulty, for us, is to know how to associate ourselves with constructive projects within the conditions provoked by the Cold War. The Cold War is a war like any other, a war that kills, even if its death toll is not as high as that of other wars. I am thinking now of what happened in China and in Greece, where in fact all of this was avoidable.

It is also the responsibility of the cultured to demand that cultural and scientific relations be possible between all people of all nations.

Now, we must admit that we could have done more in the present situation than we have done up to this point. That is our specific task. If writers are attentive to all that surrounds them, if they assume their task in full awareness of the state of the world and of the society they live in, then we will see the results of their engagement. There is certainly a difference between society and the State, but it seems to me unnecessary to emphasize this opposition. It is up to us to create conditions such that the State cannot restrict the freedoms of society.

CAMPAGNOLO: Mr. Bernal has certainly clarified the idea of the artist's freedom. Too often, we confuse the artist's freedom with a lack of awareness, that is, with the idea that the artist is not sufficiently aware of how much the pressure of concrete situations influences him and of how much he influences these situations. For my part, I would consider it very profitable for us to discuss Mr. Bernal's statements.

Mr. Polevoi made it known that, as an invited guest, he did not want to suggest the rules for conducting these discussions. I'm sorry to hear that since we all have an equal right to propose a more useful format here.

You proceeded, Mr. Polevoi, to stress that we could easily reach agreement when the discussion only concerned strictly cultural subjects, such as the writer's activity. But here, it is very difficult for us to restrict ourselves to questions of that order, questions which would too severely limit what we understand by culture. Our meeting does not take for its only theme the writer's activity as such; we will necessarily be obliged to speak of political and ideological issues. Certainly—and in this I share Mr. Silone's opinion—we do not have to pass judgment on the political situation, but we will be led by our very discussions on the present state of culture to consider, in a general way, our political experiences.

VERCORS:[16]   I would like not to enlarge but rather to restrict the discussion, by specifying a certain form of engagement and presenting another way of grasping this notion.

I have asked myself this question: If I am, by virtue of my reputation as a writer and a cultured man, generally in a position to influence events; if what I write and say has a public and social value, what would my spiritual and concrete position be before an individual injustice (for example, the Dreyfus affair) or a social injustice (for example, the oppression of a minority)? For some, the question will take the following form: Should I keep silent in order to preserve my intellectual purity or should I intervene, at the risk of endangering this purity, of being corrupted by my action and by the reactions that will follow? For others, the question will be: What will my position have to be, if I'm afraid my intervention will compromise or even endanger the institutions I adhere to by conviction?

I do not believe I'm restricting the notion of engagement here, because such questions are at the heart of any political engagement.

SPENDER: I'm afraid that what Mr. Vercors is saying does not involve the engagement of his whole being. If, in fact, you want to protest an injustice, you write newspaper articles, but it is very doubtful that you would be acting simply as a writer then. You are acting as any other citizen would. As a writer you're affected by any event, unjust or not, and that must be felt in your works. The simple fact of writing is an act of engagement, and you have to know you're doing what you can, and not grasp at the unattainable. This awareness is already an act that testifies to the freedom of the writer and the artist.

SARTRE: You're right, if you consider the newspaper article or the novel as a kind of additional, or moral, duty. But if you are passionate, if you have as much passion for a cause as you would have for the subject of a novel, there is no reason—and the proof of this is that there are political pamphlets, in French literature, for example, that are masterpieces—there is no reason why you cannot do your best work for this cause. If you are engaged, as a human being, to the point of being deeply affected by injustice, then you are able, as a writer, to do valuable work. It is precisely because you begin by deciding, as a writer, to be withdrawn from the company of people, that one day when you become indignant at something, but only feebly, you can ask yourself about fulfilling a moral duty. And your work will be bad.

SPENDER: I am often reproached for not having written enough on the subject of the Spanish Civil War. What I reproach myself for personally is not having been capable, in fact, of sufficiently exteriorizing the Spanish Civil War. But perhaps I was incapable of speaking about this experience and of what I learned of fear.

PRYCE-JONES:[17]   The question of the cultured man's engagement is evaluated very differently in different countries. In England, for example, the life of the cultured is a bit muted; it involves no engagement in political life, no ideological stance. English writers may think they hold themselves more aloof from events than writers elsewhere, but they believe they are doing so voluntarily. If they write poems, they may consider themselves pure writers, inhabiting an ivory tower. And this is perhaps the reason why many of the English I meet, and above all English writers with a sharp conscience, like my friend Mr. Spender, suffer somewhat, at times, from the belief that they are not sufficiently engaged. I believe that, for twenty years now, English writers, who do not write political pamphlets voluntarily, have nevertheless been engaged at heart; but it is a question of their discovering the form of this engagement. In England, our case is very different from that of intellectuals in other countries. For us, the most important thing is first to be honest with ourselves, which has always been difficult for some of us, and then to be right on top of current events. It is this, I believe, that constitutes engagement.

PIOVENE: I would like to ask Mr. Bernal a specific question. If we admit that the artist must be fully, consciously engaged, we can also admit that an overly abstract conception of freedom must be rejected. But in that case, another problem arises: Who can judge whether artists are truly conscious or truly engaged? I see a difficulty there.

BERNAL: Since the writer addresses himself to the public, it is the public who judges. After all, the writer is someone submitted to the public's judgment, a judgment that manifests itself either in criticism or in the greater or lesser success of books. It is obvious that writers who push their own books too hard are poorly engaged. But I only wanted to speak of an internal judgment, that of conscience, and not some tribunal that would evaluate the degree of engagement.

I would now like to take up the question Mr. Spender raised: Should writers—or any intellectuals, I would add—turn away from their own work for the sake of other activities? In my opinion, there is no ready-made response to this question. It is not possible to choose here: or rather, writers have already made their choice, by beginning a career in letters. Certainly, talent must be given the opportunity to fully manifest itself. Yet the writer also has the possibility of changing that career. One can also reject the world. And ultimately, there is also a third solution, the most difficult one, which consists in blending works having both a cultural and a social orientation. I am aware that this is not an easy enterprise.

The problem is to make it such that the social works and the personal works have a kind of unity. In another domain, we note a difficulty of the same nature between those sciences that are useful to humanity and those that are interesting in and of themselves. I believe it possible, by a wilful effort, to see where certain works lead that in appearance are not directly useful, but which nevertheless can actually lead to important results. This is certainly the case with literature. Writers should dedicate their whole lives to this kind of effort. A sufficient number of examples prove that good writers have always been involved in the great movements of their time. There has been too much large-scale suffering in recent years, which has weighed too heavily on the world, for us to speak of a desire to avoid our fellow men. This is why I can discern symptoms within English literature of a desire to abandon an evasive attitude and to re-engage in current events. In any case, for we practitioners of science, this effort on the part of people of different cultures yields a greater return than ever before.

MERLEAU-PONTY: I spoke of engagement, and of the engagement I would consider worthwhile, without thinking that in rejecting the pessimistic solution I was rejecting engagement as a whole. But I believe, as Mr. Campagnolo does, that there is not only a factual engagement, tied to the situation in which we find ourselves, but a voluntary reappropriation of this situation by us, and that engagement adds to what is a factual situation. I do not want to deny this, just the opposite.

In order to quickly clarify these ideas, a good example of an engaged book is Stendhal's *Lucien Leuwen.* You know that when Gide returned to Paris after the war, his antipathy for engagement was so great that he repudiated the entire second half of his book. The first half is a question of love, and the second, of the electoral campaign at Caen. And Gide said that from that point on Stendhal's novel was boring: "It wants to get us engaged, and that is why it's boring." It is my impression that general opinion holds the second half of *Lucien Leuwen* very highly. Incidentally, it is Stendhal himself who gives it this value, in a passage where Lucien Leuwen says to himself: "What am I? Who have I had to do with up 'til now? [Lucien Leuwen is a young man of twenty-two or twenty-three.] I have been involved with my horse, and so long as I have been involved only with my horse, even if I am a good horseman, I have not begun to live; I am still only a 'perhaps'; I will be something other than a 'perhaps' when I have been involved with men and not just with a horse."

Engagement is the coming into relation with others; and engagement succeeds when, in the course of this engagement with others, we come to extract from it a formula for living with them. In saying that engagement does not put an end to autonomy, I want to emphasize that this work must be done without adhering to an exterior discipline. If Malraux's *Espoir* is an engaged book, it is to the extent that within the book we constantly sense Malraux's hesitations, what disturbs him about the political movement he's associated with. One can say this book is not effective except when it is ambiguous, and that if it ceased being ambiguous, it would at once cease being effective and engaged.

It was not a question for me, in justifying literature about bees, of reducing literature to bees; I chose this limit-case in order to say that even such literature could have something to say about relations with others. It seems to me that a healthy conception of engagement is that within which autonomy is not separated from relations with others and all that these imply. From the moment where, on the other hand, you are told, "You will act and be involved in life" (and therefore you must lie or keep silent); or: "You will be a writer, and nothing else," then there is no longer any solution for the cultured person.

SARTRE: I would like to posit a limit-case which is opposed to that of Merleau-Ponty, because I am in complete agreement with what he just stated, insofar as he calls himself, as Stendhal did, a writer who is in a bourgeois society and who benefits from this semi-freedom we all enjoy. Someone just said—and we all agreed—that it was a matter here of contributing to the construction of the kind of State or society where the writer would be free. The State where the writer is free is the State where everyone is free, because we cannot conceive of a State where the writer is free and others aren't. Such a State does not exist. And we may suppose that in China or Russia, writers think that such a State is in the process of being built. What must writers be in this case, in a society they think is in the process of constructing the freedom of humanity, and thus the freedom of the writer—not their own personal freedom, since they'll die before having seen it, but the freedom of art and of the writer at some future time? What materialism means, what it teaches us, is that it is difficult to construct such a society; that the latter is not simply constructed by revolution but also by an immense ulterior labor.

To illustrate that the writer's convictions in these other countries are effectively different than our own, this is what was happening in China as I was leaving there: national education officials were forcefully soliciting writers to write children's stories. It's obvious that if the French newspapers had learned of this, they would have ridiculed the Chinese government and Chinese literature: "Can you imagine André Malraux," they would have said, "forced to write a children's story!" I admit, by the way, that if someone asked me to write a children's story, I would be very embarrassed. But let's consider the situation such as it is: here you have people who are responsible for culture and who are considered cultured, who are participating in a great cultural movement that is creating future readers for them and which, in addition, helps to free people, because they are learning to read Chinese. They learn with some difficulty, and since there are not yet enough professors and administrators, it is also expensive. The Chinese teach each other to read, and the children need reading manuals and storybooks, and they also need to be helped along in the reading of a certain number of books that will be appropriate for their age for years to come. We in the West have an ample supply of children's books; we don't have the problem. Would you consider it the duty of all writers, who are sustained by a cultural movement and interested in seeing culture develop, to contribute, even if it is not at all within their specialty, to the development of culture and literature by conforming as best they could to this directive? Or do you think that to do so destroys their personal responsibility and their personal value as writers? There you have a problem that seems to be a limit-case, like the one Merleau-Ponty posited apropos of *Lucien Leuwen*, and which, I think, deserves a response because it is a question here of external determination. On the one hand, they do not write children's stories because of some internal need; and, on the other hand, their work is located within a cultural movement they can at best simply accept and within which they can only deplete their energies. If I pose this problem, it is because we must always keep in mind in our discussions here the differences between states that want to create a civilization of the masses and states like our own, where the masses have not yet reached the stage where they can truly benefit from literature, even though they are beginning.

RISTIĆ:[18]   I will begin by responding to Sartre's question. First, as a writer, I firmly believe one can do nothing worthwhile on command, including a work written for children, which, if it is to be a literary work and not simply a reading manual, cannot be effective if it is done on command.

I should also excuse myself here for not being able to completely avoid politics, or propaganda, and I say this frankly, because I'm aware of not being able to do so. It might profit this discussion to introduce two more notions, which I'll take from two titles by Merleau-Ponty. One of his books is called, if I'm not mistaken, *Humanism and Terror*; the other is called *Adventures of the Dialectic*. I do not believe we've talked about humanism, and I will not say we haven't spoken of dialectic, but aside from one remark by Mr. Campagnolo, we have not sufficiently profited from the spirit of dialectic. It can be dangerous to posit certain antinomies in a way that's too absolute. For example, at the beginning of his statement, Mr. Merleau-Ponty spoke of the political interpretation of the thaw—and perhaps I'm over-simplifying here—but the dilemma is as follows: either there is a movement toward parliamentary reform or toward a renewal of dictatorship in another form. In my opinion, this is to pose the question in terms that are too absolute, because in the development of social life, in the complexity of this development, things are not distinguished in such a clear-cut manner. Furthermore, when speaking of the philosophical meaning of the thaw,

Mr. Merleau-Ponty asked this question: Can we return to internal criteria or must we hold to external criteria? Someone already said it's impossible to entirely separate these two aspects of critique, to oppose these two criteriological orders, since on the concrete level it is a matter of a kind of synthesis.

MERLEAU-PONTY: It takes two terms to create a synthesis. All I said was that we must not disqualify the internal criteria.

RISTIĆ: I will not be so brash as to remind you what dialectic is. Two terms can be involved in a non-dialectical manner; they can also be involved in a dialectical manner. All I meant is that it is not a question here of an irreducible antinomy nor of an entirely real one. I believe Mr. Bernal has also spoken of an apparent contradiction.

As concerns the question of engagement, we would also have to ask where the cultured man's engagement comes from. Because ultimately, we cannot say a priori that the cultured man is an engaged man. This is a complex problem that can be taken from a sociological, political, moral, psychological, etc., point of view. What is the motivation, what is the source of the modern cultured man's engagement? If I remember rightly, in England they called the years between 1930 and the Second World War the "pink decade." It was so named because a great number of intellectuals, who had vague liberal ideas, were focused in a more precise fashion during these years, in a social and political fashion, and for a very simple reason: because they noticed a danger that every cultured human being felt. This engagement, which in a certain sense can be identified with a political orientation—let us say leftist, or in any case anti-fascist—was both a defensive and a rebellious attitude. And Mr. Sartre has done well to point out a difference between these forms of engagement.

Poets can feel rebellious without quite knowing why . . . to be in violent opposition to the reigning ideas surrounding them. . . . After the First World War, a number of poets and artists expressed their opposition in very different artistic forms: surrealism, modernism, etc. Some of them were thereby drawn toward a political orientation and thus toward a social and political engagement. To simplify things, we can say they were rebelling, to begin with, against certain symptoms, against certain elements in the superstructure; and that, through a more or less conscious analysis of their feelings of rebellion and of the object of their rebellion, they came to realize they were revolting against consequences and not against causes. They therefore, by themselves, consciously analyzed or directed their revolt, without yet submitting to any word of command from the party or the system. This entire process has always had as its guiding theme the idea of freedom, which becomes more and more concrete for those who seek it in a more and more conscious manner. They look for ways to attain it. They realize that they will never get there alone nor by purely idealistic or anarchistic means and that they must consequently *share* the battle for freedom which, during the years when fascism menaced Europe and even more so during the years when fascism occupied Europe, had taken a very patent and clear form for all intellectuals: the form of the battle against Nazism.

In general, this fight for a materially founded freedom continues. With respect to the artist's engagement and obligations, in my country (excuse me for seeming to propagandize, but in the end I simply cannot avoid it, and you know that I consider my country as a country where a new life, socialism, is being created) we are trying to find the means that will best allow us to attain that. In our country, there is no possibility of officials demanding of writers in general that they write children's books or social novels extolling the socialist edifice or describing the construction of a public center, all the while explaining what it means to have worker-organized enterprises. It is quite natural, even normal, for our political leaders to applaud writers, art, and literature, and to help them along; but I assure you they would never directly ask writers to create made-to-order works of art.

I believe that in each country where an effort is being made to create a new life, there are enough conscious, cultured men who have, in one way or another, come to the conclusion that to participate in this effort is to their own benefit, precisely because they are men of culture. This benefit is perhaps not immediate, but it is still in our interests to collaborate on this construction, to care about it, and to be empassioned for it. And it is natural, at least in terms of what I see practiced at home, that there be writers who force themselves to participate in this work, because it corresponds to their position as writers, because it is not in opposition to their integrity as writers or to their aesthetic ideas. It is not necessary to demand this effort of all writers.

SARTRE: Because you have lots of writers and few Yugoslavians; but in China, there are six hundred million Chinese, and very few writers.

RISTIĆ: Among these six hundred million, the chances are much higher, statistically, of finding writers who write for children.

SARTRE: There are very few Chinese writers.

RISTIĆ: I am not sure writers can be created artificially, even for children, or above all for children.

SARTRE: It is not necessarily true that one doesn't write well on command. That's an illusion of our bourgeois epoch, because the writer wanted to guard his independence. But the entire classical period, and even the Renaissance period, is made up of works of art executed on demand.

Given the present state of things, asking a Chinese writer to write a children's story does not seem to attack his or her freedom.

MERLEAU-PONTY: Valéry wrote when his editor asked him for something. An editor is a much less respectable authority than a chief of state.

RISTIĆ: Yes, but he wrote for this editor what he, Valéry, wanted to write; there was an accord between Valéry's intellectual need to write something and the demand.

VERCORS: I believe we can very well satisfy a demand tied to the domain of our habitual activity. You will excuse me for citing my own case—not my case as a writer but as someone who submits to certain imperatives of bourgeois society. Writers who want to earn a living simply by writing can find themselves in a situation that obliges them to write things they do not feel like writing; they will be in the same situation as if they had received a command from the State or from an editor. But writers can also try to do something that allows them to write freely. Personally, this is what I did a few years ago; when I did not want to write any more pages I didn't feel the need to write. I returned to the art of drawing, and I created a small studio for art reproduction. I did not at all feel that this activity affected my integrity as a writer. Just as I paid a tax on supplemental income in order to earn my living, I think that writers in China believe in paying a "tax" for the construction of the country when they give part of their time to writing works ordered by the government. These works will not have the value of those done spontaneously, but they'll be good enough to participate in the necessary production of a great number of children's books. I see no antinomy there.

MERLEAU-PONTY: I will first respond to Sartre's very direct question. If I were Chinese and were asked to write a children's book, I would most certainly accept, because that would not stifle me as a writer. But if I were asked to suppress myself in my writing, that is, to write books wherein I would not say what I know to be true, wherein I would only say a small fraction of what I know to be true, I would refuse, if I were courageous enough. Why, you may ask? Because we are assuming that this society in the process of being constructed more than deserves my personal sacrifice. The issue is to know whether we can construct a mass society by such means. In reality, it seems to me the example cited is a limit-case, the case of a mass society which is the very model of an underdeveloped society, corresponding more or less to Mr. Fedin's formula, in which State and society are one. More precisely, there is as yet no society there, there is only a State in the process of constructing itself. Under these conditions, I find it absolutely defensible that politics should utilize culture, but I do not see why one would see in this the definition of culture and of the writer's function, nor why a writer who lives in an old society would take as a canon of culture what is after all just an expedient.

SARTRE: I did not want to speak of canons, but only to demonstrate that we are faced with problems which are not our own, which do not affect our own writers, but which are nevertheless concrete problems. If we had to speak of China here, we should have spoken with respect to its problem as an underdeveloped society, economically and culturally. Consequently, there are a great number of problems associated with the writer, but which we do not address because, in general, we speak of the writer because of what most of us are in bourgeois society, or in Poland, or in the U.S.S.R., enjoying a head start, living in a country with a certain level of cultural and economic development. Yet this level has been attained at the cost of a thousand sacrifices, which posed problems similar to the ones which face China today.

MERLEAU-PONTY: Yet in China the transformation of society has been effected in a few decades. The issue is to know whether they can attain, in a period of a few decades, a result comparable to that achieved by the passive history we've come through.

SARTRE: Yes, they have farther to go. But ultimately, perhaps they must go through this period.

BERNAL: It seems strange to me that we're speaking of the Chinese people in this way, when in fact the great majority of the population in our countries, or at least in England, do not read literature at all. The real writers write for a certain elite and not for the millions. The problem is much simpler than that: to find a way to allow writers in the old countries to reach their own people.

CAMPAGNOLO: We are talking about two different things here, without properly distinguishing them. When we reached the problem of engagement, we returned numerous times to the idea that it is not the cultured man who should be engaged, but the work; this, in my opinion, is a mistake. For me, cultured men can and must be engaged, but they cannot engage their work. In effect, cultured men can engage themselves politically in the name of culture, and for culture, but they are not in a position to turn their engagement into a performance. Yet they can, of course, feel an obligation to do so. In China, writing a children's book may be an expression of a cultured man's engagement, but what results from it? If people feel the need to be engaged as writers, that means they want to work so that their art produces a truly worthwhile result. It is more or less at their own bidding that the work takes on a specific direction.

We must distinguish between the engagement that manifests itself in the form of a rebellion and the engagement that can be understood through the expressions "engagement for culture" or "in favor of culture."

Of course, one can execute works of great worth on command, but only on condition that the command arrives at the right moment and coincides with what the artist or writer understands by engagement. And this was proven during those periods when society flourished under favorable conditions; while in moments of crisis, as is the case in China and in our own countries, the engagement we can ask of the cultured man does not consist in writing valuable works, but in taking part directly in political life, with a particular attitude, and in lending support to the party and the country.

That is, of course, a political act, but the cultured man's engagement is a political force that tends to transcend settled circumstances. This engagement is not without risks. We've witnessed the example of Soviet intellectuals. Mr. Bernal spoke of this problem: Do we have to carry out scientific research according to the theories suggested by the political regimes of our respective countries, or should we equally accept theories coming from other countries? You know that in the U.S.S.R., it has finally been recognized that, in the scientific domain, one cannot ask even the scientist who is most convinced of the excellence of the Soviet regime to accept a scientific theory simply because the regime prefers it. An intellectual can thus be a perfect Marxist and at the same time claim intellectual freedom.

SPENDER: The danger of this discussion lies in posing problems of imagination as if they were problems of knowledge. It's true we can know things, but not yet true that the things we know can be imagined; and I concur fully with Mr. Bernal when he reproaches writers for not being sufficiently aware of events. But when artists are forced to write, I do not see how they can transform the object of their knowledge into imaginative terms. The poet Shelley formulated this problem very well: we must, in his view, *imagine* certain truths. But imagining truths has more to do with a poet's own rationality than with a duty that can be imposed on him. As concerns the stories for Chinese children, we have to remember that these writers must please not only the children but also the Chinese government.

—Trans. by Jeffrey Gaines.

5

◆

Phenomenology and Analytic Philosophy (1960)

R. P. VAN BREDA: During a private conversation Professor Ryle has reproached me amicably for reading Husserl too assiduously.[1] I agree that this is "my greatest fault." However I am obliged professionally to do so, if only to correct the galley-proofs. You know that it is not the accepted fashion to read an author attentively. I know, on the other hand, of the remarkable study that Mr. Ryle has devoted to Husserl in the journal that he edits. All this cannot keep me from returning his compliment and reproaching him, in turn, for not having *sufficiently* read his Husserl.

In spite of all that I know of the gulf that separates Anglo-Saxon philosophers from the continent, I am unable to hide my surprise at having heard Mr. Ryle, again just now, reduce Husserlian philosophy to a philosophy of Platonic essences. I believe that the present state of Husserl studies, without mentioning the unpublished texts to which we have referred in our debates, do not any longer permit this reduction of Husserlian phenomenology to a simply eidetic philosophy, above all, eidetic in the sense of Plato.

That Husserl otherwise lacked humor, above all, in his writings I do not doubt for an instant; I have paid dearly to learn this. But for you to contend that he was completely ignorant of the sciences of his time, I find this an astounding assertion. Husserl received his doctorate in mathematics in 1882—it seems to me that Mr. Ryle could not be ignorant of this. The most intimate frequenters of Husserl's home both at Halle and at Göttingen were well-informed scholars: for example, Georg Cantor and David Hilbert. It was at the end of a lecture by Husserl at Göttingen that Hilbert proposed his famous idea of a *Definitheit*, although he was obliged to correct it afterwards. Max Planck was also one of those who came regularly to his door. To the end of his days, Husserl maintained a voluminous correspondence with men of science. Obviously, he was not the beneficiary of the distinguished privilege of living within the community of a "college," because in Germany, as everyone knows, this institution does not exist. But on the other hand, he met and was engaged with many scholars who were not philosophers. I think he is not the only one to have defended a certain priority for philosophy; even in the Anglo world certain thinkers have defended this thesis. In this matter as well he has an illustrious predecessor, namely, Aristotle. I don't think anyone would dream of ridiculing the Stagirite by referring to him as "Führer."

As to the Logical Investigations, all that you said of it in your otherwise remarkable analysis of the importance of the verb in the sentence shows that this problem had caught the attention of Husserl before 1900. A notable part of his Investigations was devoted to distinguishing this function of the verb from other functions of the parts of the sentence. One also finds in his work the incipient form, perhaps erroneously conceived, of a philosophy of Sachverhalt, which one finds again in Wittgenstein. He is not as unconscious of these problems as you say.

I know that you did not want to recapitulate the history of logic in continental Europe within your presentation, but all the same, one cannot ignore that the circle at Vienna was born in Vienna, and that around this time—which was also that of Russell and Whitehead—philosophers were enormously occupied with logic in Austria and other continental locations. This occurred less in France, where human mortality seems to be dead set against those who would construct a mathematical logic; but one could, all the same, cite Couturat, Cavaillès, not to mention Duhem and Poincaré. There is as well a school of logicians in Holland, Belgium, and Switzerland, and in the Scandinavian countries, of whose number several illustrious representatives are here.

But I do not wish to end with such negative remarks and I must excuse myself for having insisted so long upon them. I come now to those more familiar and positive aspects of your project, in particular to your admirable work on the "Concept of the Mind." I find here many descriptions that you have yourself termed, in a certain passage, "phenomenological." There is, in spite of everything, a difference. For Mr. Ryle, if I understand this correctly—and this will be the principal object of my question—all descriptions of givens, whether conceptual or discursive, as he terms them, might be philosophic. But there is a difference here between you and Husserl. Husserl might find that some "phenomenological" descriptions within your style are not descriptions of essences. Before a phenomenological description acquires a philosophical status, it is necessary that this description be devoted to some concepts that are characteristic for "more general regions." One can discuss this, and you will certainly offer me some objections. A description at this level of generality constituted for Husserl a "regional ontology." Many of your descriptions, for someone who, like myself, closely follows the lead of Husserl, are not only interesting but extremely instructive in regard to this particular region of the discursive and the conceptual realms.

It seems to me—and I will conclude with this minor point—that many phenomenologists practice in Europe, after Husserl, the same genre of analysis which occurs at Oxford; but they do not have the same temptation—pardon my use of this word—to hypostatize language [*langage*], to hypostatize expression [*langue*], to hypostatize the concept and the word; in this instance, the Oxford analysts show themselves to be excellent Platonists, which Husserl is not.

RYLE: I used the word "caricature" to qualify what I was saying about Husserl. I do not know if the caricature resembles him, and I care little if it does.

As to the question of whether we "hypostatize" language in Oxford, as Father Van Breda contends, I cannot use the term "language" in that which concerns me. I do not think that one can accuse me of hypostatizing it or of whatever else there might be. The tendency which pushes us to hypostatize concepts, whether this tendency existed in Husserl or not, is a danger which menaces all of us, but I hope to have at least outlined certain methods to guard against this temptation. Whether I myself have succeeded or not is another question.

I am happy to be able to gather here some further information on the last writings of Husserl and on his contacts with the scientific world. But I would hope that this debate does not degenerate into another colloquium on Husserl.

QUINE: Professor Ryle made a distinction between words which he told us present a meaning [*signification*] only when they are integrated into a context and those words of which one can say—according to him—that they offer a meaning by themselves, outside of a reference to any particular context. Among these words which only have a contextual sense, one finds articles, particles, and active verbs. The first part of my question is this: Ought one to include in this category only words which do not appear to refer [*rapporter*] to any object? If, according to you, this is so, I would have a second question: Ought one admit for words, which have a proper meaning outside the role that they can play in a context, that the objects to which they refer constitute in some way their meaning? Or better, as with Frege, do you keep the distinction between the meaning of a word and the reference of this word to its object? Given this last hypothesis, I would ask you if it does not seem strange that indirect meaning by reference to a context appears only for words or in sentences which do not refer explicitly to any object? Is it a simple coincidence that contextual meaning only intervenes where meaning as reference to an object ceases to play a role? I wonder for my part if this coincidence is not explained by stating that the sense of these substantive words (by contrast to the play [*jeu*] of references with objects) is just as contextual as that for words which do not visibly have any meaning by reference to objects?

RYLE: It is certain that, when I am in the process of speaking—let us say of Socrates, I can designate the person of whom I speak in several manners. I can use the name of Socrates. In certain contexts I can employ the accusative or nominative masculine pronoun as: "he" or "him." Otherwise, I can use a descriptive paraphrase: "the master of Plato," for example. I cannot say that it follows from this that there is a class of expressions that we can call referential, unless we take the term "class" in a very loose sense. There might be many things that one might be able to say in relation to a paraphrase, such as "the master of Plato," that might not apply to the proper name of Socrates. I understand by this that a descriptive phrase such as "the master of Plato" adds something to the sense of the word "Socrates"; and this contribution could be placed in evidence by varying the second term and formulating a similar expression which presents no sense in whatever context there might be. If we substitute for it, for example, the expression "the master of the moon"—"the professor of the moon"—we produce nonsense, because it is easily understood that the moon has nothing much to learn from Socrates. A descriptive paraphrase, if it presents a sense, therefore adds something to our comprehension of a word's meaning, but it can also offer no sense whatsoever. The case of the pronoun is different. We cannot assimilate it into a proper name. It serves only to designate for us a person already known to us, and the confusion between this pronoun and the proper name of this person could confuse only a stranger who might know poorly both the person and the usage of language, and who by the repetition of this pronoun comes to conclude about it that "he" is the proper name of Socrates. To know how to manage pronouns in a language is to have learned to employ a meaningful expression that takes its particular value in each instance within the sentence from the circumstances determined by its use. When we correctly employ the pronoun "he" in order to designate Socrates, nothing authorizes us to say it any more than any other descriptive paraphrase: "the man with a snub nose," for example, gives us the *sense* (*sens*) of the pronoun "he."

QUINE: And the name of Socrates?

RYLE: The name of Socrates is a proper name, which applies only to its person, and consequently the question of its meaning, the problem of knowing what it means, does not present itself. There might be perhaps some additional nuances to be elaborated here. But it is impossible for me to assert that "the man with a snub nose" or "the master of Plato" or any other descriptive paraphrase constitutes the meaning of the word "Socrates." By contrast, nothing prevents one from saying that "the man with a snub nose" that you see over there is a person that one names Socrates.

AYER: My suggestion runs along the same lines as these which Mr. Quine has attempted to trace out. It appears to me altogether evident, as is also the case for Mr. Quine—and I believe that on this point Mr. Ryle might be in agreement with us—that in no case might one be able to identify the meaning of an expression with the object or the person that this expression designates, whether it is a matter of a proper name like that of Socrates—of which Mr. Ryle reminded us that one could only say it presented a meaning—or whether it is a matter of a descriptive paraphrase. The proof of this is that the expression can lack its object and nevertheless present a sense by itself. The phrase where this expression comes into play might be able to present the same sense to several persons, whether the allusion is understood or not.

But if this is so, it seems to me that the distinction Mr. Ryle established toward the middle of his exposition, and to which he seemed to attach a certain importance, is poorly founded. I refer to the paragraph in which he stated: "We can say true or false things in relation to Socrates, but we cannot say true or false things about that which 'not' [*ne pas*] and 'or is' [*ou est*] express. All attempts to say what is true or false about what these words express lead us necessarily to absurd assertions." By this he implied that the expressions which designate objects distinguish themselves from other expressions, in the sense that one can speak of what the former can signify, but that one can say nothing about what the others signify. This distinction, in my understanding, does not hold. It appears evident to me that one can justly speak about all sorts of expressions which do not designate objects. One could speak of Socrates, to wonder whether he was a good philosopher or a bad one; but one can also speak of sleep or of boredom, and if one cannot say much about "and," particularly about *"and"* so placed in quotation marks, there remains much to say about the whole ensemble of processes, of manners of being, of actions, of sensations, or of impressions that one cannot consider as objects. And this fact tends to give again a certain luster to the much-denounced notion of intuition of essences. I am in agreement that the expression is not a happy one, that it drags us into all sorts of difficulties, if we wish to reintroduce it without precautions. But it seems to me nevertheless that one can legitimately pose some question about—let us say—the memory: in what does the memory consist? Is it essential to reserve this notion to designate only those experiences that are our own? Here are questions to which the answer might be found by looking in the first place at the analysis of the genre of sentences in which the words of memory [*memoire*] and of recollection [*souvenir*], or locutions, such as "to remember" [*se rappeler*], "to evoke" [*evoquer*], "to reflect on one's past" [*se pencher sur son passé*], can come into play. And it is not impossible that this is the genre of research that certain disciples of Husserl recommend, in which case their curiosity seems to me perfectly legitimate.

I would like Professor Ryle to make clear exactly what he understood when he established this distinction.

RYLE: In the paragraph which you mention, I tried to express my interpretation of what Wittgenstein argues in his *Tractatus Logico-Philosophicus*. Since logical objects do not exist, he tells us that substantially none of the propositions that the traditional theories of concepts or of propositions present to us can be considered as descriptions of these objects. He adds, going much further, that since no genuinely philosophical object exists, none of the propositions contained within traditional philosophy hold any sense, since the philosophers have nothing in particular about which to speak. This is not a point of view that I share. But I see here an important point to put in relief, not only from a historical perspective but also from a philosophical one.

In fact, it is perfectly evident—and I agree with Mr. Ayer on this point—that we can legitimately speak of all sorts of things such as the memory, perception, sleep, or boating—and that a part of what we say about these different subjects will have its repercussions upon the manner in which we broach philosophical problems. But what counts here is that, in order to explain what philosophical elucidation involves, it behooves us to characterize this notion clearly and exhaustively and to try to give a description of a new type of entity. I believed, perhaps wrongly, that the analysis of Wittgenstein helps us to see this distinction more easily. It also shows how, for him, one can say that propositions contained in traditional philosophy, just as those that logicians in their area offer us concerning logical objects, are empty of all meanings since they have no object. I think that Wittgenstein pushes things a little too far when he affirms that one cannot use a phrase such as "to speak of . . ." or "to think about . . ." without producing a descriptive statement of the object about which one speaks or about which one thinks. I think for my part that one can utilize phrases of this genre in a much more liberal sense. And I no longer see any contradiction between what I just said and the fact that one cannot say false or true things in relation to words such as "and," even when one can say false or true things in relation to Socrates. This still means that one cannot treat the word "and" as if it were related to an object, even when the contrary is the case for the word "Socrates."

In summary, all that I tried to do, in the disputed passage, was to explain why, in the spirit of Wittgenstein, the propositions stated by philosophers are empty of sense, because they are empty of any particular object, just as are those propositions stated by logicians, although not in the same way. I do not necessarily share this view, but simply wished to illustrate the difference between a philosophical proposition concerning, for example, the memory, and such a descriptive statement of ordinary language concerning, for example, Socrates.

AYER: Do you think that Wittgenstein lays out a sufficient criterion to determine what is an authentic object? Can you yourself give us one?

RYLE: No, certainly not. I think that all he was hoping to do was to limit their field of action, while having recourse to the analysis of propositions which he had already decided were meaningful, and perhaps to come one day, on Easter or Trinity Sunday, to the authentic object to which these meaningful propositions refer. Such at least was his overall program.

AYER: And for you, if I have understood, the choice of propositions supposedly significative of an authentic object is more or less arbitrary?

RYLE: Yes.

MERLEAU-PONTY: I have also had the impression, while listening to Mr. Ryle, that what he was saying was not so strange to us, and that the distance, if there is a distance, is one that he puts between us rather than one I find there. But naturally, there is perhaps here an illusion fostered by optimism, and it is necessary to make precise how far our agreement goes, or what has appeared to me to be our agreement. I would like Mr. Ryle to help us here, by responding to some questions that I am going to pose on the margin of his account.

He seems to admit, at least at the beginning of his account, as something already given and which has no need to be discussed, the distinction between factual and conceptual research. He did not take responsibility for this distinction, but in the end he does not raise any criticism against it. Now, I was wondering, while listening to the end of his account, if he really maintained this distinction the entire time. I would like him to explain several details concerning this point.

I would also like to ask him if he admits that *signification* (meaning) can always be considered as a synonym of the verbal meaning, *Wortbedeutung*. He criticized Husserl by claiming he had padded his theories of meaning—as if Husserl had first conceived meaning strictly tied to language and then in turn had wished to make all enter into the *Wortbedeutung*. But, in fact, from the start, from the time on of the *Logical Investigations*, Husserl was concerned with the difference between *Wortbedeutung* and *Bedeutung*. Does Mr. Ryle himself admit this distinction, and does not the end of his account authorize us to say that he largely exceeds the inventory of meanings—I might say: *langagières*?

I have been consistently struck, while listening to Mr. Ryle, by the fact that he himself enlarges—by the development of his own reflections—the limits that he at first presented to us as the limits of English analytic philosophy. This is constantly visible, not only in his own work, but also, for example, in the researches of Wittgenstein. Mr. Ryle has underscored very readily that there is an insufficiency in conceptual analysis of language. He employed this excellent expression, that there is "after all in language, the living force of that which we in fact say." He underscored, with Wittgenstein and other authors, that it is not possible to give a conceptual translation of all the words of language. In addition to this conceptual content that one can try to give them, the words do, in language, a type of *work* [*travail*]. The work of a term such as "if," for example, might not be rendered by a conceptual analysis of the term "if." And, along with Wittgenstein, he showed the possibility of a type of clarification of these terms which is not a description of objects. On hearing this, I told myself: I do not see much that separates us.

Finding oneself in the presence of this valuation of the employment of language, a valuation of an employment that is not reducible to a simple conceptual definition, one wonders if Mr. Ryle admits that in order to determine it, we must have recourse not only to the reflections of analytic philosophy, but also to an immanent study of linguistic phenomena for which certain parts of linguistic science might be the rough sketch?

In a more general fashion, does Mr. Ryle accept that the thinking with which a philosopher concerns himself is always, for example, interrogative thinking? Or does he consider an investigation of, for example, indicative thinking legitimate as well? Is it his opinion that philosophy or logic can be reduced to a study of correct and incorrect sentences? Is correctness and incorrectness for him the cardinal virtue of thinking? German writers distinguish readily between *Richtigkeit* [correctness] and *Wahrheit* [truth]; they say that a proposition can be *richtig* [correct] without giving us the *Wahrheit* [truth] of the matter, which is what would occur if we were to give a full and complete account [*saisie*] of it. Does Mr. Ryle admit a distinction of this order, or does the study of the conditions for the correction of verbal expressions appear to be for him a sufficient definition of philosophy?

Finally, does he admit that there is *invention* in that which has to do with thinking? Because it seems to me, in listening to him, that the limits of philosophy, such as he has traced them, leave no place for an inventive function. In truth, the question for a philosopher is not so much to know *if* God exists or does not exist, if the proposition *God exists* is correct or incorrect, as to know what one understands by God, what one wishes to say in speaking of God. Does Mr. Ryle accept this distinction? Does he also accept the necessity of accounting for much more than the correctness or incorrectness of a proposition? I would say that one must account for its *richness*, that which the proposition brings us and the manner in which it organizes our field of thinking.

In the last part of his exposition, Mr. Ryle gave us some glimpses of his own research which, for me, is not absolutely a surprise, since I have worked with his *Concept of Mind*. I found here some indications which completely satisfy me, for example, when Mr. Ryle said that the task of a philosopher is never simply to make the inventory of a concept, that the philosopher, when he examines that which is hidden in a word, is led into a complex spider-web of concepts. This appears to me to be profoundly interesting and true. Does this conform to the program of philosophical investigation that Russell posed or that even Wittgenstein posed? This is the question that I asked myself. I submit it to Mr. Ryle, certainly not as an objection, but as a demand for clarification.

Mr. Ryle opposes concepts of disposition to concepts of action. For me, when one speaks of "dispositions" I ask all the questions that Mr. Ryle asks, but I also ask some others. I would like to know if Mr. Ryle holds these latter questions to be philosophic. For example, in regard to these concepts, I raise the problem that one terms "actualism." Some philosophers think there is only the actual, and whatever is not actual has only a mental reality, taken as a second reality in relation to the actual. There are also some philosophers who question the value of the notion of the possible, the notion of the possible which is strictly tied to that of dispositions. Does Mr. Ryle think that when we deal with dispositional concepts it is only a matter of knowing the regular usage of these concepts at play in a public language, or rather does he accept that philosophy can question the legitimacy of such concepts, the legitimacy of the notion of the possible and of its relations with that of the actual? Does an investigation of this subject appear purely and simply to him as "non-sense," or rather does it appear to him to be philosophical?

When he speaks of the imagination, it seems to me that his position is perfectly clear: his own research is not a conceptual research in the sense he gave this word at the beginning of his exposition. In his studies of the imagination, he does not limit himself to addressing only the treasure of the common language, which employs the word *imaginer* and the word *imagination*, in order to see in what non-contradictory senses this term can be used. It seems to me that he refers—I dare not use taboo words, but finally I must—to the experience that we have of the imaginary. And this experience is mute. He refers to this experience before its formulation. And he tries, precisely, he, a philosopher, to formulate verbally an experience which is no longer set in propositions. Do I deceive myself, or does Mr. Ryle agree?

Finally, in what Mr. Ryle says of the *Cogito*, at the end of his statement, and which is very interesting, I see the occasion for a final question.

Mr. Ryle says that there are propositions in the first person and propositions in the third person. But if we are to speak of grammar (since he does), does he accept that there are also propositions in the second person, and that according to him one can pose philosophical problems in regard to them? Said otherwise, is the following a legitimate philosophical question: For what reason does it happen that the altogether extraordinary property [*propriété*] of those propositions in the first-person is in some manner shared [*participable*] by other propositions besides the ones we ourselves pronounce? When I hear Mr. Ryle, he is quite certain that I consider him as a first person who is not myself. Does this transference of the first person outside of ourselves raise a problem requiring philosophical elucidation? If yes, then truthfully our positions are not as distant as Mr. Ryle has been saying. But I do not wish to go on any longer, and I am sure that everyone is impatient, as I am, to know Mr. Ryle's position on these different points.

RYLE: I hope that Mr. Merleau-Ponty will refresh my memory if I forget any points in my response to him.

The first question touched upon the distinction that I make, after others, between empirical and conceptual research. Mr. Merleau-Ponty asked me if I had indeed followed my distinction, if I see here a clear distinction and how I demarcate it. I fear it will be quite difficult for me to give a definition so precise that it applies to all research of fact. But the demarcation is made by a distinction which is familiar to us. We all know that the chemist or the astronomer does not resolve the problems with which he is engaged while meditating in an armchair—at least not all, nor all the time. They use some instruments, they employ some techniques which for them are appropriate. For one, a telescope, a spectroscope, the examination of photographs; for another, a balance, test tubes, and a Bunsen burner. See here what comes to my mind when speaking of research of fact. Nothing very mysterious, as you see. But what matters is that the questions of fact of this order are not the province of philosophy. One will never say that so and so is a better philosopher than so and so because so and so knows facts of which the other is ignorant. In any case, and in order to respond to your question, the difference is sufficiently clear to fulfill what we expect from it.

Your second question involves the notion of meaning. Do I limit the use of the term to those sole cases where one can discuss the sense or non-sense of a verbal expression? Will I accept hearing of a usage much more general, as that which applies to such and such a natural phenomenon—for example, when one says that a halo around the moon means rain for tomorrow; or that the footprints on the sand mean, for Robinson on his island, that he is no longer alone in his kingdom? Be it far from me to prohibit whatever usage of the words "to mean" [*signifier*] and "meaning" [*signification*] in this larger sense. What I simply wish to say is that I limit the usage, for my account, to the case where we find ourselves in the presence of an option between a meaning value, or a non-meaning one, the sense or non-sense of an expression; this is to say when we wonder what it wishes to say, if it wishes to say something. As to knowing if the halo of the moon or the piling up of black clouds on the horizon mean rain for tomorrow, this is not a question which interests the philosopher. However, to know if the sentence of Lewis Carroll, telling us that the cat disappeared while leaving his smile behind him, presents a sense or not, even if the philosophical question posed here is not very important, puts us on the trail. In all discussion relating to conceptual research, in philosophy or even more generally, it is important not to stretch excessively the sense of the term "meaning" to the point where we include sentences of the type, "the black clouds mean that the rain will fall." Otherwise the discussion strongly risks losing all philosophical interest.

If I remember correctly, the third question involved invention. Can human thought create new meanings? I might respond that from all evidence, this is so. We have an arsenal of new significations which our ancestors did not have at their disposal. Each progression of the sciences, each footstep in knowledge, which concerns not a point of detail but an essential point, renders answerable, debatable, refutable—therefore meaningful—a whole ensemble of things that had not been before. To choose only one example, before Freud the notions of consciousness and unconsciousness were relatively limited. One said of someone that he was engulfed by the unconscious, if he was sleeping, if one administered an anesthetic to him, or if he fell into a coma. The development of Freudian theories led to the enlargement of the meaning of these concepts and to the introduction of intermediary concepts, such as the subconscious, which Freud used in order to give an account of the new problems that he was studying. At the same time, new conceptual problems can crop up for the philosopher, insofar as new concepts come into the light of day. The same thing goes for each forward bound of science, whether it concerns a matter of mathematics and the natural sciences or of grammar or of whatever else there might be.

In the fourth place, Mr. Merleau-Ponty asks me—he kindly transcribed his question for me into English—if I am still strictly in agreement, in my research, with the program outlined at the beginning of the century by Russell and refined by Wittgenstein and some others. My response is: *I certainly hope not!*

I do not mean by this to say anything disagreeable concerning Russell, Wittgenstein, or anybody else. But the simple idea of being totally in agreement with someone or another about some problem, this seems to me to be a death blow to all philosophical enterprise. If the last word had been said, the only thing which would be left for us to do would be to sit ourselves down in our chair and twiddle our thumbs. We would be reduced to silence.

The philosophical importance of Russell, as of Wittgenstein, appears to me to reside precisely in this, that they have opened some pathways, without giving the solution to any problem. So much so, that the notion of being in agreement with their program does not raise within me even an echo of sympathy. I am aware of owing them much, of having learned much from my contact with them, and perhaps most importantly, at least I hope so, by their failures. We would not have known that certain directions in which the thought of Russell was engaged led to a certain failure, if he had not himself pursued those directions. While generalizing, I might say that to learn something from a philosopher is to learn to recognize those points on which one disagrees with him.

I have just come to the interesting point that you raised—I do not know if I am following exactly your order, but this is not important—in regard to the second person. Mr. Merleau-Ponty takes a particular interest in the case of statements "in the second person," which is to say in the case where a person converses with another. I recognize that in the short passage of my exposition which I devoted to the *Cogito*, I did not give any particular attention to this case, to which I attach some importance in the examination of all sorts of questions. If I have passed it by in silence, this is because I insist above all in responding to a very particular problem, which was to know why some propositions in the first person, of a certain type, of a certain class, appear to us to occupy a privileged position in the order of knowing. In this sense, they seem to present affirmations that their author would be unable to doubt or think false. This privileged rule that our mind confers upon some propositions which seem outside the possibility of doubt, outside the possibility of error, which distinguish them therefore from all other affirmations that we can enunciate, does not exist anymore when we apply the same propositions to the second person or to the third. It is this very particular grouping of propositions in the first person concerning consciousness [*connaisance*], certitude, etc., which aroused my curiosity and which I was moved to analyze. They are strange [*étranges*], in fact, for the reason that I have given: if a person cannot say that he or she is depressed or suffers and wonders at the same time if what he or she says is true or false, it is not any less absurd to treat this genre of propositions as we treat propositions concerning consciousness, certitude, conviction, etc. I do not know which place I can give them in the epistemological order. They embarrass me. Now, this difficulty does not exist, it seems to me, for propositions in the second or third person.

Certainly, in a general manner for quite another sort of problem, the fact that a subject A speaks to another subject B and that this other can respond to him is one of the most important facts that one can consider when one speaks of "persons."

You have also questioned me, for a moment I no longer know when, about the problem of the "correctness" or "incorrectness" of language; this problem is neither remotely nor particularly important to me. This concerns the grammarian. It might be incorrect to place a singular verb in agreement with a plural subject. To say, for example, "French men *is* fond of wine" (I do not speak of the character of the truth or falsity of such a proposition) is incorrect—but this is only a matter of syntax. Inversely, one can say in a very correct manner of speaking from the viewpoint of good usage, in answer to the question, "From what did he die?", something like "Oh! because it was written in his destiny that he should die at this moment." Grammar is followed, the words are used according to their grammatical categories. It is not a matter of correctness. What it is a matter of, by contrast, is the philosophical outrage which occurs when one answers a question concerning the physiological reasons for a death (cancer, pneumonia, old age, or accident) while invoking the intervention of the forces of destiny. I say intentionally a philosophical "outrage" because it is not simply a matter of an error concerning the cause (let us say of the attribution of a death to cancer when it was actually due to a fall on the stairs) but of a slipping from the plane of causality to an entirely other level. It goes without saying that the analysis of such a philosophical blunder has nothing to do with the question of knowing if the proposition in which it is formulated is grammatically correct or incorrect.

There remains a last question, which again turns around the expression of linguistic analysis. I have carefully abstained from utilizing the word "language" [*langage*] or the adjective "linguistic." Not that I find it repugnant to use these terms occasionally, but because I believe that one has only too much a tendency, at Oxford as well as other places, to use the words "language" and "linguistic" in a sense so lax and vague that one introduces confusion everywhere. I know of what I speak, when I consider what someone says in English or in French in determinate circumstances. But recently the fashion has been to utilize the term "language" as if it came from an inexhaustible spring from which gushes, as if by a miracle, opinions and beliefs, or thoughts, and this will simply not work at all. In matters of truth and falsity, one does not say that there are English truths or French errors, or vice versa, except in an extremely limited sense in which one might be able to say that there is a truth or error concerning English or French. Whatever it might be, if one utilizes before me the word "language" I am always the first to ask: Of which language are you speaking? English?

French? In a philosophical context, the word "language," in the vague and indeterminate sense of the term, does not seem to me to have any application. It is without interest in relation to the problems which concern us. . . .[2]

—Trans. by James Hatley.

PART II

◆

Texts

6

The Nature of Perception: Two Proposals (1933)

I. STUDY PROJECT ON THE NATURE OF PERCEPTION

It has seemed to me that in the present state of neurology, experimental psychology (particularly psychopathology), and philosophy, it would be useful to take up again the problem of perception, and particularly perception of one's own body.[1]

A doctrine inspired by critical philosophy treats perception as an intellectual operation through which non-extended data ("sensations") are related and explained in such fashion as to finally constitute an objective universe. So regarded, perception is like an incomplete science, a mediating operation.

Now, experimental investigations carried out in Germany by Gestalt theorists seem to show on the contrary that perception is not an intellectual operation. The "form," on this view, would be present in sense-knowledge itself, and the incoherent "sensations" of traditional psychology would be a gratuitous hypothesis.

The development of neurology has, on the other hand, clarified the role of the nervous system, whose function seems more and more to be "conduction" of the neural input, and not the function of "elaboration of thinking." While relieving neurologists of the task of looking for decals of mental functions in localized anatomical functions, and in this sense freeing psychology from "parallelism," this conception brings out the role of "nascent movements," which the nervous system functions to provoke, and which have to accompany every perception. Perception is thus set into a motor framework. The correlation between visual data and those of touch or of muscular feel, which is established, according to the viewpoint prompted by critical thought, by intellectual activity, memory, and judgment, seems on

74

the contrary to be ensured here by the very functioning of the nervous system. And here, too, the psychologist should perhaps give up his image of a universe of non-extended sensations which "the education of the senses" would convert into a voluminous space by the progressive association of visual data with tactile data.

One would especially have to study the recent literature on the "perception of one's own body." If it seems difficult in a general way to distinguish a matter and a form in sense knowledge, it appears even more difficult regarding perception of one's own body, where extendedness seems obviously to cohere with the sensation.

These observations, and others like them, if a thorough study of the documentation confirms them, would mean going back on the classical postulates of perception. Indeed, the realist philosophers of England and America often insist on what is irreducible to intellectual relations in the sensory and the concrete. The universe of perception could not be assimilated to the universe of science.

In summary, in the present state of philosophy there are grounds for attempting a synthesis of the results of experimental psychology and neurology with respect to the problem of perception, to determine through reflection its precise meaning, and perhaps to recast certain psychological and philosophical notions currently in use.

II. THE NATURE OF PERCEPTION

A new study of perception seems justified by contemporary developments in philosophical and experimental research:

- — by the appearance, notably in Germany, of new philosophies which call into question the guiding ideas of critical thought, until then dominant in psychology as well as the philosophy of perception;
- — by developments in the physiology of the nervous system;
- — by developments in mental pathology and child psychology;
- — finally, by progress in a new psychology of perception in Germany (*Gestaltpsychologie*).

During my research this year, such an attempt seemed to me all the more justified because, since the analyses of Lachelier (*L'Observation de Platner*) and Lagneau (*Célèbres Leçons: Cours sur la perception*) which underlie the theory of perception in Alain, works published in French (for example, the two theses by Duret entitled *Les Facteurs pratiques de la croyance dans la perception* and *L'Objet de la perception*, Alcan, 1929) take almost no account of recent German work.

A. PHYSIOLOGY AND PATHOLOGY OF PERCEPTION

Nevertheless, it has not seemed possible to broach this study of perception by way of the physiology of the nervous system nor by way of mental pathology. It seemed to me that both ought to allow us to specify the relation between sense-knowledge and intelligence, by specifying the connection between "projection" and "association." Though the views of C. von Monakow (summarized in Monakow and Mourgue, *Introduction biologique à l'étude de la neurologie et de la psychopathologie*) and the notion of "chronogenic localization" furnish guiding concepts for experimentation, they do not yet seem to have yielded specific investigations capable of throwing light on the psychology of perception through brain physiology. It is significant that the overview of H. Piéron (*Le Cerveau et la pensée*), so precise with regard to "projection," can make only hypothetical points regarding associative phenomena and their relation to the zones of projection.

As for pathology, at least in France, it too cannot provide a guiding thread. The thesis by P. Quercy (*Études sur l'hallucination*, v. II: *La Clinique*, Alcan, 1930) finally leaves unanswered the question—essential for us—of whether hallucination is a seeing without an object or merely an "attitude" favored by a degradation of beliefs. We can therefore find in it nothing presumptively favorable to a psychology which would make of normal perception a brute given, or, on the contrary, a construction involving the totality of mental activity. Nor can the thesis of H. Wallon (*Stades et troubles du développement psychomoteur et mental chez l'enfant*, 1925—since published under the title *L'Enfant turbulent*) furnish, in other ways, a decisive orientation. The author reconstitutes the normal development from the subjective to the objective by the method of pathology. But the genesis of external perception remains hidden: it is not yet present, it seems, in the "sensori-motor stage"; in the "projective stage" which follows immediately, it seems fully constituted. For this projective stage is known to us only by analogy to certain epileptic states of mind; now, to be sure, the world of the epileptic child may well be marked by instability and incoherence, caught up as it were in a tyrannical activity—yet it is a world, or rather a mass of external things, and we have not been privy to the genesis of this externality.

Nevertheless, neural physiology and pathology should be able to provide some very important information on two points. On the one hand, there are "localized reflexes" (Piéron), and on the other hand, astereognosias and more generally agnosias. But even in those cases where the nature of the injuries particularly favors the localization of lesions (bullet wounds or small shell explosions, Gelb and Goldstein, *Psychologische Analysen hirnpathologischer Fälle*, v. I, ch. 1), we should notice that the conjectures always move from the observable sensory or psychic disturbances to merely presumed localizations. Gelb and Goldstein thereby conclude that the first task, before any attempt at physiological interpretation, is to give as exact a description as possible of the disturbed behavior. But the experiments to be undertaken in order to analyze the consciousness of the patient will obviously be suggested by the guiding ideas of a psychology of normal perception (for Gelb and Goldstein, by those of *Gestaltpsychologie*). We are thus brought back to the psychology of the normal—provided always that its conceptions remain subject to the strict control of the facts of pathology.

B. PHILOSOPHY OF PERCEPTION

Psychology of perception is loaded with philosophical presuppositions, which enter in through the seemingly most innocent notions—sensation, mental image, recollection, understood as permanent beings. . . . Even apart from any intention of looking into the furthest problems of perception—into the meaning of truth in sense knowledge—the psychological problem could not be completely elucidated without resorting to the philosophy of perception. A part of our work this year has therefore been devoted to it.

The phenomenology of Husserl is doubly interesting to us. First, taken in the strict sense assigned to it by Husserl, phenomenology (transcendental phenomenology or "constitutive" phenomenology) is a new philosophy. Its primary problem is not the problem of knowledge, but it gives rise to a theory of knowledge absolutely distinct from that of critical thought (E. Fink, "Die phänomenologische Philosophie Husserls in der gegenwärtigen Kritik," in *Kantstudien*, 1933).* Second, it is said that Husserl is indifferent to psychology. The truth is that he maintains his earlier criticism of "psychologism" and continues to insist on the "reduction" whereby one passes from the natural attitude, which is that of psychology as of all the positive sciences, to the transcendental attitude, which is that of phenomenological philosophy. This difference in attitude suffices to establish a very definite line between phenomenological analyses of perception, for example, and psychological analyses dealing with the same theme.

But, in addition to the fact that he himself has provided an example of a properly psychological analysis of perception (*Ideen zu einer reinen Phänomenologie und phänomenologische Philosophie*, sec. II), Husserl explicitly compares (ibid., sec. I, ch. 1) the relations of phenomenology and psychology to those of mathematics and physics, and looks to the development of his philosophy for a renewal of the principles of psychology (cf. *Ideen*, I, II, and the Fink article cited). The properly phenomenological analyses, for example, those of memory and image, which have been published in the *Jahrbuch* (for example, Fink, "Vergegenwärtigung und Bild," *Jahrbuch fur Philosophie und Phänomenologische Forschung*, XI) are not lacking in consequences for psychology.

---

* [Note added in margin of written text:] Cf. Lévinas, *La Théorie de l'intuition dans la phénoménologie de Husserl*; G. Gurvitch, "La Phénoménologie de Husserl," *Revue de Métaphysique*, 1928; J. Hering, *Phénoménologie et philosophie religieuse*; and Husserl, *Méditations cartésiennes*.

But one must insist on the fact that in no way do they aim to *replace* psychology. The renewal in question is not an invasion. It is a matter of renewing psychology *on its own terrain*, of bringing to life *the methods proper to it* by analyses which fix the persistently uncertain meaning of fundamental essences, such as "representation," "memory," etc. (Linke, "Phänomenologie und Experiment in der Frage der Bewegungsauffassung," *Jahrbuch*, v. II; and by the same author: *Grundfragen der Wahrnehmungslehre*, Munich, 1918). Phenomenology definitely distinguishes "eidetic" method and "inductive" method (that is, experimental method), and never challenges the legitimacy of the latter.

We should not be surprised that the phenomenological movement has even inspired experimental research (for example, Linke, "Die stroboskopische Täuschungen und das Problem des Sehens von Bewegungen," *Psychologische Studien*, v. III, p. 499). It has been maintained (Gurwitsch, "Phänomenologie der Thematik und des Reinen Ich," *Psychologische Forschung*, 1929) that the analyses of Husserl lead to the threshold of *Gestaltpsychologie*. Finally, all "descriptive" psychology is called phenomenology in a very broad sense.

The importance of the phenomenological movement for psychology is scarcely indicated in France by anyone but M. Pradines (*Philosophie de la sensation*, v. I, especially the "Introduction"). He reproaches the philosophers, from Hume to Bergson, with having too often reduced consciousness to a sum of "impressions" (even in Kant, the "matter" at least of knowledge is something of this sort). As a result, spatiality and in general "signification" are secondary and acquired for consciousness, among the more consistent of these philosophers. Now, for M. Pradines, the appearance of higher senses, essentially different—in the structure of their apparatus—from senses mingled with affect, would be a biological absurdity if from the start it did not pertain to them to be "distance senses," to signify an "object." This philosophy of sensation could be considered a psychological application of the theme of "the intentionality of consciousness" advanced by Husserl.

Phenomenology and the psychology it inspires thus deserve maximum attention in that they can assist us in revising the very notions of consciousness and sensation, in conceiving differently the "cleavage" of consciousness.

C. PSYCHOLOGY OF PERCEPTION

A large part of our work this past year has however been devoted to *Gestaltpsychologie*. The older psychology postulated sensations as primary data of consciousness, supposed to correspond item by item to local excitations of sensory apparatus, such that a given excitation always produced the same sensation (*Konstanzannahme*; cf. Helson, "Studies in the Theory of

Perception; I: The Clearness-Context Theory," *Psychological Review,* January 1932; also Köhler, *Gestalt Psychology,* New York and London, 1929). To get from these alleged "givens" to the scenario of things as we actually perceive them, it was necessary to conjecture an "elaboration" of sensations by memory, by knowledge, by judgment—of "matter" by "form"; a passage from the subjective "mosaic" (Wertheimer) to the world of objects. The school with which we are concerned explains for one thing, by the psychological factor called Gestalt, what the older psychology referred to interpretation and judgment. The Gestalt is a spontaneous organization of the sensory field which has supposed "elements" dependent on "wholes" which are themselves articulated within more extensive wholes. This organization is not like a form imposing itself upon a heterogeneous matter; there is no matter without form; there are only organizations, more or less stable, more or less articulated. But these definitions only sum up abstractly experimental investigations which can be followed up in two main directions:

1. *Object* Our everyday perception is not of a mosaic of qualities but of an ensemble of distinct objects. What makes one part of the field thus set off and differentiated, according to traditional psychology, is the memory of prior experiences, knowledge. For *Gestaltpsychologie,* an object does not stand out because of its "signification" ("meaning"), but because it possesses in our perception a special structure: the structure of "figure-ground." One determines the objective conditions—independent of will and intellect—which are necessary and sufficient to engender the "figure" structure (for example, the maximum and optimal distance at which several points are *seen* as a figure, a constellation—Wertheimer). This very structure is analyzed, is definable by certain *sensible* properties: for example, the differential threshold is higher for the background colors than for the figure colors. According to Gelb and Goldstein, *certain* psychic blindnesses, which had been interpreted as an inability to "project" the appropriate memories on the sensation, would be instead a perturbation of the structural processes just noted (W. Köhler, *Gestalt Psychology,* London and New York, 1929; "An Aspect of Gestalt Psychology," by C. Murchison, in *Psychologies of 1925*; K. Gottschaldt, "Über den Einfluss der Erfahrung auf die Wahrnehmung von Figuren," *Psych. Forschung,* VIII, 1927; Sander, "Experimentelle Ergebnisse der Gestaltpsychologie," in *Bericht über den X Kongress für experimentelle Psychologie,* 1927; Gelb and Goldstein, op. cit.).

This "figure-ground" structure is itself only a particular case of the spontaneous organization of sensory fields. In general, it must be said that primitive perception bears rather on relations than on isolated terms— *visible,* not *conceived* relations (Köhler, "Optischer Untersuchungen am Schimpansen und am Haushuhn," 1915; "Nachweis einfacher Strukturfunktionen beim Schimpansen und beim Haushuhn," 1918). These conceptions render Weber's Law more understandable and, by the same token, are thereby confirmed: the discontinuity of the conscious changes corresponding to a continuous variation in the stimulus is explainable by certain structural laws (the law of levelling, the law of accentuation), and finally appears as a particular case of the general law of "pregnancy" established by Wertheimer (Koffka, "Perception: An Introduction to Gestalt Theory," *Psychological Bulletin*, XIX, 1922; Sander, op. cit.).

2. *Space and Movement* The perception of space is a prime site of intellectualist elaborations. The distance of an object, for example, is referred back to an instantaneous judgment which is based on signs, such as apparent size or a disparity of retinal images, and which concludes how many steps we would have to take to touch the object. Space is no longer an object of vision but an object of thought. Now, a penetrating critique of "disparity of images" (Koffka, "Some Problems of Space Perception," in *Psychologies of 1930*) leads to the admission that the disparity of images, even if it is a condition of depth perception, is not the occasion of a judgment, but the cause of a neural process of which we know only the conscious outcome, in the form of an impression of depth. In reality, the phenomenon of depth perception has a structure analogous to those just noted. This is particularly well demonstrated where an object is seen through a nearer transparent object: the seeing of depth can be produced or cancelled by modifying the color of the surrounding field (cf. Koffka, ibid.; Tudor-Hart, "Studies in Transparency, Form, and Colours," *Psychologische Forschung*, 1928). Here, once again, Gestalt psychology is in a position to interpret important findings previously made: those of Schumann and his school which disclosed a sort of space-quality in perception (Schumann, Fuchs, Katz, Jaensch, de Karpinska, et al. in *Zeitschrift für Psychologie und Physiologie der Sinnesorganen*). Although this research may have had some influence on the work of Lavelle (*La Perception visuelle de la profondeur*, Strasbourg, 1921), and although Pradines has supplied a bibliography, they themselves remain unknown in France, and the thesis of Mlle. R. Déjean (*Étude psychologique de la distance dans la vision*, Paris, 1926) does not deal with them, even though she also tends to posit distance as inherent in seeing.

Supposing that we always judged what we saw by what was painted upon the retina, and that points stretching into depth were projected onto a single plane, one indeed had to suppose that the subject reconstituted the depth, got to it by means of a conclusion, but did not see it. By contrast, and for the very same reason, the immediate perception of width and height presented no difficulty. But we no longer have any reason to consider depth to be derived and ulterior. Perhaps it should even be seen as a more simple mode of perception than perceiving surfaces. Gelb and Goldstein (op. cit., I, pp.

334–419, "Uber den Wegfall der Wahrnehmung von Oberflächenfarben") show that seeing surface colors is a relatively fragile organization, easily altered in certain pathological cases, when it gives way to a seeing of "thick" colors [*épaisses*]—all the "thicker" as they are less pale [*clair*] (on the relations of paleness—or more exactly, of *Eindringlichkeit*—and apparent "thickness" [*épaisseur*], see Ackermann, *Psychologische Forschung*, 1924, and Tudor-Hart, loc. cit.).

Moreover, direct study of our perception of space in terms of height and width had already uncovered structural phenomena. The characteristics of "vertical," "horizontal," or "oblique" are conferred upon the lines of the visual field, declared the earlier psychology, by a mental reference to the meridian of our retina, to the axis of our head and our body. For Wertheimer, on the contrary, certain important points of our sensory field ("anchor" points) determine a sort of "spatial level," and the lines of the field immediately feature the indices "upward," "downward," without judgments or comparisons ("Experimentelle Studien über das Sehen von Bewegung; Anhang," in *Zeitschrift für Psychologie*, 1912). Experimentation shows disruptions of this equilibrium or changes of this level, and shows that in such cases there is no question of an intellectual operation, of a change in a system of coordinates.

Similarly, in a series of methodical experiments, the same author disclosed, in so-called stroboscopic movement, a "pure movement," a movement without a moved. Our perception of movement could not therefore be assimilated to an estimate of increasing distance between two points which alone are perceived, that is, to movement as defined by the physicist. It should be stressed that in this analysis, as in the preceding ones, the whole concern of the Gestalt psychologists is in experiences which their principles render possible and which are not otherwise accounted for. Nothing could be less like a hasty appeal to something *sui generis* (Wertheimer, loc. cit.).

These remarks do not claim to exhaust the analysis of perceptual space according to Gestalt psychology. We have mainly drawn on new findings which fall under traditional considerations. But it has also opened new chapters, for example, that of the statics inherent in our perception (Köhler, *L'Intelligence des singes supérieurs*).

3. *Gestalt Psychology and Child Psychology* The idea of a "syncretic perception" in children (Claparède, 1908), confirmed by more recent research, and in particular by a study of stroboscopic movement in relation to children (Meili and Tobler, *Archives de psychologie*, 1931–32), collided with research which indicated on the contrary a highly sensitive perception of details among children. The notion of Gestalt seems capable of doing justice to both lines of investigation. For syncretic perception (of a uniform bloc) and analytical perception (where only juxtaposed details exist), rather than

conflicting, as often supposed, together contrast with the structured perception of the adult in which the ensembles are articulated and the details are organized.

The child's perception is nonetheless already organized, but in its own fashion. And a principle offered by Gestalt psychology to psychogenetic theory is that development does not occur by simple attachment or addition but by reorganization (Koffka, *Die Grundlagen der psychischen Entwicklung*, 1921; *Journal de psychologie*, 1924). For perception, a world of connected objects would not appear out of a mosaic of impressions, but better articulated ensembles would appear out of poorly or otherwise related ensembles. One could thus join up with certain observations by Piaget (*La Représentation du monde chez l'enfant*) which Piaget's own formulations do not always express accurately. If one says, for example, that the child's perception of the world is "egocentric," this is true enough, in the sense that the world of the child ignores the simplest criteria of objectivity of the adult. But precisely to be unacquainted with adult objectivity is not to live in oneself, it is to practice an unmeasured objectivity; the notion of egocentricity should not be allowed to suggest the old idea of a consciousness enclosed in "its states." Observations by P. Guillaume (*Journal de psychologie*, 1924) point on the contrary to the precociousness of behavior adapted to space. It is significant that H. Wallon, who seemed to conceive the genesis of objective perception along traditional lines, as a passage from the internal to the external (Wallon, "De l'image au réel chez l'enfant," *Revue de philosophie*) implicitly restricts this thesis in his latest work, *Les Origines de caractère chez l'enfant*. He sees the child—from the age of three or four months, it seems, that is, "when there begins the myelin joining of the interoceptive and proprioceptive domains, on the one hand, and the exteroceptive domain on the other" (p. 176)—"turned toward a source of excitations, toward a motif in motion, and bent on experiencing its various possibilities" (p. 180).

4. Gestalt Psychology and Theory of Knowledge This wholly new conception of the content of consciousness has important consequences in the theory of sense knowledge. These consequences have not yet been clearly shown. Within Gestalt psychology the issue is hardly discussed. The usual attitude of psychologists is adopted: the distinction between a world of things and an immanent consciousness. The organization or structuring of consciousness is explained by central physiological phenomena (Wertheimer's "transverse" phenomena, cf. loc. cit.), whose existence is, moreover, much contested. Those outside Gestalt psychology have maintained that its problem of knowledge is couched in the same terms as Kant's (Gurwitsch, op. cit.). We must look, we believe, in a different direction, for a very different solution.

BOOKS AND ARTICLES (IN THE ORDER CITED):

Lachelier, Jules. *L'Observation de Platner*, in Oeuvres, II, 65–104 (Paris: Alcan, 1933).

Lagneau, Jules. *Célèbres Leçons: Cours sur la perception* (Nîmes, 1926).

Duret. *Les Facteurs pratiques de la croyance dans la perception* (Paris: Alcan, 1929).

Monakow and Mourgue. *Introduction biologique à l'étude de la neurologie et de la psychopathologie* (Paris: Alcan, 1928).

Piéron, H. *Le Cerveau et la pensée* (Paris: Alcan, 1923; 2nd ed.).

Quercy, P. *L'Hallucination*; II: *La clinique* (Paris: Alcan, 1930).

Wallon, H. *L'Enfant turbulent* (Paris: Alcan, 1925).

Gelb and Goldstein. *Psychologische Analysen hirnpathologischer Fälle* (Leipzig, 1920).

Fink, E. "Die phänomenologische philosophie Edmund Husserls in der gegenwärtigen Kritik," in *Kantstudien* XXXVIII (1933), 319–83.

Husserl, E. "Ideen zu einer reinen Phänomenologie und phänomenologische Philosophie," in *Jahrbuch für Philosophie und Phänomenologische Forschung*, I (1913), 1–323.

Fink, E. "Vergegenwärtigung und Bild," in *J. für Phil. u. phän. Forsch.* II (1930), 239–309.

Linke, "Die stroboskopische Täuschungen und das Problem des Sehens von Bewegungen," in *Psychologische Studien* (Leipzig: Engelmann, 1907), II.

Gurwitsch, A. "Phänomenologie der Thematik und des Reinen Ich. Studien uber Beziehungen von Gestalttheorie und Phänomenologie," in *Psychologische Forschung* (1929), 279–381.

Pradines, M. *Philosophie de la sensation* (Paris: Les Belles Lettres, 1928–1932).

Helson, "Studies in the Theory of Perception. I: The Clearness-context Theory," in *Psychological Review* (1932), 44–72.

Köhler, W. *Gestaltpsychologie [Gestalt Psychology]* (New York and London, 1929).

Köhler, W. "An aspect of Gestalt Psychology," in C. Murchison (ed.), *Psychologies of 1930* (London: 1930), 163–95.

Köhler, W. "Some Tasks of Gestalt Psychology," in ibid., 143–60.

Gottschaldt, K. "Über den Einfluss der Erfahrung auf die Wahrnehmung von Figuren," in *Psychologische Forschung* VIII (1927), 261–317.

Sander, F. *Experimentelle Ergebnisse der Gestaltpsychologie* (Jena: Fischer, 1928).

Köhler, W. "Optische Untersuchungen am Schimpansen und am Haushuhn," in *Abhandlungen der Königlichen preussischen Akademie der Wissenschaften*, 1916.

Köhler, W. "Nachweis einfacher Strukturfunktionen beim Schimpansen und beim Haushuhn," in ibid., 1918.

Koffka, K. "Perception: An Introduction to Gestalt Theory," in *Psychological Bulletin* XIX (1922), 531–85.

Koffka, K. "Some Problems of Space Perception," in C. Murchison, op. cit., 161–87.

Tudor-Hart, B. "Studies in Transparency, Form and Colour," in *Psychologische Forschung* (1928), 255–98.

Lavelle, Louis. *La Perception visuelle de la profondeur* (Strasbourg, 1921).

Déjean, R. *Étude psychologique de la distance dans la vision* (Paris, 1926).

Ackermann, "Farbschwelle und Feldstruktur" in *Psychologische Forschung* (1924), 44–84.

Wertheimer, M. "Experimentelle Studien über das Sehen von Bewegung," in *Zeitschrift für Psychologie* LXI (1912), 161–265; "Anhang," 253–65.

Köhler, W. *L'Intelligence des singes supérieurs* (Paris: Alcan, 1927; tr. P. Guillaume).

Meili and Tobler. "Les mouvements stroboscopiques chez les enfant," in *Archives de psychologie* XXIII (1931–32), 131–56.

Meili. "Les perceptions des enfants et la psychologie de la Gestalt," in ibid., 25–44.

Koffka, K. *Die Grundlagen der psychischen Entwicklung* (Osterwick am Harz, 1921).

Koffka, K. "Théorie de la forme et psychologie de l'enfant," in *Journal de psychologie normale et pathologique* XXI (1924).

Piaget, J. *La Représentation du monde chez l'enfant* (Paris: Alcan, 1926).

Guillaume, P. "Le problème de la perception de l'espace et la psychologie de l'enfant," in *Jour. de psych. norm. et path.* XXI (1924), 112–34.

Wallon, H. "De l'image au réel chez l'enfant," in *Revue de philosophie*.

Wallon, H. *Les Origines du caractère chez l'enfant* (Paris: Boivin, 1934).

—Trans. by Forrest Williams.

7

◆

Christianity and
Ressentiment (1935)

I

The description of *ressentiment* which Scheler borrows from Nietzsche[1] reminds one of the "traumatic reminiscences" of Janet or the complexes of Freud or Adler. It is a question of one of the "segments of life" or of one of the "types of behavior" which is the object of a concrete psychology. The desire for revenge, hatred, and envy give rise to *ressentiment* only when they are not successfully released or expressed and when they clash with the repressed force of an impotent sentiment. Although hatred leaves the man of clear consciousness unscathed, it paralyzes the man of *ressentiment*. The man of *ressentiment* dreads every attitude, all speech, and each act in which hatred might be expressed. From that point, a state of anxiety spreads quickly. One might say that hatred has forgotten its *raison d'être*, that it exists for itself; nothing can satisfy it once the initial act is repressed. *Ressentiment* wills nothing; it accomplishes nothing. It is henceforth an attitude so essential and so little connected to the event from which it is born that its analysis will everywhere uncover the latent under the most varied manifest content.[2] Many alleged "gratuitous" acts are, in reality, only "defective acts"; the leveling process involved in *ressentiment* traverses a state of apparent serenity—conversation, work, a friendship or an attachment sometimes of long-standing. The body mimics consciousness and physiological anguish is united with a feeling of incompletion and interior emptiness. It happens that this animosity which no longer aims at anything is then turned against the self and personal, individual weaknesses: "hatred of self, disgust of self, and the desire to take vengeance, upon oneself."[3]

But precisely because it weakens and destroys that which supports it, *ressentiment* devises a kind of recovery; it draws near a reaction and a genuine solution just as an injured organism makes use of "substitutions."

85

And it is here that it almost becomes creative, because it obtains, as Nietzsche said, a "falsification of the value tablets." Unable to escape the sight of values of which he is incapable, the man of *ressentiment* denies them in order to free himself from them. Henceforth, "the man of *ressentiment* can no longer justify, understand, or realize his own existence and sense of life in terms of positive values such as power, health, beauty, freedom and independence. Weakness, fear, anguish, and a slavish disposition prevent him from becoming master of these things or of these qualities. Gradually his sense of values shifts; he leaves no stone unturned in coming to decree that 'all this is vain anyway' and he discovers that the necessary elements for the salvation of man lies in the opposite phenomena: poverty, suffering, illness and death."[4] Submission to the ever-growing blindness regarding the values which he is incapable of attaining; doing the best he can to attain a measure of goodness and beauty; denying the existence of value because it escapes him: such is the consolation of the man of *ressentiment* and such is his "organic mendacity." Having corrupted the hierarchy of values, he will be sincere with regard to his new scale of values by ardently embracing that which he idolized. Scheler's diagnosis is profound: having lied once and for all, "the man who has so deceived himself no longer has any need to lie."[5]

This reversal is condemned precisely because it is the motive for impotence and it is not suitable to a positive perception of new values; what makes this recovery a perverted and deceitful recovery is that it is not a return to completeness. When the value of illness is affirmed because the healthy individual has lost it, the infirm individual does not positively see the value of the illness: he successfully overlooks the value of health. The man destined to *ressentiment* is the one who cannot perceive the values of others without reference to himself. He wants "to be worth at least as much as the others." If he cannot truly equal them, he will—and this is characteristic of *ressentiment*—make a virtue of necessity by viewing his weaknesses as the very highest values. These assertions only indicate the same weakness under another name; they preserve the character of a *reaction*. "Whereas every noble morality springs from a triumphant affirmation of oneself, says Nietzsche, slave morality is from the very first a 'negation' of everything which is not part of oneself, or whatever is different from oneself. . . . This negation is its own creative act. This reversal of the perspective of valuation—this viewpoint which is *necessarily* determined by the exterior world rather than by oneself—this appears to be typical of *ressentiment*."[6] That which the man of *ressentiment* lacks in order to effect a true recovery is not the triumphant affirmation of oneself—which could be but another illusion—rather it is patience with oneself, an acknowledgment of the shortcomings which are his; if there is a question of injury, for instance, a genuine pardon is in order. Such acts leave the value of others intact and make us share joyfully in all their nobility.

II

For Nietzsche, pardon and sacrifice are the "same flower of *ressentiment*." Christianity follows the two epochs which are described: first, slavery wherein the impotence of man is asserted in force, vengeance, and impatience—in a word the "impoverished life." Then envy and hatred of the masters find a reaction in spiritual vengeance and a reversal of values, wherein weakness becomes a "worth," impotence "goodness," meanness "humility," restraint "obedience," and cowardice "patience." Suffering becomes poverty, and failures come to the fore as if they were the most noble qualities; exuberance and triumph of life are dubbed worthless. Those who participate in life are the unfortunate whom it becomes necessary to "pity" and to "love." And just as "the slaves influence the masters," the "bad conscience" is seen to appear: the masters are ashamed of their own power. It is good that they mistrust themselves, Nietzsche thinks. Impotence becomes the greatest success of hatred because it is the most subtle means of offense—it is the "sublime vengeance" of the weak. So, "out of the trunk of that tree of revenge and hatred, of Jewish hatred—the most profound and sublime which the world has yet known— ... from this hatred, there grew something equally incomparable, a *new love*; the most profound and sublime kind of love. . . ."[7]

In the eyes of Scheler, the analysis of *ressentiment* is a discovery of prime importance for the explanation of morality. It is a question for him, then, of knowing whether Christianity is only a kind of justification for those who are not able to live. But it is indeed true that he reverses the idea of love which the ancient philosophers have known. In the works of Aristotle, for example, love is a need or a lack, proceeding from the inferior to the superior, from the imperfect to the perfect. On the other hand, in the writings of Augustine, love "beautifies beyond all reason," it is an act which descends from the superior to the inferior, from God to the world, from the strong to the weak, and from the rich to the poor. But if it is so directed, is it necessary to say that it tends to the "less living"? Quite to the contrary, it is a super-abundance of life. "Its action arises from a powerful feeling of security, strength, and inner salvation, of the invincible fullness of one's own life and existence. Furthermore, its action arises from a clear awareness that one is able to share one's existence and possessions. . . ."[8] Love and sacrifice cannot appear as contraries in life unless one imagines life in the fashion of a preservative system—mere self-preservation. In reality, observation suggests more the idea of an expansion or a prodigality. Egoism and fear of death, which many ancient philosophers sought to overcome, belong to the viewpoint of degenerative facts, while on the contrary, indifference with regard to one's life has "vital value."

It is true that "the history of Christianity is . . . filled with terrible instances of contempt of the body, especially of anything regarding sensuality."[9] It is, however, not proper to contrast Christian asceticism with other varieties of asceticism. Its meaning is not hatred and contempt of the body; its value is not in itself. Without speaking again of spiritual liberation, it ought to assure the living an autonomy in regard to "all the particular external stimuli which come to him."[10] This is why asceticism is found outside religion, in certain techniques of education which prepare for war or for sports, as, for example, with the Spartans. There is a purely biological asceticism which seeks to deliver the *vital* from the *agreeable*, and it could be said that the very greatest success in life is not to abound in pleasure but to preserve oneself and to advance "with a minimum of mechanisms."[11] The Gospel gives us the same analogy: "The ravens with neither storehouse nor barn" and "the lilies which do not toil and spin" and yet "they are arrayed more gloriously than Solomon."[12] Christian poverty is not *against* life, since there is within that kind of life a spontaneous indifference in regard to its own circumstances. It is not that the Christian is uninterested in the greatest freedom of existence and living every moment of his life to the fullest. But, just as the life of plants and brutes is ignorant, in its naive force, of obsession with their welfare—so Christianity seeks to render to man a confidence and spontaneity which is beyond the natural in the average, tormented intellect. What Christianity outlaws is precisely, and in the strongest sense of the word, "a vital weakness."

It becomes quite clear—and this is an immediate evidence that one can demand Nietzsche to reconsider—that when the "new love" inclines toward sickness or toward poverty, it is *from* the sickness and *from* the poverty that a man wishes to be rescued. *Behind* the suffering which has no value in itself (the value is found in the act through which one accepts it by himself) is the spiritual pulsation of the man who is loved. This is his power of recovery. Through this *act* of love, one will see that the living are united not in suffering, but in *recovery*. Love of the poor and the unfortunate does not—as has been said too frequently—multiply the amount of evil. It wishes to reduce it. And the triumphant affirmation of oneself which Nietzsche wishes to put in its place might well be called the "fear of life" if it is not capable of regarding the suffering which exists.[13] Scheler, however, does not forget those passages of the Beatitudes found in the Gospel according to Luke which are a malediction of riches; and of those who "laugh today." In these passages, it would seem that unless one is poverty-stricken and held in low esteem by men, it becomes impossible to enter the Kingdom of God. One will see that such a version of Christianity, as alien to *ressentiment*, is more of an interpretation than a complete morality, and Scheler supposes that this text of Saint Luke can perhaps be so interpreted.[14] But moreover, the Evangelist wishes to introduce through a vital principle the idea of a New Spirit, of a Kingdom of God incommensurate with all the earthly distinctions which men have invented; the ridicule of earthly values has no other meaning, perhaps, than of indicating negation in the face of God. And finally, even though it is disconcerting, the entire question is one of knowing if, according to the Gospel, these negations are of the very essence of sanctity. But it suffices to think of all those texts where Jesus announces Life—and thence to those who follow him—in order to recognize that that which is aspired to from the very beginning is beatitude. Riches and good fortune are a delusion to those who can be noble, but it is only if the rich are complacent, self-assured, and unable to see beyond the present moment. Poverty and misfortune are in no sense a means of justification; they can be just as terrible a delusion to the poor and unfortunate. When Jesus told the rich young man that he should give all his wealth *to the poor*, was He not really saying that if it is necessary to despise the delusion of riches, it is likewise necessary to relieve the poor of their poverty?

If these remarks are justified, then Christianity entirely escapes *ressentiment*, since these negations are nothing other than the opposite of a fundamental affirmation: love, which is the unique precept of Christianity. It is the *raison d'être* and very truth of all law. If this new love demands a "holding in suspense"—rather than a repression—of the natural reactions of violence, does it not really want our actions to be independent of the attitude of others and never to have the character of a reaction? Does it not really accomplish the promises of a Will to Power which is but a triumphant affirmation? Because it is only a negation, *ressentiment* is an interior poison, but what is certainly essential to Christianity is honesty of heart. "Action ought to emanate vitally from the profundity of personal individualism, as the fruit from the tree."[15]

III

These remarks, however, even if they are justified, do not carry the weight of a definitive solution. If acts of sacrifice *are not against life*, it is necessary to add immediately that they are enacted in a world "essentially transcendent to the life and the fortuitous incidents of the life of a Christian";[16] the assurance of the Christian is of its very nature analogous to the vital confidence of natural existents. But, Nietzsche will ask: Can one lay claim to both natural life and supernatural life at the same time? To use the old adage: Can one hold with the hare and run with the hound? Either one attends to the supernatural sense of Christianity, but then can one without equivocation say that Christianity is not contrary to life? From all the evidence, according to the Christian, there is "a sacrifice of life itself to those values prized more highly than vital values."[17] Or else, Christianity is really in accord with biological values, in which case it is necessary to establish the relation between Christianity and biological values and to determine their perpetuation and interdependence. Scheler has good reason to show that the Christian directly aspires to neither suffering nor poverty. Before all else, he seeks the Kingdom of God. But this life to which he tends is a new life, another life. It is then established that Christianity is not a fact of gross *ressentiment*, because it does not begin with an explicit negation. But might it not be a fact of subtle *ressentiment*, since it searches for a transcendent life? Does not the mere wish of going beyond earthly values suppose a "tedium with life"—nowadays it could be called a weakening of "the function of the real"—does this not lead ultimately to a devaluation of the earth?

But the thought of Nietzsche can surely be detected: it is granted that Christianity *presents itself* as an affirmation, that law wishes to be only a preparation for joy. But to believe in this appearance would be just to reduce it to the artifice of *ressentiment*: Christianity wishes and claims to be first of all an affirmation; the question is whether Christianity can be anything but a negation. And that is because every positive act is immanent to life, derived from the psychophysiological energy of man. In regard to this biological monism, every tendency toward a super-nature can be nothing but an illusion. "Life," a unique substance, does not admit of "another life," or a "new life." The sole problem revolves around knowing through what mechanism it has produced a doctrine which denies it—just as evolution begets excessive organs and eventually they become useless. And Nietzsche thought that he had resolved the problem through the discovery of *ressentiment*, understanding it as one of the phenomena of "substitution" which compensates for a vital failure. There is no longer a question of knowing how Christianity is presented. Rather it is a question of knowing precisely if the affirmation of values which exceed human psychophysiology, and which ones, if it becomes necessary, ought to be sacrificed. Perhaps, in reality, it is an epiphenomenon of life; the aberrant product of vital degeneracy.

It is here that French readers need to discover the principal works of Scheler, which are as yet unpublished.[18] It is necessary to explore his phenomenology and his theory of knowledge in order to give an answer to the previous question. To admit, as does Nietzsche, that everything which manifests itself to consciousness is a direct or indirect product of physiological and vital causality, is an unjustifiable postulate according to Scheler—just as empiricism is a predilection for Husserl. Empiricism[19] wants every judgment to rest on a sensible intuition, without pointing out that the genus of intuition required for each judgment depends on its nature, which it is first necessary to consider. To take for granted that there is no other mode of being than sensible existence, without simultaneously having explored the positive content of consciousness, is, in spite of all claims to radicalism, a prejudice of empiricism. The first task of reflection is to make an inventory, a description of consciousness, without giving to sensible existence a priority which naturalism surreptitiously concedes to it. And likewise, if as Scheler wants it, we extend this exploration and this survey to the emotional and sentimental sector of consciousness, we will guard ourselves from giving, through a postulate, a privileged reality to the acts and functions which have a biological interpretation. It will be necessary for us to describe consciousness without prejudice as it immediately appears: the "phenomenon" of consciousness in its original, manifold diversity. Yet the claims of a phenomenology of the emotional life ought not to be reduced to those of a descriptive psychology. The "suspension" (*epochē*) of the natural movement which carries consciousness toward the world, toward spatio-temporal existence, and which encloses it—this phenomenological reduction does not merely tend to a more faithful introspection: it is truly an introduction to a new mode of knowledge which moreover manifests the world as well as the self. But, however, if we no longer give any thoughtless priority to things, to states of consciousness engaged in space and time, and to causal explications than are to be admitted, and if we follow the articulations of "phenomena" in living consciousness, then the characteristics and connections which manifest themselves with evidence will allow new laws to appear to us. There is no question of a physical necessity to follow this approach: it is essential to do so.

But, if we direct this new attention toward the content of emotional consciousness, we shall discover in it two essentially different strata. On the one hand, *affective states* (*Gefühlzustand*), which are whole in themselves, like anger, rage, rapture; on the other hand, sentiments or emotions (*reines Fühlen*), like sympathy, love, and hatred, whose proper nature is to pursue some term *other* than themselves—to which, in this sense, "intentionality" is essential.[20] The same character pertains in general to cognitive acts, for example, to perception: it points beyond itself to an "object." But intentionality of the emotions has the unique character of being unable to be expressed in intellectual significations. The contents toward which they tend can be determined only secondarily through the intelligence. Their essence, therefore, is "a-logical"; it is this which is expressed in calling them values. Phenomenological exploration penetrates several regions of such values, and it is impossible to reduce the one to the other, because they are apprehended with an evidence which, from the phenomenological viewpoint, is the final argument:[21] values of the agreeable and the disagreeable, vital values, spiritual values (those of truth and falsity, of the beautiful and the unbecoming, of the right and the unjust), in a word, values of the sacred and the profane, aim "towards specific acts of love and of hatred."[22] Moral values, which particularly interest us here, are nowhere situated in this hierarchy. It is because the good act strives to realize some degree of value on all levels of being previously described. Moral value therefore exists on each level. But absolute moral value has the character of an act which tends to realize the very highest degree of values.

Across the spectrum of concrete objects and creatures, for example, in a man whom we meet for the first time, in the inner circle of the family, in an instantaneous smile, we immediately seize value, and this perception cannot be explained through a previous experience of pleasure or pain lying in similar objects. In that which concerns moral values, there is some justification for saying with Kant that the Good is not the result of an induction recapitulating our experience of good things. The error would be to believe with Kant that because it is not empirical, the good ought to be formal and ought to express autonomy of the will. There are some "a priori materials," that is to say, some objects of concrete intention which manifest in their properties an essential and extratemporal necessity. The realization of the greatest values, in which the moral act consists, is therefore a participation or a full perception—not an heroic affirmation of an empty form. That which is called will has no other capability than of disposing and awakening us to the perception of values. It is "blind as regards values" (wertblind).[23]

A rigorous description of the content of consciousness brings to light a "moral apprehension" (sittliches Erfassen) which manifests itself to us as irreducible to immobile affective states or to inclinations and desires. It opens one's mind to an objective hierarchy of values which are no less valid when they do not attract us. The act of preference through which we seize a spiritual value is phenomenologically distinct from the tendency (Streben) which it sometimes establishes, as knowledge is distinct from desire. In place of exploring in its total variety the emotional life of man, philosophy sometimes endeavors to reduce the intentional part to the affective part. Its horizon is thus incredibly limited. Spinoza defines the good as "that which is or can be desired,"[24] as one might say, a permanent possibility of happiness; it no longer means objective valuation, but consists only in a relation of things to us. The object of "moral relativism" in all its varieties ought to be described as the successive emergence of the values in history. In fact, just as morality has been reduced to a tendency toward happiness, so the "moral relativism" of Comte, Mill, and Spencer has merely been able to record the various ideas of happiness according to the types of society. Nietzsche has pointed out the following with strong conviction: moralities do not differ solely through the manner of conceiving happiness; they differ more profoundly through the position which they accord to it. But, could this reproach not be turned against Nietzsche himself? The very nature of the works of Nietzsche proves that riches and ancestry establish "moral relativism" completely. But doesn't his biological monism[25] appear, in the perspective of Scheler, as the final degree of the collapse of values? But, the characteristic of *ressentiment* is denial and restraint. . . .

It is at this point that Scheler's approach can be discerned with precision. His philosophical attitude can be defined in general as an effort to restore to consciousness the variety and the diverse intentionalities which *ressentiment* has removed. A philosophy of *ressentiment* is explicated through *reduction*. Men have therefore been witness to these systematic reductions in the theory of life, the theory of emotions, the theory of knowledge, as well as the theory of morality. In the evolution of life, Lamarckism and Darwinism tend to minimize the role of the factors of growth for the benefit of preservative factors: having given, once and for all, a principle of creation in the form of fortuitous, congenital variations, Darwinism becomes interested principally in the factors of selection. The question of knowing how life develops tends to be transformed into the question of knowing how the aberrant forms, supposedly given, are eliminated. The metaphysical dualists, who refer the phenomena of life to a mechanical causality, clearly indicate in man a sort of divorce between the soul and the body. The body is considered "dejectedly as a distant object,"[26] and this finally gives way to a "weakening impulse." But the same dualism manifests his vindictive turn of mind when he substantially reduces all the spiritual to the intellectual. By paying heed to the intentionalities of the emotional life, the real nature of value can be discovered. This can no longer be overlooked. Empiricism and subjective idealism explain consciousness as a composition of impressions. These "pathetic" philosophies[27] deny that a content of consciousness can naturally have a *meaning*; consciousness is a fact of states which receive secondarily a signification, spatiality, for example, through means of association of ideas. Love, hatred, sympathy are no longer orientating acts but states of pleasure or sadness enclosing oneself, *accompanied* solely, says Spinoza, with the idea of an external cause. The perception of others as such, very often inherent to these acts, re-establishes an interior reconstitution of the states of consciousness of others. All this occurs with the aid of my own, unique experience. But just as the region of the vital is reduced to that of the mechanical, so the region of the spiritual is reduced to that of the vital, for all that which is not intelligence. "The clear, almost cool spiritual enthusiasm of Christian love[28] is interpreted as an 'affective hallucination' or an 'affective induction.' "[29] A psychology of history reveals in all these reductions the rhythm of *ressentiment*. These philosophers no longer know "through a direct intercourse with the world and things."[30] The step of prime importance is no longer a recognition of the evidences which are given, but a search for the "criteria" which arrest doubt and resist it. By way of contrast, Scheler's constant attitude is specified as a "profound confidence in all that which is immediately given"; "it is not a wish to dominate the world, but a joyful impulse of one's existence, of greeting towards the expansion of vital plentitude."[31]

Such is the response which the philosophy of Scheler gives to the naturalism of Nietzsche. A direct intercourse with things, creatures, and consciousness makes this sphere of life manifest itself where *ressentiment* has wished to imprison spiritual values and religious values under the mask of truth. If Nietzsche were able to situate Christianity in the presence of a dilemma and give it a choice between naturalistic immanence and illusory transcendence, it would be only by virtue of a philosophical affirmation: that of biological monism. If, inversely, "a logic of the heart reveals, beyond the vital exigencies, an objective structure of spiritual and religious value, Christianity can no longer be accused of depreciating the terrestrial life through the sole fact that it aspires to something else: transcendence can no longer be the sublimation of a vital weakening."

IV

But the same philosophical light which makes evident the specificity in religious acts also makes apparent the degradations or distortions which are suffered throughout history. Against the distortions which are the inner product of Christianity and then become manifest outwardly, the criticism of Nietzsche is the sharpest. The criticism is directed to a "bourgeois" morality which "after the 13th century gradually disintegrated Christian morality."[32] It remains for us now to note the connections of the religious acts and life of true Christianity so as to better comprehend the degradations.

When the "new love" demands sacrifice of a natural movement, it is essential to remark that value is recognized therein. Christianity has never recommended a sort of autosuggestion in the manner of the Stoics, where pain would lose the character of an evil. There is no question of creating a race of "tamed modern gregarious animals" *incapable* of hostility, but rather a race capable of performing acts superior to those of instinct.[33] The affirmation pronounced on the level of the "spiritual person" permits subsistence beyond the realities of nature. Nature is "admitted" and completely transfigured. Jesus never spoke of a new political order or of new institutions which would distribute riches otherwise, or of a stoic "cosmopolite." "He calmly admitted the differences of condition which are in force between masters and slaves, the domination of an imperial power, and even natural instincts capable of creating relations of hostility between men". . . .[34] It is neither the struggle of the classes nor war which is proscribed; it is hatred. "This is not to say that struggles ought to cease or that the instincts which are their points of departure ought to be destroyed . . .; the main point is that the true and genuine enemy—he whom I know to be my enemy and whom I combat with all means at my disposal—is my "brother in the kingdom of God." In the midst of the struggle, hatred should be absent, especially that ultimate hatred which is directed against the salvation of his soul."[35]

Nevertheless, nothing would be further from the thought of Scheler than imagining a religious life *"plated"* on the life of nature and which would communicate nothing of itself. It is precisely because it is not a phenomenon of the biological, political, and social order and precisely because it does not directly aim at these orders that Christian love can impregnate them. And it is precisely when, with Luther, he wishes to be conscious of himself as an affective state, that he deserts society. If justification through faith precedes and conditions justification through works, and if one counts the number of works even to the act of love of men, it can no longer be the road of justification. Primary attention is given to "the proper work of salvation," which no longer does more than join "each soul and its God." Luther also notes that there is nothing which favors less the idea of a Church than where the responsibility is collective, or salvation is not the work of the individual himself. From there, one is easily led to abandon love of one's neighbor, to resort to a sensible sympathy for other men in place of true love of one's neighbor and to invest the moral functioning of society to "authority." There is perhaps not a necessary sequence here; it appears, however, that such an effective passage has occurred in history. But it is just where religious values tend to be confused with affective states, and one might say, to be humanized, that they cease to control the economic relations of men. By indicating the non-temporal character of religious acts, one refuses to identify them with a specific form of social or political organization; this is by no means to separate the religious from the sphere of the socioeconomic. It is, perhaps, to prepare one to be more faithful to it. The kingdom of God or this new society between men which creates love without speaking is not to be interpreted, as suggested by the Platonic phrase, "in heaven," and less of the earth. It should not be thought of as a negation of the earth, as an overthrowing of the earthly life, a backdrop, so to speak, contrasted with center stage. In periods of great faith, the kingdom of God has never been the occasion of compensation. *Because* it is not a world overthrown—but *another thing—precisely because* it is transcendent, it is not a means of postponing justice until after death—a means of making the poor patient. . . .[36]

By carefully studying Scheler one will see that what he sets up as a distortion of Christianity is its inattention to the economic conditions of men. This is to disguise in love a "very human" *ressentiment*. There is a "love" of others which is nothing other than a hatred of oneself; there is a "love" of the poor which is nothing other than a hatred of the wealthy and which loves in them precisely that which it is necessary to heal. This kind of love condescends to the "life of the humble people" and the "stench of the sickroom."[37] It is this pretended love, and it alone, which exposes Christianity to the criticism of Nietzsche, who reproaches it for loving suffering too much, just as it is exposed to the criticism of Marx, who reproaches it for deceiving people. Christianity ought to render its adherents more exacting, more acute, and more fully aware of the matter of social politics; love of men has nothing in common with a "social esprit," which would be but a decadent flavor of suffering men—this is a perpetual danger for Christianity.[38]

Another exigency of *ressentiment* will distort it even further: that of a sort of spiritual equality among men. For Scheler the idea of a "human nature," of a specific difference which equalizes men among themselves and distinguishes them radically from the animals, marks the irruption in Christianity of pagan thought and bourgeois humanitarianism. For that which definitively elevates man above his race is the "new birth," the accession to the superhumanity of grace. In this sense, the anti-humanism of Nietzsche is of Christian ancestry.[39]

An even greater reason makes it necessary to attempt to trace the development of humanitarianism. It shows how, in preserving words sometimes, *ressentiment* has substituted in Christianity a totally new morality. The Gospel as well as the Old Testament can be summarized in the one commandment: love God with your whole soul and your neighbor as yourself. We will be unsuccessful in directly explaining the enigma of this commandment: the union of love of God, love of one's neighbor, and love of oneself. But this communication of the threefold love becomes evident through the counterproof of humanitarianism. All humanism is essentially Promethean and begins with hatred—the hatred of the wisdom and goodness of God: wretched men find themselves in the milieu of a hostile universe. Their ingenuity which little by little and in spite of nature invents houses, boats, arts, sciences—their incertitudes, their efforts, their defeats, their final successes, their earthly nature gradually emerge from the light and shadows of animality—that is the religion of humanism. Nature immediately loses in value since man is only worth as much as he separates himself from it and withdraws from it. One will see then the psychologies of the nineteenth century explain systematically the love of nature, of animals, or of plants by transferring on them the sentiments which are normally addressed to man. Suppressing the love of God is simultaneously a suppression of the world; one wants to see that they withdraw also from one's neighbor. For the appeal henceforth is addressed to "every member of the human race" or, as is said, "to all mankind."[40] One finds in mankind so much more dignity than one finds in the greatest number of individual men. But through this immersion in the "human race" love of self is lost. One will think without doubt of the words of Pascal: "*le Moi est haissable*"—Pascal is a "man filled with *ressentiment* as few others, who was a genius in hiding the fact and in interpreting it in Christian terms."[41] But this word is not a pledge to Christianity. The commandment continues—to love one's neighbor "as oneself." But humanitarian "altruism" doesn't want love of oneself. "Love your neighbor *more than* yourself," says Auguste Comte. This is where the essence of love is forgotten. Because one no longer sees in it anything other than an affective state, one can no longer see in love of self anything other than self-complacency.

Humanitarianism has thus invented a sort of asceticism which no longer has anything in common with Christian asceticism. It refuses all value to *gifts* in every sense of the term. The only good acts are those which a man performs through his own proper powers, through his own *work*. To speak of solidarity in evil as in good no longer makes any sense. The "human race" has replaced the invisible church and the human race does not make gratuitous gifts: each man, according to Comte, ought to return as much as he can according to what he has received from society. In this spirit the idea of a sort of treasury of moral value in which men can participate as though they do not have merit—the idea of a Communion of Saints—becomes incomprehensible. But like the gifts of Grace, those of nature have lost all value. The religion of utility, the cult of labor, while favoring the production of good things, forbids their enjoyment.[42] All the essential notions of morality—those of Christian morality in particular—were impregnated little by little with value judgments proper to a mercantile civilization. If one does not find satisfaction in these words and if one goes to the root of the problem one will see what a difference there is and what a debasement of evangelical poverty and voluntary sacrifice there has been to bourgeois economy, the "virtue of the rich."[43]

Thus, according to Scheler, Nietzsche is not mistaken in his description of *ressentiment*; also, he is not mistaken when he believes that it can be recognized among certain Christians; but he is entirely mistaken when he believes that Christianity has been founded upon it. Bertram has written a good book, recently translated,[44] and it serves to confirm the judgment of Scheler. One reads in it that almost all the enemies of Nietzsche were internal enemies: Schopenhauer, Wagner, Socrates, and St. Paul. These men, whom he detested, were nothing but phantoms conjured in his own mind, and through them it is he himself, according to his own unique disposition, which he is attempting to injure.[45] It is to be presumed that in the same manner Christianity which he tramples underfoot is none other than an aspect of himself. He wrote in 1868: "That which I appreciate in Wagner and that which I appreciate in Schopenhauer is the moral atmosphere, the fragrance of Faust, the Cross, death and the tomb."[46] The Christianity which he defiles, and that which he bears within himself, is it not precisely a "moral atmosphere" of death and the tomb? And if, as Scheler has luminously pointed out, true Christianity, which is the Cross, is not a "fragrance of Faust," "death or the tomb," one understands that he is uninjured by the criticism of Nietzsche. Bertram indicates that perhaps the final letters which Nietzsche signed as "Dionysius" and "the Crucified" signify "the everlasting nostalgia of an aspirant to a life of Christianity elevated to the highest power, and seen, no longer in the mirror of obscure speech, but face to face."[47] Both Scheler and Bertram make us understand that instead of looking for a Christianity of life in Luther, Nietzsche should have found it in the pristine origin of Christianity. This might have happened had Nietzsche not read the Gospels in the atmosphere of Faust and death. As it was, Nietzsche was not even aware of the extent to which he was impregnated with this atmosphere.

V

There ought to be no question, after having followed Scheler so long, of posing every single question which this essay raised. We have chiefly insisted on the analyses, incontestable from our point of view, where Scheler admirably shows the difference between Christianity and its "counterfeits." The complex description of humanitarianism will be surprising perhaps—if anyone can still be surprised—warned through the previous French lectures of Curtius and Sieburg. They make one conscious, perhaps, that prometheism, the religion of civilization, is far from being indispensable to "human dignity." They penetrate French education in an incredible manner. Far better to teach intercourse and friendship with nature than that which these proud citizens risk living without knowing it. But to how many Christians is it necessary to recall the life of St. Francis of Assisi? In order to understand certain violent animosities which the mere word Christianity raises, nothing is more important than to be conscious of all that which customs, the contingent proprieties of the "milieu," and above all the hypocrisy of *ressentiment* interposed between us and the faith of the fishermen of Tiberias. The vindictive atmosphere has certainly made our approach to the problem more difficult. If Scheler limits himself to bringing to light the pure motivation of Christian acts, their intentionality, their expression, that which renders Christianity incomparable to other ideologies which recommend *similar acts*, the true nature of sacrifice which involves a knowledge of what is sacrificed—if Scheler limits his exposition to an explanation of these, no one can object. It is especially in this order that we have placed our exposition.

But, in our consideration of this essay, and in the French text, we believe that we perceive in the passages something else. "In the name of humanity, one comes little by little to proclaim universal peace."[48] It is no longer a question of noting that which really distinguishes Christian pacifism from a pacifism of vital depression. Scheler, it seems to me, sets one to thinking that pure Christianity does not tend to develop in a regulation of life, to combat war and develop vital value. But, according to the same reasoning, why combat sin if it is chivalrous, if hatred is not implied in it. Whatever is the decisive importance of one's intention and whether justification is ever "experienced" or not, it is always characteristic of Christianity to admit that there are some acts which affect the "spiritual person," although performed in solitude—there is a bond between that which we do and that which we want, a substantial connivance of the "spiritual person" and sensible consciousness. In this sense, Christianity in all its purity *"militates against"* sin, just as it militates to wrest the poor from their misery. While every observable consciousness is occupied in violence without hatred, the "spiritual person" can rest intact, his transcendence assures him a kind of metaphysical salvation: we do not have to escape from ourselves, we have already escaped. The concrete relations of the "spiritual person" and sensible consciousness evidently pose a question of the religious order, just as those of intentionality and affectivity pose a philosophical question.

With regard to the method of Scheler, of which we have been able to give but a ridiculously brief glance, it will be for French readers a significantly worthwhile reagent. M. Fernandez wrote as the most natural thing in the world: "It is not only his language nor his interests which truly indicate his philosophy; it is his disposition of not believing anything which is not affirmed through an effective *act* of intelligence, in giving to each word his own unique meaning. From this angle, if one penetrates to date the subterfuges of passion, every philosopher is an intellectual at birth and an idealist by instinct; and every anti-intellectual philosophy reduces itself to an intellectual act through which the spirit bestows the right to yield to the most secret complacencies."[49] For M. Fernandez, whose formation in this regard is entirely critical and French, the effective act of intelligence excludes in principle that which restrains or shocks it; to understand is never to seize the object of thought as it is; it is constituted from the chaos of the world, and the thinking subject has the right of imposing his rules on that which is given, because without them there would be no object, but only the meaningless illusion of "sensible diversity." The norms of physics become the laws of being. The universes of perception, art, emotions, religious acts are considered as sketches or even debasements of the universe of science. There is no doubt that the philosophy of science has done a good job in pointing out that no one has yet conceived a scientific analysis which exhausts that which is given here and now. Even in the future, the *object* of science cannot be co-extensive with all that *exists*. The criticism of M. Brunschvicg will accord without difficulty, but he will respond that, of that which has not been reduced to an object of science, we are able to say nothing, to think nothing, not even that it exists. However, if the scientific coordination of the given does not show us how things "are facts,"[50] if objectivity cannot exhaust existence, will it not be the act of the philosopher to try a rediscovery, a description of existence in all its forms? Such is the purpose of M. Wahl or M. Marcel. And it is also the claim of a descriptive philosophy which Scheler has made worthwhile. But there is question of a description of essences. The constitutive act of philosophy would not be to grasp consciousness of the creative activity of the subject, but to grasp knowledge of objects of thought and to follow the articulations which they impose on us, for example, describing the life of the emotions such as this life really is. Where M. Fernandez speaks of "secret complacency," it is very true that every philosopher knows where he wishes to enter philosophy. The whole question is one of knowing whether he truly has the right of going in. If the classical analysis of the emotions, of perception, of religious acts has changed as easily as cloud formations, then it is the philosopher's right to dissolve the classical analysis. In reality philosophy has not yet rendered an account of their intentional nature as it is compatible with evidence. It is deficient from the first in offering a correct analysis which explains an appearance as it really is. Is there not therefore a necessity and a right of attempting another? If one could give to philosophy an essential definition of intelligence which would put an end to all future discussion, two consequences result: first, it would give to philosophy a certain lucidity fostering a protected atmosphere; second, it would perhaps surrender all claim to knowing what is.

—Trans. by Gerald Wening.

8

Being and Having (1936)

Philosophy as well as common sense has taken our contemplation of inanimate objects and indifferent things as representing the model and ideal of human knowledge.[1] When I look out my window and see people walking along the street, "I am in the habit of saying that I see people . . . and yet from this window I see only hats and coats which could be coverings for phantoms and automatons. But I judge that they are people. Thus I understand, by the sole power of judgment that resides in my mind, what I thought I was seeing with my eyes."[2] My perception of other people can thus be broken down into two elements: on the one hand, that which is properly seen—clothes, the shapes of bodies, a human shell—which Descartes would doubtless reduce to a set of colored patches and lines, and on the other, a judgment through which I confer upon these inert givens a living meaning. Let us now turn our attention to the knowledge of one's own body and let us question the psychologists of the nineteenth century. They will tell us that our body is a set of visual and tactile sensations which are distinguishable from foreign bodies on the basis of several characteristics. This mass of privileged sensations is constantly given to me, and it is accompanied by particularly strong affective impressions. And these special characteristics give rise to a judgment by which I circumscribe the limits of my body. In a word, in both cases, we are used to setting out from a certain type of knowledge considered *normal*: the contemplation of a set of qualities or characteristics that are scattered, meaningless. Against these givens, this spectacle, a subject is posited, who interprets and understands them and who is consequently no more than a "power of judging," a *Cogito*. And since that analysis is easily applied to scientific knowledge, philosophers are convinced that knowledge is a dialogue between a "subject" and an "object" in the sense that we have just specified.

Marcel's first essays spoke in protest against these reductions and against the theory of knowledge they contain. Perhaps the people I distractedly

101

observe walking by in the street do not look any different to me than clothed mannequins. However, we must bear in mind that, by taking a kind of "defensive market position"[3] ["*spéculation à la baisse*"], what has been taken as the model for our perception of others is a distracted sort of knowing, one in which it is in fact the case that I do not perceive human beings but rather human shapes vaguely moving about. By contrast, a human being who is *present* to me, the one to whom I address myself, who is truly a second person before me, this "you," cannot be reduced to a set of characteristics I could coolly catalogue. And by the same token, when I consider my body as it is given to me, it is clear that the knowledge I have of it cannot be assimilated to the supposedly normal type described above. The striking fact that my body is precisely *my* body cannot be accounted for by merely adding affective impressions, or "double sensations," as they were called, or even judgment and an entire body of knowledge, to a mass of visual and tactile sensations. My body does not appear to me as an object, a set of qualities and characteristics to be linked up with one another and thus understood. My relation to it is not that of the *Cogito* to the *cogitatum*, the "epistemological subject" to the object. I and it form a common cause, and in a sense I *am* my body. Between it and me there cannot properly be said to be a relation, since this term designates the behavior of one object in reference to another. Here it is more a question of presence, adherence, and intimacy. But similarly, to the extent that I really believe in objects and grasp their physiognomies rather than their "characteristics," their presences rather than their essences, they become something like the extension of my body. It is not on my body as I experience it, nor on objects as understood by people who live among them, that philosophers have carried out their analyses. They have positioned themselves in the "spectator's point of view,"[4] which stripped the object of its human aspect, of its hold on us, while freeing the subject from involvement in such situations as hope, despair, promises, or prayer, in which it strains forward toward the other to the point of inseparability. In order to apprehend himself as a pure, unattached "I," the philosopher had to treat himself as an object; he had to assume toward himself that spectator's point of view that we first learn to assume toward others. In this sense the *Cogito* is far from being the first principle, the condition of all valid certainty. The root of the ingenuous affirmation is rather the body's consciousness, which may well underlie all affirmations of the existence of physical objects. "Embodiment, the central given of metaphysics . . . is the given on the basis of which a fact is possible (which is not true of the *Cogito*)."[5]

Marcel's more recent works make it possible to ascertain the philosophical significance of these remarks. It is not just a matter of marking off, alongside the physical world and the scientific universe, certain regions—one's own body, the domain of the "you"—that could not in fact be annexed. It becomes increasingly clear that the analyses of one's own body and of the "you" were the first trial applications of a general method, the first examples of a new type of knowledge. It seems that what phenomenology offered Marcel in this instance was not fully formed truths but a way to draw out and justify what his first reflections implied. For even when those reflections took on the more definite form of an opposition between existence and objectivity,[6] the casual reader might still have held that after all the author was merely making a distinction between two "contents of thought," just adding a new chapter to the psychology of knowledge. Phenomenology, insofar as it refuses to conjure up, behind the actual or virtual object of our thoughts, *things* that might not bear any resemblance to it, immediately confers undeniable value upon distinctions established between "contents of thought." In this sense Marcel can adopt a "transcendental"[7] or "phenomenological point of view."[8] Existence and objectivity, therefore, can no longer appear as two phenomena in the restrictive sense of the term: they are henceforth two regions of being. A phenomenological method—at the same time that it brings being closer to the subject, for the simple reason that the only being we can discuss is the one we know, albeit inadequately—binds the subject closely to being by defining the former as a tension or an intention oriented toward an end point. From that moment on, a new field of research is opened up, one which stretches beyond the body proper and the domain of the "you," to embrace all the "involvements" of the soul. Themes for analyses will involve the person engaged in perceiving, thinking, wanting, hoping, and praying as well as beings that are perceived, known, wanted, loved, adored, prayed to *as they are intended or at least sensed in these acts themselves*. With *Being and Having*, Marcel's philosophy has been enlarged, so to speak. It tends to become an understanding of life, of the entire set of situations lived through by human beings, each with its own atmosphere. To an increasing degree the center of the perspective shifts from the body to the soul. If my body is indeed more than an object that I own, it is equally true that it is not me; it is "at the border of what I am and what I have," at the line of demarcation between being and having. The central fact of metaphysics is clearly no longer thought of, as stated a moment ago, as the presence and the remoteness of my body: it is rather, in Marcel's new book, the presence and remoteness of my life, the adherence of my life to myself, and at the same time my power to sacrifice it, my refusal to become indistinguishable from it.

The point here is to conceptualize what most philosophers have held to be insignificant. For we are not "equipped" to conceptualize existence, and all the work remains to be done. It is striking to see how prudent or timorous philosophers have been about coining new terms for the very aspects of existence most vital to them. They have tried, for example, to analyze the Christian soul, using Aristotelian notions, which is a kind of paradox, since in Christianity life must be at stake and the soul must be able to be lost or saved. Between that soul and Aristotle's soul as "form of the body," it is impossible to see how a union could be brought about. "Form is eternally saved, it cannot even be threatened."[9] Occasionally the matter it contains might overflow its borders, so to speak, but form itself remains intact and merely withdraws temporarily in order to leave room for material causality. Now, within the soul, there may in fact be a "desire for perdition."[10] And similarly, the salvation of the soul, if it is the "form of the body," is nothing more than the preservation of a natural hierarchy, the normal functioning of a metaphysical mechanism. How can one pretend that the Christian notion of salvation is reducible to good health, or the religious life to hygiene? We must therefore recast our categories.

We should also become accustomed to considering "proof" as a secondary mode of thought. "Proof can only confirm for us what in reality has been given to us in a different way."[11] It consists in "bringing to the discursive level of thought an act that is entirely different."[12] It does not entirely embrace what it has been created to prove; it delineates the schema or prepares the way for an act of which it is not exactly the equivalent. When it is a question of what exists in the truest sense, reflection is less concerned with seeking its *nature* than with bringing out the reasons why there is no nature to be known. It will locate the boundaries that separate *problems*, in which an unknown is determined by its relation to known terms, from *mysteries*,[13] in which the enigma (for example, the meaning of suffering) cannot be resolved by a combination of notions but only by acts of sacrifice or despair. In this way the philosopher prepares a path for hope; but he does not demonstrate, he does not prove, he only points out an irreplaceable experience by showing why it is so. If proof is secondary, certainty is not necessarily expressed in explicit judgments and clearly circumscribed concepts. And that is why "I myself do not know what I believe."[14] As for matters of faith, can one speak, if not of proof, at least of verification? To verify is always to appeal to a more accurate or less prejudiced observer (whether that observer is ourself or someone else), to eliminate whatever personal element our first observation might have had. Hence, such an operation loses all significance the moment our object is to see what, by hypothesis, is inaccessible to the indifferent gaze and is only revealed at the cost of personal involvement. To require a "rectifying experiment" here would be to postulate that truth is what can be verified by all.[15] Certainty, then, becomes indistinguishable from a kind of "efficient intuition."[16] "Is it not perhaps the essence of the ontological that it can only be borne witness to?"[17] There is only one way to confirm that witness: to show that, by essence, it is more valid than any confirmation.

Analyses of promises, commitment, and having, far from describing a few "states of consciousness" borne by an organism that is itself based on the physical world, introduce us into a new world that contains the physical world and is not contained by it. All the perspectives are reversed. Temptation and faithfulness are no longer "inner events" within the arena of a consciousness enclosed in time and space. Rather, space and time are the "forms of temptation,"[18] extreme cases of absence, just as being is "the place of faithfulness," the extreme case of presence. And this presence and this absence should not be thought of as modalities of proximity and distance in time and space. On the contrary, the modalities of proximity and distance have to be derived from presence and absence. According to Marcel, a new theory of time needs to be developed. In a certain sense, a deceased friend who is present to my thoughts is more truly alive than a "living" person I don't like.[19] Time is normally conceptualized as a piece of wood that is burning up: the past is that ash that no heat will ever bring back to life; it is *something* about which nothing can be changed. But if I think of a dead friend, he must be. If he is present to me, why should I hold back from saying that he exists? What proof, what criterion shall I ask for, since this sort of existence by definition has neither proof nor criterion? "There is no historical sedimentation,"[20] and nothing is irrevocable. We can act not only upon the present, but also upon the past. Similarly, we can act upon the future, and what proves it is commitment. I promise a sick friend to come back and see him. "At the moment I make the commitment, either I arbitrarily posit an invariability in my feelings that it is not really in my power to impose, or I accept in advance the obligation of accomplishing at a given moment an act that will in no way reflect my inner disposition when I execute it. In the first case, I lie to myself; in the second, it is to others that I agree in advance to lie."[21] Yet no analysis will cause me to discover, in a promise that is a true promise, one of these lies hidden away. And since appearance and reality merge here, these two lies are not present. What is a promise, then, if it is not the act of an I who remains distinct from the psychic states I witness or own? What is it, if not a manifestation of my being, that my becoming does not have the power to annul? In a sense, just as the entire past once again becomes a present the moment it is present to me, all promises are as if kept the moment they are sincere. If tomorrow I do not feel the same urge to be at my sick friend's side, that betrayal does not mean that my promise did not exist nor that it does not continue to exist in my being, if not in my life. Such are Marcel's efforts to sift out spiritual acts in their purity, to contrast them with imitations that resemble them,[22] and to ascend continually from the domain of having to that of being. This movement between having and being, this border zone, defines the human condition.

The objection that comes to mind in the presence of such a philosophy is that it somehow lacks *binding* force. "There is something called living, and something else called existing: I have chosen to exist."[23] That is a choice, and it cannot be otherwise. But we must ask ourselves whether reflection cannot monitor that option more closely. Specifying and discovering criteria that can stand up against the assault of doubt, and taking an inventory of the objects of thought, these favorite philosophical activities are far from constituting the definition of intelligence itself. They represent a certain use of the intelligence, nothing more, as Marcel well knows, and his philosophy never takes an "anti-intellectual" tone. Nothing could be more in keeping with reason than this rejection of a certain type of reason. But cannot the intelligence, once "retooled," be good for anything but clearing away obstacles that obstruct the decisive intuition? "One can only proceed in this domain by calling out to others, like Karl Jaspers in his *Philosophy of Existence*; if, as I have had occasion to observe, certain individuals respond . . . then there must really be a path. But this path can only be discovered through love, being visible only to love."[24] The author feels more distinctly than anyone else how small a place there is here for philosophy proper. Once we have reached that point, if "I saw" is an argument beyond further questioning, does that philosophy not authorize to an equal extent any pseudo-intuition whatever? How will we distinguish between an authentic intuition and an illusion? That is a question the author brushes aside, because we are asking for a criterion for something that, not being of the order of the "it," cannot have a criterion. Yet we *know how* to tell the difference between true lyricism and delirious raving, for example. And when it does occur that the words of a child or a madman strike the note of pure poetry, our surprise and the kind of shock we feel are ample evidence that those two realms are totally distinct. We are therefore invited to clarify that immediate distinction between what is above and what beneath reason. If all intuition were sufficient in itself, if there were no path, no dialectic leading from inadequate knowledge to more adequate knowledge, how would each being, locked up in his or her own imperfect intuitions, feel the need to go further, to move toward more reality? Do not the existences we come to know have a certain structure, and do they not present partial aspects that are felt to be just that—facets, each of which is an invitation to go farther? Marcel doubtless believes this to be the case, since, somewhere in his work, he maintains the possibility of a dialectic and speaks of a "hyper-phenomenological" method.[25] We are, in fact, not dealing here with a completed philosophy. I have occasionally found myself presenting what in the book was a "proposition" as a thesis. Nothing could be more foolhardy or unfair than to meet suggestions with "refutations."

—Trans. by Michael B. Smith.

9

◆

On Sartre's *Imagination* (1936)

Descartes, Leibniz, Spinoza, and Hume may all have had different conceptions of the relationship between thought and image, but they all agree on an implicit definition of the image: a perception reborn is in all regards comparable to perception.[1] The image is a sensible content. Whether thought of as a modification of thought or as an impression received from without, it is a real part of the thinking being. In a word, it is an internal object. Experimental psychology never questioned that conception, never challenged it with the givens of our inner experience. At times the realm of images, with its quasi-physical attachments, was assigned a subordinate role, but its existence was not questioned. Taine's psychology was dominated by a certain conception of the image that he did not come to by direct analysis but rather introduced a priori, as early as in the preface to *The Intelligence*, in order to give psychology the element it needed if it wanted to resemble physics. In Ribot's works, psychology took biology as its model. Consequently he never failed to stress the unity of psychic operations. But when Ribot wished to analyze the creative imagination, for example, the dissociations, associations, and synthetic factors of which he spoke, they were never anything more than *constructions*. "All this creative mechanism is pure hypothesis. Ribot was no more concerned than Taine was with describing the facts. He begins with explanation" [41, 36].[2]

Shall we say that the idea of the image was corrected by Bergson on the basis of the immediate givens of consciousness? Bergson did indeed expressly claim that a difference in nature had to be acknowledged between images and sensations. But in point of fact we will soon see that his philosophy forced him to abandon the distinction. For he does not get to the problem of the image until he has already established his conceptions of consciousness, the object, and the body. The examination of these metaphysical presuppositions and their consequences with respect to images takes up, in Sartre's book, twenty very dense pages which deserve reflection. Here we can only bring out their general meaning. Sartre's first critique concerns the notion of the subject. Bergson's intention is to break with the conceptions that envelop consciousness in its "states," and to make sure that perception has direct access to things. We do not blame him for this. We blame him for having, in a sense, sought less a solution than a compromise. The world, in preparation for its becoming representation in the subject, is called pure perception; things, prepared to become thoughts, are called "images." But either these terms are taken in an extremely vague sense, and "images" and "pure perception" are nothing but other names for "world" (and in that case consciousness remains to be deduced, since the *esse* does not imply the *percipi*), or in calling things "images" one invests them with a kind of diffused consciousness, from which personal mind is obtained by degradation. But what is a consciousness without an I? "Consciousness appears . . . as a quality, a given character, almost a kind of substantial form of reality" [44, 39]. If at this point one were to object that it is the living body and the "center of indetermination" it envelops that account for awareness, "then it would be abusive to label 'consciousness' those passive realities that consciousness can apprehend, and we would be going back to a metaphysics based not on the world as conscious, but on consciousnesses confronting a world" [47, 41–42].

The transition of matter to mind, of pure perception to memory, and Bergsonian concordism are once again the object of Sartre's second critique. If, for the Bergsonian image, to be conscious is nothing more than to be isolated, how is it that memories can continue to lead an individual life in the Bergsonian unconscious? How can this be, when, the moment I cease perceiving an object, my body stops generating the nascent acts that circumscribe, within the world, the objects of which I am cognizant, so that as soon as the act of perception is completed, the conditions of knowledge are no longer assembled? How can the present retain a lasting psychic existence that will become a past that I can recall? "A present that is pure action cannot, by any manner of reduplication, produce an inactive past, a past that is pure idea" [51, 45]. We could indeed establish the past without further ado by simply declaring that the mind *is* memory, which would amount to waiving all explanation. Let us then make the supposition that the present is continuously duplicated in the memory. Restored to consciousness through the reproduction of its motor framework, memory is brought back to life: the former scene reappears before our eyes. But how does it differ from an act of perception? It can only be recalled by being reintegrated into actual behavior, but if it is thus reintegrated, it is the present. How do we know that it refers to the past? That is the real problem of memory. It is not enough for copies or photographs to be kept or even reproduced; the essential thing is for them to be understood as allusions to the past. But as long as the memory is made into a vision that is preserved, even if in a state of "virtuality," we have deprived ourselves of any means by which we might understand how this subsisting present could ever look like the past—how it could assume its proper place within the perspectival ranks of the ever-receding past. In order to understand the *presencing of the past*, which is indeed the essence of memory, we must reject the mythology of memories that keep, like physical objects, and replace it with the rigorous analysis of the acts in which "I" know the past. These memories in the third person are, however, precisely Bergson's memory-images. They want to "thrust themselves into the light of day"; they "set themselves in motion" [55, 49]. We are very close, here, to the images of associationism: fragments of the past endowed with their own causality. And as a matter of fact, though he placed intellectual effort above the associationist mechanism, Bergson let the "level of imagery" subsist beneath that of the schema. Associationism remains a partial truth, the truth of moments of release. Now, we must understand that it cannot be given its due. If we accept images in the sense intended by associationism, we will never understand the intentionality of mental operations. The materialism of images will contaminate it. We will speak in terms of attraction and repulsion between schemata and images. Thought will be conceived of in the third person, as a force acting upon things, and not as the apprehension of a meaning.

But let us take up for its own sake the classical notion of the image, and we will see that it excludes any valid solution to two essential problems: that of the "true characteristics of the true image" and that of the relationship between thought and images. When the classical conceptions do not treat the image as a "reduced" sensation (Taine), they admit at least that perception and image are constituted by the activity of judgment on the basis of neutral representations. The image is, per se, indistinguishable from the sensation: what determines whether it is to become perception or image is whether or not it can be integrated into the logical context of the true world. But in fact the perceptual field is at every moment overrun with accidents of lighting, strange noises, snaps, pops, and sudden apparitions that are at first inexplicable but that we do not, nevertheless, attribute to images. However astonishing the perception may be, it is always its own proof, appearing as "a primary source of knowledge" [107, 99]. Our judgment deals with the situation the best it can. Conversely, our images, for the most part, have nothing of the fantastic about them; "What we imagine only precedes a little what is going to happen, or follows by a short interval what just took place." Were they to be referred back to the "infinite system of reference" of the real world, they would fit in rather well. "Under these conditions, perception would at every moment be a conquest of the territory of the dream. We would continually have to risk denying the reality of such-and-such an appearance, based on simple presumptions, and asserting, for no definitive reason, the real existence of another appearance. The sensible universe, so painfully constructed, would be perpetually invaded by perfectly plausible visions which we would nevertheless have to reject, as best we can, without ever being absolutely sure of doing so rightfully. Clearly the world thus described, a world in which we would never be finished correcting appearances, a world in which all perception is conquest and judgment, in no way corresponds to the world around us" [108–9, 100]. Nor is the classical conception of the image any better equipped to explain the role that the image plays in thinking. If images are sensible contents that appear and disappear on the basis of associative attraction, thought has no hold on them; they are not at its disposal, no more than are the physical objects in the world, of which images are the "interior" equivalent. If relations can be grasped, if a judgment is successfully formed, it will be in an instantaneous act of thought that will immediately be interrupted. At every instant, the flux of images will break away from the "directive theme" [116, 107] of thought. That is why it will not suffice to admit, as many writers do, that the image, a sensible content, also has a meaning. As a sensible or quasi-sensible content, the image would still remain opaque to thought, resisting with its own inertia. Consciousness does not admit any pure givens within its precincts.

This proposition is obvious, if we take the trouble to think carefully about the nature of consciousness, rather than be content with a confused notion that would depict it as "the world of psychic facts," a world parallel and similar to the world of physical objects. As we inventory the existences we know, we see that they can be reduced to two types: spontaneous existence, which is self-engendering (and which is the existence of consciousness), and conditioned existence, independent of my will, which is that of physical objects in the world, and also that of sensible contents and the classical version of the image, since I have to "wait" for them, "decipher" them, and "observe" them. To say that consciousness exists spontaneously is tantamount to saying that it knows itself at the same time that it knows. If it were nothing but a power of knowing, unaware of itself, it would be given to itself like a fact and thus would enter into the second category of existences. It might be objected that the acts of my consciousness are themselves conditioned—by my bodily states, for example. These facts are without force against the patent givenness [*évidence*] of our point of departure. To relinquish that patency would be to give up knowing what one is saying. There is no fact that can establish that Euclid's propositions are not true for Euclidean space. By taking as our point of departure the spontaneous existence of consciousness, attested to by the *Cogito*, we must attempt to grasp the apparently transitive action of the body upon the soul. In any case, we can no longer admit "contents" such as the classical image into consciousness without committing a logical contradiction. Nor can consciousness, if it is self-engendering, recall or select images, since these opaque, inert contents cannot be called into conscious existence or sent off to the unconscious except by a *force* of the same nature as themselves; and consciousness is not a force [125–26, 114–15]. We are led to a reform of the concept of image, and most of the concepts psychology uses uncritically should similarly be reconsidered and reassessed in light of the actual workings of consciousness. This appears to be the object of Husserl's eidetic psychology, and here we can sense the hesitancy on the part of the psychologists. For Husserl, as we know, not even an eidetic psychology can give us the whole truth about consciousness. That truth can only be reached via the abandonment of the natural attitude, the realism of knowledge common to all the sciences, in favor of a transcendental viewpoint from which all *things* become *meanings*.

Understandably, psychologists show scant enthusiasm for (what they believe to be) a new metaphysical flight from reality. But, in the first place, neither eidetic psychology nor transcendental phenomenology claim to *replace* experimental or inductive psychology. Husserl has said more than once that the relationship between the former and the latter is the same as the relationship between mathematics and physics. Physics made progress from the moment it began using that spatial eidetics known as geometry, while awaiting other eidetics that were to complete the determination of the physical object. Similarly, "psychology is an empiricism still seeking its eidetic principles" [142, 130], without which no experiment is univocal, because the psychologist does not know *what he is dealing with*. Thus it is obvious that eidetic psychology is by no means a pretext for neglecting experiments but, on the contrary, the way to understand their meaning. Secondly, there is nothing optional about having recourse to the analysis of essences or even to the transcendental viewpoint. The contradictions inherent in the classical conceptions of the image oblige us ultimately to ask the question, "What is an image?" and to inquire into the nature (or essence) of the image. Similarly, if we refuse to break consciousness down into conscious events and to endow it with a type of causality comparable to physical causality, we do not move arbitrarily toward a transcendental viewpoint. We do so because the very nature of consciousness rejects the treatment to which we subjected it, and because we are invited to forge, for psychology, concepts and modes of explanation that are at last befitting its object.

Thus, for this new psychology, the image will no longer be an internal thing. It must not only be "conscious," as we obscurely say, but also "consciousness." The image of that sheet of paper that I just perceived is not a simulacrum that I carry away inside myself, and through which I can grasp the object of my perception a second time. Alain is quite correct in saying that I do not have this picture of the past. (And besides, if I did have it at my disposal, how would I identify it, if not with the help of a second image, and so on, ad infinitum?) But Alain is wrong to conclude that imagination amounts to no more than a false belief that has taken advantage of an ambiguous perception. If that were true, the imagination would always be affirmative, and always an illusion. But it is precisely the distinctive feature of the imagination not to affirm the real presence of its object [136, 124]. My sheet of paper, which I imagine after having seen it, is the same one I saw, but "[i]s it really it in person? Yes and no. I do in fact say that it is the same sheet of paper with the *same* qualities. But I am not unaware of the fact that that sheet is still *over there*: I know that I am not experiencing its presence" [2, 2]. The supposed image is not *seen*, it does not thrust itself upon me the way things do in perception. When I think of my friend Peter, I do not have a duplicate of my former perceptions beneath my "mental gaze." "That 'reduced Peter,' that homunculus swept along by the stream of consciousness, never was *consciousness*. It was an object of the material world that strayed in among psychic beings" [148, 135]. That which is called an image is an act in which consciousness focuses directly on the same object that was given in perception. "There is but one selfsame Peter, the object both of perceptions and images," and "the image is but a name for a certain way consciousness has of intending its object"; the image of Peter is only "one of the possible ways of intending the real Peter" [148, 134]. The specific structure of these acts, according to Sartre, remains to be studied, but this can only be done by an analysis of the acts of consciousness in general, followed by that of their modalities. This task is just begun in Husserl's published works. Sartre proposes to follow through, in what touches the imagination, in a second book.[3]

The book that he has just published will undoubtedly win him an attentive readership. It would be an exaggeration to say that Sartre is always fair. It is possible, for example, to find a deeper significance in the "images" of Bergson's *Matter and Memory*. It is possible to be of the opinion that Bergson, by presenting the world as a set of "images," wished to suggest that the "thing" should neither be broken down into "states of consciousness" nor sought beyond what we can see in a substantial reality. That would be precisely, though in far less precise language, an anticipation of the Husserlian *noema*. Likewise we may find that Sartre judges harshly the distinguishing of matter from form in the image, when he finds it in certain psychologists [89, 82; 126–27, 116], and that he is too quick to grant Husserl [146, 133] his distinction between *hylē* and *morphē*—one of the points of his teaching that has been challenged in Germany itself, and that does in fact present the most difficulties. But these inequities, if they be such, pale before the work's rare qualities: the rigor and vigor of its critical thought and its uniformally felicitous expression.

—Trans. by Michael B. Smith.

10

◆

On Sartre's *The Flies* (1943)

The publication of *The Flies* is timely.[1] It goes without saying that a text written for the theater was written to be performed, and the audience is the only real judge. But the audience has to be listening. Many of us in the audience who were attentive (and had neither relatives nor career plans within the theater world) think that there were a certain number of critics who neither looked nor listened on this occasion. It is not at all surprising that these same critics should express alarm at this publication. Confronted with the written text, it is harder to be cagey. The public has the evidence before its very eyes; let us examine it together.

First, in the theater as in reading, it is obvious that the critic is wrong in seeking the theme of *The Flies* in Orestes' "character," in Electra's "state of mind," or in the famous revenge of the orphans. There is hardly any psychology in Aeschylus, or even in Sophocles, and surely it could not have been the plot, taken from myths already known to the general public, that captivated the audience. The Greeks founded a type of theater that was meant to show a hero in a tragic situation: an imperiled freedom. "Another Electra," says one critic. Why not, since the Greek legends are the best possible scenario for a drama of freedom?

Freedom is a word that appears at least ten times in the play, and not once in most of the reviews. Is freedom, then, devoid of dramatic value? One might think (and Orestes himself thought so for a long time) that being free means not being committed to anyone or anything. Without homeland or family, made aware, by the Pedagogue and by travel, of the relativity of right and wrong, Orestes floated about in the air, impalpable, without convictions, open to any suggestion. But a moment comes when he wearies of that kind of freedom. He would like to really exist, feel the earth beneath his feet, and be a man among men. Will he abdicate his freedom, return to his accursed race, assume the burden of criminality of the house of Atreus? When one no longer wishes that kind of freedom, is there nothing left but to serve the powers that be? It is at this juncture that Orestes discovers a third path, between the freedom of indifference and the fatalism of tradition. He will slay Aegisthus and he will slay his mother; he will become once more a man of Argos. Everyone will know who he is. We are not free when we are nothing; we are free when we are what we have chosen to be. Orestes will take a stand. But he will not do so half-heartedly and, like Electra, in humiliation and envy. Ordinary people only half want what they want: they are not fully engaged. They are not one with what they do; they are divided within themselves. They hate themselves, do not attempt to live, and are in league with death. They lose themselves in the powers that be, in regrets, and under the protection of the gods, because they are afraid of their freedom and seek only to rid themselves of themselves. But if a man truly wills what he does, if he acts without any holding back, neither the passions nor the laws nor the gods have any power to thwart his loyalty to himself, his love of self and of life. Orestes breaks the old cycle of the passions at the very moment he seems to be entering it. Nor does he break it for himself alone. Since his crime is a pure crime, issuing from freedom, it only leads to freedom. Orestes did not kill to reign but to give the people of Argos the courage to live. Yet that exemplary act is the only gift he can give them. No one can opt for life for them: everyone is alone in that endeavor. Even if Electra were to follow Orestes in going through with the crime, each would feel responsible for himself or herself. There are then, ultimately, "memories that one does not share." When Orestes was invaded by a true freedom, a certain ease, a certain animal good spirits left him once and for all—precisely that peace people seek in the earth and in the dead, in the forgetting of their own newness and their own lives. Once his decision has been reached, he feels his youth flowing away, or rather, his childhood. He is cold. Freedom is contrary to nature. It calls into question the forces that tend toward repose. It separates him violently from the world in which all things move toward their end: the plant toward the plant form, the harvest toward the harvest form. As Jupiter says in a sublime scene in the last act, all of creation is against Orestes. Worse yet, his own flesh is against him. "Do you think I will ever forget our mother's face?" he says to Electra. Standing up against the gentle might of forces lulling him to sleep, the free man is like a flaw in the diamond of the world, like a splinter in nature's flesh. He is awkward, grimacing, and helpless on the surface of the perfect earth. That is the way the world is: nature's grace and innocence are impossible in humans. If they are not free, they will be slaves to the passions and remorse. We must therefore desire to be free. The choice is between that difficult freedom and the peace of tombs. This is the pathos of *The Flies*. The naturalists and

Dostoevski, whom one critic feels duty bound to drag in, obviously have nothing to do with it. The free individual has his own letters of nobility. He is Socrates refusing to flee, and proving his freedom at the cost of his life; or Count Mosca in *The Charterhouse of Parma*, proving his freedom by testing it against the labyrinth of jealousy. So much the worse for those who do not understand that kind of pathos.

How can one understand the performance if one understands nothing of the drama itself? In a very beautiful scene in Act Two, the Great Priest calls the Dead, who once a year rove the city to bring the living back to them. At the Cité theater, this scene is staged in the style of Black African ceremonies. This sets the critics to laughing and to saying that it must be a retrospective exhibit of African art: the esthetics of 1925. They forget that African ceremonies did not begin in 1925. They still thrive in Black Africa, and they are everywhere, even in our mores. They were probably in Argos. You don't have to be a "realist"; it is enough to have paused for an hour at Thebes, for example, in the stupor of an August afternoon, feeling the sun's weapons on your body, remembering the dirt, the stench, and the flies of the market-place, to understand all of a sudden, as Nietzsche did, that the Greeks made freedom appear against a background of terror and cruelty. After that, the fact that a critic talks about latrines and compares Sartre to Zola . . . it helps us take it in stride if we remember that another critic, in 1905, called Cézanne a "besotted wine-grower."

But the errors of the critics, however frequent and well known they are, pose a question. How can it be that the work itself is able to draw a public that the critic would like to turn away? It must be the case that there is, over the head of the "cultured" critic, a felicitous complicity between the sincere author and the naive theater-goer. A certain sort of minor culture—adroitness, nice turns of phrase, a lively pen—does not increase understanding, and, on the contrary, the onlooker who gives himself up to the drama can "perceive" the greatness of a theme and grasp the author's intentions in one deft move.

—Trans. by Michael B. Smith.

11

◆

Apology for International Conferences (1947)

La Nef and *Fontaine* have done a superlative job of commentary on the *Rencontres Internationales de Genève* but they must now be defended against the criticism of the Communists.

Frankly, at the *Rencontres*, as in all conferences of this sort, many things were said (and often applauded) that were vague, rash, or silly. Guéhenno had just made a sweeping statement about America being the country of freedom without justice, and the U.S.S.R. the country of justice without freedom, knowing himself how vague such declarations are, whereupon my neighbor, an Englishwoman, noted feverishly on her notebook: "Guéhenno's splendid statement."[1] As Hegel was wont to say, looking at the mountains, "That's the way things are." Discussions between intellectuals have something of the ceremony or the show about them as soon as there are more than two participants: how much more so when the public is let in.

There is not the shadow of a doubt that the public in this case was not keen on communism, and understood little about it. They all rushed to the Bernanos lecture, which I happened to miss, and which was, I am told, impossible. It was held in a room ten times the size of the amphitheater of the university where all the others were held. It was undoubtedly the most flamboyant event of those ten days, even though it was a fringe event of the *Rencontres*, along with the theater and the concerts. Not a word was said about it in the public *Entretiens*, though these were intended for discussion of the lectures. There were a few bitterly anti-Communist words by André Rousseau on the "politization of the Resistance by the Communists," energetically and justly pounced upon by Guéhenno. There was also a brief anti-Communist intervention (of the allusive, witty variety) by Rougement—a Rougement transformed by the presence of his hometown audience: not smiling and elegant, as in Paris, but severe and muscular, like a

118

popular leader. Let us also mention, to be quite thorough, the famous *vibrato* of the end and the means, performed by Guéhenno—in a rather unconvincing way to tell the truth. For, scarcely had the orator trampled upon violent and devious means, when he added that while it was true that the democracies were not all pure, the principles remained within them, and virtue was "saved by that hypocrisy"—which is a strange way to defend the purity of the means. That was the sum total of the anti-Communist argument at the *Rencontres*. It did not amount to much. The essential, for those who attended the conference, was the discussion between Jaspers and Lukács, and Lukács, with the help of a few lesser figures, didn't come off that badly.

Even if you think (as I do) that the Communist participation was not numerically sufficient, the impartiality of the administrators was obvious. Aragon forgot (or did not forget) that Hervé was invited. He did not know that the organizers had struggled, not with the Hungarian government, but with the Swiss police, to obtain a visa for Lukács. How could a man who was a minister under Bela Kuhn and remains the most important intellectual of the Hungarian Communist Party be admitted onto Swiss soil? A Frenchman from Bern, well placed to know whereof he speaks, told me that a particularly energetic phone call from *Rencontres* to the seat of government was the only thing that was able to lift the police block. Lukács, like the others, had been invited for a one-hour lecture; he spoke for almost two, despite the tight schedule . On the evening before a public *Entretien*, a Spanish Loyalist submitted a written request to speak, which was granted, in conformity with the practice of liberal societies. But the secretariat immediately sought and found a Spanish Republican to represent the other side, and the former declined to speak. A Soviet citizen asked for the floor and got it for a half hour.[2] Such was the spirit of the conference. If the Communists find it unbearable, it is because they can't stand being confronted by the others, and I wonder why. Lukács defended their positions bravely and energetically. At first, the public was not for him. But his merit compelled recognition. In matters of ideology, that is the only kind of victory there is. What Voltaire said about books should be repeated, apropos of *Rencontres*, to the Communists: that they can't do any harm. "Trumpets have never won any wars, and the only walls they've brought down were at Jericho. You are afraid of books the way some villages used to be afraid of violins. Let people read and dance; these two pastimes will never do the world any harm."

But, getting back to the subject, there are better and more serious things to say. The good thing about the *Rencontres* [literally "Meetings"] is that they are meetings. They will not change the course of events, but they are a dialogue, and if it is true that the thoughts of men can sometimes play a role in history, this dialogue adds its slight weight to our chances of having peace.

At times we say to ourselves: What is the use eliciting talk from writers, who were born to write, and what hope is there that they will achieve clarity through improvisation, when they haven't succeeded in doing so in their most thoughtfully composed writings? What is the use in bringing the representatives of communism and liberalism together, since the texts and the governments are there, and we already know they are incompatible? This reasoning only seems solid. Provided we know how to observe, and block out of the picture the fortuitous elements of fatigue or emotion (or sometimes to interpret these supposedly accidental aspects), by seeing the authors we learn something about the ultimate meaning of their works. A man—the writer *and* the bachelor, the husband, the professor, the man of letters, the revolutionary, the conservative—is one unified way of interpreting the world and other people, a constant accent or style. Again, as Hegel said, correcting an old proverb: No one is a great man for his valet—not because the great man is not a great man, but because the valet is a valet. For the attentive and generous spectator, to meet with a writer is to experience his or her thought in the nascent state, before it has become *other*. And as it happens, speaking and living writers all belong to one sole universe, that of human concern, whereas finished works, and regimes seen from a distance, seem to divide that universe into impenetrable cantons. In all dialogue there is an element of concrete universality. There was, for us, a positive gain in seeing Jaspers and Lukács, as there was for each of them in seeing the other. Jaspers has become known through a philosophy of situation. His opposition to Nazism has been steadfast. You would have expected to find a man for whom the outer world counted most. What you do find is a fine example of the German professor—grave, thoughtful, pastoral, admirably scrupulous, open to truth; but, apparently, a man of interiority, more accustomed to seeking intellectual stimulation in reflection or the fervor of personal relations than in rough and tumble communication with the ignorant or the primitive, or in the chaos of history. On one question addressed to him, he began by making a firm distinction between philosophy and politics; his philosophy would entail no political conclusion. He raised the objection to Lukács that man cannot be explained by exteriority—as if that were enough to refute marxism. He applies his philosophy of situation and communication only to private relationships, which are at the same time "spiritual" relationships; his philosophy does not appear to take into account the concrete ties of coexistence, nor to follow communication to the point at which it becomes common, general history. He relies rather upon meditation and religious elevation to establish a valid communication between individuals, beyond the "all-encompassing" within which they are, however, enclosed, and which, in Jaspers, seems an obstacle and a destiny far more than an inalienable dimension and the very element in which we live our lives. He asked in a conversation whether Sartre would accept the Ten Commandments, and ended his lecture by advising Europe to reread the Bible. But, since he is perfectly well aware of the problems of others, he took their answers seriously. He admitted, in conclusion, that the fundamental idea of marxism was an historical totality rather than a reduction of history to its economic framework. We must not give ourselves over blindly to the all-encompassing, and it is up to us to think our historical situation through as best we can. I dare say this dialogue may have brought Jaspers' attention back to certain implications of his own philosophy and to the tasks it must take up if it wishes, in keeping with its own spirit, to differ decisively from philosophies of the Ego and pure interiority.

It was known that Lukács participated in the Budapest Commune, and that, when an impertinent reporter asked him what would happen to the newspapers that wouldn't go along with the party line, he took a revolver out of his pocket and simply placed it on the table. We were expecting to see a violent individual appear. In fact, what I saw in the great hall of the university was a man rather similar to our scholars: short, pale, wearing a navy blue suit and glasses, a bit stunned by the noise and the transition, a bit isolated in that corner of the amphitheater with Mrs. Lukács and a fellow countryman. But he raised his glasses to take notes; then you could see the power and brilliance of his gaze. It is always a renewed pleasure to see the same things, transcending the differences of language and milieu, make the eyes light up with an attentive gleam. In the conversation, the central questions were quickly identified and this sociologist soon began to sound like a philosopher in full possession of his certainties. ("In a sense, everything is absolute," he said. "This passing moment is absolute.") I only wondered whether this first-rate mind was not lifted to its full level of effectiveness by the curiosity, the questions, and the resistance of an unaccustomed environment. As for us, we learned by listening to him that certainty does not lessen freedom of thought. To us, and even to our French Communists, the U.S.S.R. remains an idea, hearsay. We meticulously examine the bits of information that reach us, we frown, analyze, interpret, and whether we are apologists or critics, it is probable that in two out of three cases we do not understand. To someone born there or who, like Lukács, has lived there (one of his sons is an engineer there), the U.S.S.R. is a reality. You don't disprove a mother or a son, even when examining them with lucidity. There is a *real* assent that can only be given to things we have seen or experienced in life, and that, once given, leaves the freedom of judgment intact.

All talk about the U.S.S.R. in the West has a dream-like quality about it. We speak of the U.S.S.R. the way provincials speak of Paris, whether they love it or hate it. International meetings at which Soviets were present would make the U.S.S.R. become a part of the world. In ceasing to be a myth, it would lose the favor of a few fanatics (whose enthusiasm would not survive a trip there, as so many examples have shown), but win the status of things that exist. The official line of the U.S.S.R. since 1941 has been to establish harmonious relations with the democracies. It is an optimistic policy, and the Communists make important concessions to that optimism. (*"Es handelt sich nicht um Sozialismus,"*[3] he exclaimed at a public session, speaking of the Communist policy in the West.) Why shouldn't they grant that minor concession of accepting the dialogue and keeping bad company?

—Trans. by Michael B. Smith.

12

◆

The Founders of
Philosophy
(1956)

Other peoples have encountered philosophy or brushed up against it briefly by chance, but the Greeks founded it. They practiced and defined the basic attitude that gave rise to everything subsequently known as philosophy. While throughout the world many civilizations were producing many thoughts and customs that indeed interest us, but are only accessible to us through interpretation or as tokens of the past (witnesses to bygone days, historical documents), it is the Greeks who, almost without preparation or transition, produced formulations of the philosophical concerns that were to come down through the ages on their own strength. They touch us not in our memory or our "humanism," but in our most present thought. When we take up their texts, after twenty-five centuries, it is our very life that pulsates in their words, our manner of interrogating the world. Within these texts, a language exists that translates term for term, and there are movements, reiterated pathways of reflection, silences, that are our own. We stand on equal ground with them.

One might respond that our admiration is in fact the gratitude of the heir, and that it is not surprising that we should recognize ourselves in them, since we come from them. But the extraordinary thing is that what they discovered has retained an undiminished stimulating power. The fact that philosophers down through the ages identify what is best in themselves with the Greeks . . . that in itself is a credit to the Greeks and qualifies them as founders.

Of course they did not establish all the themes of philosophy. They did not have the idea of a world in movement. They often contented themselves, a few humanist concessions notwithstanding, with the division of the world into barbarian and Greek, slave and freeman. Even when they were in favor of it, they did not anticipate how revolutionary the freeing of the slaves nor the statement "There are no longer Greeks or Jews"[1] would be. They did not anticipate the immense potential public that was waiting (and is still waiting) at the doors of culture and of the State, the problem that was to be brought about by a world in which all the peoples of the globe want to live full lives, nor the anxiety of a science and an art that no longer rest on any principle and must continually redefine space, time, rest, and movement. . . . They did not possess a certain sense of history and of subjectivity. However, these accomplishments still stand within the horizon they opened up, because they created and understood the kind of question that constitutes philosophy.

With them, for the first time, and definitively, philosophy is the quest that brings to light all the presuppositions of life and knowledge, the desire for an unconditioned knowledge, absolute transparency. The philosopher is defined by the distance that he takes from the world, society, and himself as an empirical entity.

What is more, they went so far as to understand that the extreme point of that kind of reflection is the rediscovery of the abrupt upsurge of being prior to reflection, and that radical knowing rediscovers unknowing. The philosopher is therefore not only the one who cuts himself off and returns to himself. The distance he places between himself and the too familiar world of things that are taken for granted is but the means of a greater attentiveness; the doubt cast upon "beings" is but the revelation of "Being." They not only dreamed of an absolute knowledge, they understood that the absolute inhabits the "relative."

Thus they invented the dialectic, that is, the overcoming of skepticism, the truth that issues from paradox, the power of truth inseparable from the power to go astray, the being-oneself in the being-other. They invented immanence, since every idea of its own accord leads us to others, but an immanence that functions by reversal is therefore also called transcendence.

Reason can be a phantom as terrifying as those of the imagination. The Greeks created a type of reason that knows that, in being no more than what it is, it would not be reason. They found a type of reason that allows the rest of man to speak, that even consents to myth, provided it is the imagination that saves from the imagination. Such is the myth of reminiscence, which seems to be a reverie on the soul's prenatal past, and in which generations of philosophers read that all knowledge is recognition, that nothing absolutely external to us ever befalls us; in short, the pure principle of interiority.

They created philosophy, because in the areas of nature and freedom, existence and idea, finality and mechanism, the negative and the positive, reason and unreason, justice and power, optimism and pessimism, humanism and anti-humanism, they defined the antagonisms that are our perpetual coordinates. Most essentially, they are the founders, because they understood that the antagonists produce and reproduce one another unstintingly, and that Apollo, as Nietzsche said, would have nothing to do without Dionysus, nor Socrates without Oedipus.

—Trans. by Michael B. Smith.

13

◆

The Discovery of History
(1956)

"Discoveries" in philosophy are always at the same time "inventions." When philosophers formed the concept of history, this "realization" was a shaping and not the simple notation of a prior fact. Humanity would not *live* a history if someone had not one day *spoken* of history. . . . However, it was at a certain moment, in a certain historical context that history was first spoken of. It is in reality-history that the consciousness of history makes its appearance; it is not born out of nothing. As Marx says, it is the product of its own product. Truth is not ready-made in things, and yet, by a "retrograde movement," it presents itself to us as existing prior to our act of knowledge. We encounter reality: that is the cause *and* effect of the knowledge we have of it. This circle is the definition of history, and it is up to the philosopher to learn to live with it.

In all societies, humans know that there were humans before them, and, vaguely or precisely, they also know what they did. When they begin living and thinking historically, it is not a new object that their consciousness annexes, but rather a new time-structure (a new relation to others, a new idea of meaning and truth) is established. Nothing in the literature of the Greeks shows that they had caught a glimpse of the thickness of the generations to come and, even as confused forms, of the *other* worlds that would be born. The *centuries of centuries*, the *possible worlds* that were not realized, and the still possible transformations of this world—these thoughts, familiar to us, scarcely appear there. They appear attentive only to what is. One has the feeling they repressed their rapture and their dejection, relegating them to their myths. Chronos devours his children; at the center of the earth there is a force that grants being only to take it away again. The "time" of the Greek philosophers is more akin to a force that destroys being only to recreate it, a scintillation of being, an uninterrupted surge that

126

creates being upon being, imitating immutability as best it can. With the possible exception of a few passages in *Parmenides*, in which the instant rends the fabric of time, they do not conceive of time as departure. Like the cycles of nature, time recreates rather than creates, and its disjuncture is a "return."

Perhaps the "people of history" think no more of the future than do others. But what is new in historical time is that what we do opens up a field, founds, institutes, takes up a tradition, and anticipates a future. An exchange takes place, and a secret consonance occurs between what has been, what is, and what will be. Time is no longer the natural surge that comes from before we were. Even in our efforts to understand the past, we are borne by the feeling of something that is to be done, and, just as the body when we awake gathers itself around an object in order to become "behavior" again, so the most ancient time is summoned to be present to what it will become in us. Our present is itself an "enterprise." Whatever we may think, our institutions and our plans encroach upon the future, they count on its continuation, they only function in an historical milieu. They are, as we say, "conditioned" to history.[1] They install people, unbeknown to themselves, in the atmosphere of history.

This change in the structure of time is a phenomenon that we try to conceive of as inexpensively as possible, without modifying our familiar categories of thought. We try to conceive of history as a second nature superimposed upon the first. Progress as a fatal consequence of good, or simply the conviction that the inventions of mankind are immediately and inevitably compatible with human life, are ideologies that postulate a power that oversees the changes of history just as nature looks out for our permanence. Even the incomparably more elaborate notion of a *logic of history*, if understood as immanence of what is in what was, or of our future in our present, is tributary to the same preconceived ideas. The moment we think, for example, that the old world carried capitalism within itself as a plant carries a seed, the moment we treat the past as a rough sketch of the present, and prehistory as approaching an ineluctable history, and the moment we view history as the announcement of the end and consummation of history, we are reducing historical time to natural time. History, precisely because it is not nature, refuses to be treated as a second nature. It does not establish itself by substituting, in place of natural causality or finality, another order of causality or finality that annuls them. History slips in quietly, making the former adopt its language, artfully leading them away from themselves. That is why it is essential for history not to be "absolute history," a universe of immanence in which the dimensions of time collapse inward, overlapping one another. Greece was what it was: it was possible for nothing to have come of it, or something quite different than what did in fact emerge. The logic of the development that leads from it to us was only thought, *only came into existence*, because the West created the type of society, the material and intellectual conditions, that made the idea of an economic universe possible, and therefore the idea of Greece as a "pre-capitalist" society. Retrospection does not retrace the steps of a pre-established causality and finality, and it must not be said that pre-capitalism produced capitalism as if it contained its entelechy within it. One should only say that pre-capitalism degenerated of its own accord, leaving the field open for something else. Thus, the new system was not necessary, even if the preceding one was no longer possible. Similarly, our time does not carry its future within itself, except to the extent that it excludes certain impossible restorations. Perhaps one day it will appear in history under the name "pre-socialism." If that happens, it will happen because socialism will have been instituted, and not because it waited, hidden within the heart of capitalism. And that will occur through channels and developments that are not necessarily those that an analysis of nineteenth-century capitalism predicts. Perhaps such a future is underway within our system in sectors to which we are not paying attention. We might already be able to spot those sectors if we took a freer look at the present, in order to divine what its definitive appearance will be in the eyes of the future.

The concept of history represents a major acquisition for philosophy, provided it is not used as an anti-metaphysics. Far from replacing metaphysics, it sheds unprecedented light on the most fundamental metaphysical issues. What is this truth that is born and will die? What is this meaning that takes hold of its antecedents, without being able to close its grip on them or on the future? What is this affinity that makes humans of interest to humans both simultaneously and in succession? Not in the sense that animals are of interest to animals, because they resemble one another or complete one another, but in difference and rivalry; not in the monotony of nature, but in the disarray of history. There is a discovery of history, but it is not the discovery of a thing, a force, or a destiny; it is the discovery of a questioning and, you might say, a kind of anguish.

—Trans. by Michael B. Smith.

14

◆

The Philosophy of Existence (1959)

I would much rather speak to you of the philosophy of existence than of existentialism, for reasons that you probably already know.[1] The term "existentialism" has come to designate almost exclusively the philosophical movement which arose in France after 1945, chiefly as a result of Sartre's instigation. In reality, this philosophical movement has its antecedents: it is tied to an entire philosophical tradition, a long and complicated tradition, since it actually begins with Kierkegaard's philosophy, and following this, is derived from philosophies such as Husserl's and Heidegger's in Germany, and in France, even before Sartre, from philosophies such as that of Gabriel Marcel. Thus, it is extremely difficult to isolate Sartre's attempt in relation to the other well-known efforts just mentioned. For me, Sartre's work was undeniably original. But since he was rebuilding an entire style of thought, it was truly impossible to grasp his philosophical efforts, his veritable philosophical politics, by separating it out from the rest. Bearing this in mind, I propose to discuss the beginnings of existentialist thought in France.

This beginning occurred in the years from 1930 to 1939 (the ten years which preceded the war). And since it is, as you know, especially in 1944 and 1945 that existentialism in the Sartrean sense appeared and established itself, I am talking about the period which immediately preceded its birth. However, it would be lengthy, difficult, and tedious to examine all of the writers who contributed to this period, so I propose a simpler manner of proceeding. I will examine a few of the ideas which formed the French philosophical landscape during the years—around 1930—when Sartre and I finished our studies. Following this, I will attempt to show how this landscape was disrupted or at least profoundly modified by the intervention of the authors who may be grouped under the heading of "philosophy of existence," which will then open up a perspective upon Sartre's attempt; and to see exactly how this attempt was related to the others, and how, conversely, it is tied to Sartre's more personal and more original talent.

Around 1930, when I finished my philosophical studies, how did things appear in France, from the philosophical point of view? It may be said that two influences, and only two, were dominant, and that the first of these was much more important: the key philosophical thought of the epoch in France had been that of Léon Brunschvicg. I do not know if Léon Brunschvicg is very well known today by philosophers outside of France. He was, among us students, absolutely and justly famous, perhaps not so much because of the philosophy he advocated and taught us, but because of his quite extraordinary personal qualities. He was a philosopher who had access to poetry and literature, who was an extraordinarily cultivated thinker, and his knowledge of the history of philosophy was as profound as possible. He was a man of the first order, not so much because of the conclusions of his doctrines, but because of his personal experience and talent, which were considerable. But then, exactly what doctrines did he propound, and, in short, how did he orient us? Without being philosophically technical, it can be explained in a few words: Brunschvicg transmitted to us the heritage of idealism, as Kant understood it. For him, this idealism was flexible, but it was nonetheless for the most part Kantian idealism. We became acquainted with Kant and Descartes through Brunschvicg, which is to say that this philosophy principally consisted of a reflexive endeavor, a return to the self. Whether pertaining to the perception of the objects that surround us or to scholarly activity, his philosophy in all cases sought to grasp both exterior perception and the constructions of science as creative and constructive activities of the mind. This was the truly constant theme of Brunschvicg's thought, for whom philosophy essentially consisted in the fact that the gaze—which scientists turn toward the object—is brought back to the mind which constructs the objects of science. Such was, in short, the allure of this philosophy, though it must be mentioned that its content is quite meagre.

Brunschvicg had an admirable knowledge of the sciences, the history of the sciences, and the history of philosophy. But what he had to teach us as a philosopher nearly always consisted of a Cartesian reflection, by means of which he returned from the things to the subject which constructs the image of things. As regards pure philosophy, his essential contribution consisted precisely in informing us that we must turn toward the mind, toward the subject which constructs science and the perception of the world, but that lengthy philosophical descriptions or explications cannot be made of this mind, this subject. He said—and this was a formula that he readily employed—that human beings participate in the "one," that the "one" is the mind. He meant, by saying that this "one," this mind, is the same in everyone, that it is universal reason, but in describing it as such he wanted to oppose it to all other types of being. There is not your mind and my mind and the minds of others. No, there is a quality of thought in which we all participate, and philosophy begins and ends by returning to this unique principle of all thought. The entire history of philosophy, which Brunschvicg pursued, was the coming to consciousness of this spirituality. According to him, philosophies were worthwhile to the extent that they succeeded in being conscious projects, and he judged them according to this canon, this rule.

There was quite another philosophical influence at the same time as Brunschvicg, but it remained in the background for diverse reasons: this was the influence of Henri Bergson. Consider the fact that Bergson stopped teaching in 1930: he retired in order to devote himself entirely to his work. Also, he never taught in the university nor at the Sorbonne; since 1900 he had been a professor at the Collège de France. And it must be said that, for quite a long time—though this was about to disappear just as I began my studies—there was a certain hostility toward Bergson on the part of the Sorbonne, which was more rationalist in orientation—or so it was understood at the time. Did this hostility stem from the fact that for us Bergson was fully established when we began our philosophical studies? Was this why we tended—as is customary for students—to search for something else? The fact remains that Bergson's influence was not very important around 1930.

All the same, let us say a few words about this influence. If it had been exerted upon us, it would have been very different from the Kantianism and Cartesianism we received from Brunschvicg. Indeed, as you know quite well—nearly everyone knew Bergson, more or less—Bergson's philosophy is not at all an idealism. It by no means begins with a return to the *Cogito*, to the subject of thought. It begins with a very different approach, one which involves a return to what Bergson called the immediate givens of consciousness. This is to say that I grasp myself, to begin with, as the first truth of philosophy; but I grasp myself not as pure thought, but as duration, as time. Bergson's analysis in *Matter and Memory*, for example, shows that if we consider time, we must necessarily center our consideration on the dimension of the present. For Bergson, the dimension of the present subsumes all consideration of the body and the exterior world. He defined the present as that upon which we act, and we clearly act with our bodies. So it is immediately apparent that this duration which Bergson calls to our attention implies a relation to our bodies: a completely carnal relation, as it were, to the world through the body.

Thus if we had been careful readers of Bergson, and if more thought had been given to him, we would have been drawn to a much more concrete philosophy, a philosophy much less reflexive than Brunschvicg's. But since Bergson was hardly read by my contemporaries, it is certain that we had to wait for the philosophies of existence in order to be able to learn much of what he would have been able to teach us. It is quite certain—as we realize more and more today—that Bergson, had we read him carefully, would have taught us things that ten or fifteen years later we believed to be discoveries made by the philosophy of existence itself.

But finally, since we are not really indebted to Bergson, let us come precisely to the period 1930–39, when we finished our studies, began to teach in the provincial lycées and to write doctoral theses. This period was the moment of our great initiation into the philosophy of existence, when we discovered Husserl, Jaspers, Heidegger, and Gabriel Marcel; and in particular, the review *Esprit*—a review which still exists and which you doubtlessly know—which at that time, under the impetus of Mounier (also a philosopher), was often oriented toward themes of philosophy of existence. I wish to briefly characterize these themes.

In reaction against philosophy of the idealist type—both Kantian and Cartesian—the philosophy of existence is primarily explicable by the importance of a completely different theme, that of *incarnation*. In the first writings of Gabriel Marcel, his *Metaphysical Journal*, for example, this theme was presented in a striking fashion. In philosophy, the body, my body, is usually considered to be an object, for the same reason that the bodies of others, animals, and, all told, even a table, are only exterior objects. I am mind, and opposite me there is, therefore, this body which is an object. What Gabriel Marcel maintained was precisely that this is not so, and that if I attentively regard my body, I cannot pretend that it is simply an object. In some respects it is me: "I am my body," he said. Yet it is not only the body that intervenes, for through it a general aspect of the sensible world was put under the scrutiny of our mind. Gabriel Marcel had quite long ago published an article entitled "Existence and Objectivity," in which he rightly opposed things which exist to objects, as in physical objects, objects construed by physicists. Sensible things, as they come under our scrutiny at the same time as the body, become the philosopher's themes for analysis. As Husserl said, through the perception we have of them, things are given to us in the flesh—carnally, *leibhaftig*. These philosophers set out to examine this sensible and carnal presence of the world, whereas previously, particularly under the influence of Kantian critique, scientific objects were what philosophers sought to analyze.

Undoubtedly, one has the feeling that in certain respects this position rejoins the Bergsonian one. But this is not yet something we could manage; we had to await the reading of these new writers in order to understand the significance of the theme of incarnation that we might have been able to learn from Bergson. In reality it is not only a theme, not merely a subject or an object of reflection that he proposed—it was a style of philosophizing. For example, Gabriel Marcel said that philosophy presents a particularity which differentiates it from all other sorts of disciplines: it deals with mysteries, not problems. This is the distinction which he made between the two. A problem is a question which I pose to myself and then resolve by considering different givens which are external to me. For example, if I wish to know how to construct a bridge or how to solve an equation, I consider the givens of the problem and then try to find the unknown. In philosophy it is an entirely different phenomenon, because, as Marcel said, in philosophy we must work out a very singular type of problem. In these problems, the one who poses them is also engaged. This person is not a spectator in relation to the problem, but is rather caught up in the matter, which for him defines the mystery.

If you think about this, you can see that, after all, what is expressed here in an abstract and general fashion was broached by my earlier examination of the sensible world. For it is precisely in the sensible world that we come to recognize such a strange sort of knowledge. I consider this sensible knowledge of the world completely paradoxical, in the sense that it always appears to me as already complete at the very instant that I pay attention to it. When I reflect, when I pay attention, my interior gaze bears upon my perception of things. This perception is already there. Thus, in the actual and concrete perception of the world, I am myself the subject, the one who speaks. I am already caught up in the game at the very moment that I attempt to understand what is happening. It is therefore the model of the sensible world that was used here. But finally, this philosophy far surpasses the simple emergence of a new theme of analysis: a new style of thinking was proposed to us at a time when it was necessary to consider philosophy as a mystery rather than as a problem.

A third theme which this philosophy presented to us for the first time— and which moreover still has great importance for all contemporary thought—is the theme of one's relations with the other. It is quite striking that this theme had not explicitly appeared in philosophy before the nineteenth century. Consider philosophers like Kant or Descartes: a philosopher reasons, and it goes without saying that his reasoning can be precisely reconstructed by another person, another reader. This can be accomplished so accurately that the philosopher and his readers parallel and reflect each other. There is no problem passing from one to the other. When Kant writes the *Critique of Pure Reason*, for example, he speaks of everyone's rationality and not only of his own. What the philosopher begins to understand, after Hegel in particular, is that in reality this is a much simpler matter than we had thought. For my relations with the other are not such that I can immediately affirm or postulate that what is true for me is also true for him. That is the problem. How is it that I know that there are other thinking beings entirely comparable to myself, since I know them only from the outside, while I know myself from the inside? Hence our third problem.

And with this problem of the other—to which we shall return—arises a theme which has increasing importance in French thought up through the present: this is the theme of history, which is essentially the same as the theme of the other. What simultaneously attracts and scandalizes philosophers about history is precisely man's given condition of not being alone, of always being considered in the presence of others, in an extraordinarily complex relation with them. The result is that we are no longer concerned simply with juxtaposed individuals, but with a sort of human tissue which is sometimes called "collectivity." History was not a subject often spoken of when I was a student. The history of thought was above all the history of philosophical systems. The moment that philosophy became interested in human and general history and joined the history of philosophy to human history in general, something had evidently changed. I simply wished to indicate how we were directed toward the explosion of 1945, and I now arrive at the main subject of this talk, which is an examination of Sartre's endeavor, what it had in common with its predecessors, and its originality.

Sartre knew all the philosophers of whom I just spoke; all of them are philosophers of existence in some respect. He discovered their works in the course of a stay at the Institut Français de Berlin during the years that preceded the war. I recall very well that upon his return he made us read Husserl, Scheler, and Heidegger, for example, all of whom were already slightly known in France but whose works were not widely read at that time. This philosophical education which he gave himself contributed to guiding us to these points of view in 1945.

But we must add that our time in occupied Paris during the war, the circumstances of the war and of those events resented by us all, also contributed to calling his attention to concrete problems and to orienting him toward a concrete philosophy, though they in no way altered his style of thought.

I recall quite well that in the years before the war, as we were talking one day, he offered an argument that seemed to have a paradoxical air to it, but which at bottom really didn't, at least not from the point of view of a certain philosophy. He said: "After all, there is not really any difference between a catastrophe in which 10 or 15 people die and a catastrophe in which 300 or 3000 people die. There is the difference in numbers, certainly, but for each dying individual, it is a world and a meaning that dies, and whether there be 300 or 3000 that die, the scandal is no greater. The scandal is exactly the same." This idea, to which he did not especially hold, struck me deeply. In retrospect, it struck me because I realized that such an idea reveals to what extent during the prewar years Sartre was removed from the political and historical point of view, from the perspective of heads of government. From the point of view of someone who has authority over other human beings, there is a great difference between an accident in which ten people die and an accident in which a thousand people die. From the statistical point of view, which is that of social and political life and history, there is an enormous difference. Only from the philosophical point of view, which considers each consciousness as a whole, there is no absolute difference between the death of one person and the death of a hundred people.

When one has lived through those years as we all had—I mean he, I, and all of our friends in Paris—with the presence of the Germans and all that it entailed, it can certainly be understood how it was natural for us to become increasingly oriented toward what happens, toward events, the exterior, toward political and social life. Consequently, the historical course of events played a role in orienting us toward the world, just as the philosophy of existence did, for its part, though by abstract philosophical means.

This combination of circumstances, plus the maturing of our own personal reflections, led Sartre to write his major work, *Being and Nothingness*, published before the end of the war. And all of our ideas formed in that period were to find their expression in the review *Les Temps modernes*, founded in October 1945.

The themes dealt with by Sartre's philosophy are the same ones to which I just alluded, but they were transformed by his unique style of dealing with them. For example, the theme of incarnation, more generally spoken of as "situation": human beings, as Sartre presents them in *Being and Nothingness*, are situated beings. This theme existed before Sartre wrote of it, but he transformed it in the following manner: in *Being and Nothingness* he presents an extremely rigorous analysis, destined to show that what philosophers had called the "self," the "subject," "consciousness," or whatever else could not in reality be designated by a positive term. If I were to try to see what I really am, I would finally discover that nothing could be said of the self. Descartes already said something similar in his *Meditations*, when he said: I am not smoke, I am not subtle matter, I am thought, and a thought cannot be touched, cannot be seen, in a sense it is nothing, which is to say, it is not a visible thing. The "nothingness" in question in the famous book of which I speak is such that the subject, or what is usually called the subject, must be considered as nothing.

But naturally, nothing cannot rest upon itself. Nothing, that which is no thing, needs to be supported by positive and existing things. Thus we may say that the nothingness which we are drinks the being of the world, just as, in the legends of antiquity, the dead drink the blood of the living in order to come to life once again. Nothingness drinks being, and it thus assumes a place, a position, in the world. Why do I have a body? Because this self which I am and which is nothing needs a positive, existing apparatus to come to the world—it needs a body. This description of humanity as simultaneously "being and nothingness," as a nothingness which assumes a situation in the world and which comes to the world through this situation, is a uniquely Sartrean element which had nothing to do, I believe, with what authors such as Gabriel Marcel had previously presented through the same terms, "situation" or "incarnation."

One may say that this self which is nothing is freedom. For what is it to be free if not to have the power to say "yes" or "no"; that is, not to be this thing or that beforehand, but to be what one wishes? Freedom—to repeat what we just said in other terms—consists not in living in non-being and indifferentiation but in opting for something, in choosing to do something. And this freedom—which is in itself an illusion, non-being—is only truly practiced when it sets itself a task and accomplishes something. We are free, Sartre said, to engage ourselves, meaning that even what is most free in us—our total independence with respect to all that is present—really can be spoken of only thanks to an act in which, on the contrary, we resolve ourselves, which we choose and through which we become something.

There is something equivalent in Sartre to what Gabriel Marcel called the mystery of being, but with an entirely different accent. The accent for Gabriel Marcel was, strictly speaking, religious. Yet it cannot be said that Sartre is, in the broad sense of the word, an irreligious philosopher, since to the contrary there is a domain where certain Christians have found themes in his work with which they agree. But for Sartre, all the same, what is called the mystery of being becomes in some respects a limpid mystery. There is a self which is nothing; there is the world which is made up of positive things; and the only task for the self which is nothing, for the self which is freedom, is to somehow make this world be. There are two entities face to face—if we indeed wish to separate them, for strictly speaking one cannot say face to face, since they are not separable; there are two entities, neither existing by itself, neither self-sufficient. Being needs humanity as witness, and humanity needs to enter into the world in order to be. The mystery which Gabriel Marcel calls the mystery of being becomes a sort of strangeness of fate that compels us to relate to a world that is profoundly alien to us. Since in the final analysis we are nothing, there will always be a distance between me and what I see, between me and what I do. Sartre called this distance a "channel of nothingness" (*manchon de néant*). For example, what is there between me and this carafe I see? There is nothing; my gaze goes out to grasp it where it is. In a sense, therefore, it is as near to me as possible. Yet there exists this impalpable distance, which means that the carafe is an object and that I who perceive it am not an object, and I am not part of this object.

With this idea of nothingness, the problem of the other, for example, for which Sartre has provided an extraordinarily acute analysis, becomes yet more difficult, a problem which will naturally continue to concern us. For I obviously see the others, I see their bodies, but I do not see them from the inside. I do not see the center, since it is nothingness and is therefore not visible. According to Sartre, consequently, I no longer perceive them as others, and I can know that there are other people only when they gaze at me. For I find myself frozen by their gaze, transformed into an object by this exterior gaze. Hence I feel the other's presence within me in the form of a sort of loss of my substance, a loss of my freedom, hence I become an object under the other's gaze. This means that my relation with the other is by definition tragic, since I cannot grasp the other as he feels himself and as he exists as interior freedom. According to Sartre, I see a face, and it is frozen, a sort of destiny. Likewise, the other sees only my exterior, yet this entirely negative relation between us is fully effective and preoccupies us at every moment.

These two points of view provide the titles to the book's two parts, as well as the rubrics which have remained famous: the point of view of the *for-itself* and the point of view of the *for-others*. The *for-itself* is me just as I see myself, or you just as you see yourself. The *for-others* is me just as you see me, or you just as I see you. There is no possible coincidence between these two perspectives. I cannot be exactly in the eyes of the others as I am in my own eyes. This is impossible, even if I am as sincere, as frank as possible: by sheer position we could not coincide. Yet this image which you have of me bears upon my own regard, it strikes me, effects me, defines me, concerns me. This is precisely how the problem of the other—which certainly predates Sartre's philosophy—is revealed and becomes yet more urgent in his hands.

Finally there is the problem of history, to which we alluded earlier: this is a problem which poses the limit-case of the other. The problem of history is reinvested with an absolutely dramatic character, on account of the urgency of the questions themselves from the philosophical point of view, as well as on account of historical circumstances. For we must not forget that, in the France of 1945, we had a country which was governed by a political coalition, part of which was the French Communist Party, which is to say a lot. That signifies—political life itself being quite alien to a philosopher or a director of a journal as was Sartre—that it is not simply a matter of personal politics and French assemblies: it is a question of something quite different. It stemmed first of all from a camaraderie that existed during the period of the war and the resistance. And it also stemmed from the fact—evident to all French people of the time, even to those who were politically far to the right—that nothing could be accomplished without the contribution, the participation of the Communist Party. This posed the problem of coexistence, as it were.

Sartre never was a Marxist. He was quite removed then, as now and always, from all types of materialism in the Marxist sense of this word. For Marx, there are causes which act upon consciousness, upon humans. For Sartre, there are no causes which can truly act upon consciousness. Consciousness is total, absolute freedom. The only point, which is not exactly a point of agreement, but which may be a point of convergence, is that for Sartre, if indeed I am non-being, absolute freedom—and therefore escape from all types of external determination—I bear responsibility for all that occurs outside of myself. For example, I bear responsibility for the image that others have of me. I abide by it, it matters to me, and I assume it. However, one finds a vast difference, you will note, between a philosophy which makes the subject, consciousness, humanity, depend upon exterior circumstances, and a philosophy which says that human beings, free subjects that they may be, cannot dissociate themselves from—and must take upon themselves—what occurs outside. This second attitude, which is Sartre's, is quite another matter. It is profoundly different from the Marxist philosophical point of view. This is the essence of the divergence expressed as far back as 1945 in *Les Temps modernes*, by Sartre's article on the question "Materialism and Revolution."

On the problem of history, Sartre's contribution consists in trying to lead the Marxist or Communist readers of his journal to sway their thought, their philosophy, in his direction. It cannot be said that this attempt succeeded, an attempt which may retrospectively be considered very naive, but which was indispensable, considering the circumstances of the era. This attempt was still stressed during the most critical period of the Cold War, between 1952 and 1954, at the exact moment that I found it necessary to leave *Les Temps modernes*, despite the friendship which tied me to Sartre and which continues to bind us together. It was at that moment, in fact, that he most distanced himself from the Communists. For this was the period when anti-Communism appeared to some people as the alpha and omega of politics, when it seemed sufficient to be anti-Communist in order to be political. Thereupon Sartre, who had never been a Communist and who was not always well understood, considered it necessary to oppose such an attitude and thus to support the Communists. Not that he thought the Russian regime could have done any better, but because he thought that the others were wrong in using Russia as a symbol of evil.

This period of extreme proximity to the Communists ended with recent events, in particular the Hungarian uprising. At that time, Sartre completely broke with the Communist Party. And in his journal, what actually appeared (*Les Temps modernes* still existed) was somewhat derivative, a foreign literature of Marxist tendencies, principally from Polish publications or from publications which in a general manner reconsidered Stalinism and the entire system.

This was the adventure of 1945. Naturally, it may be asked: What remains of it? Apparently not much! Sartre himself renounced, so it would seem, dealing with political subjects, and devoted himself to several other works. In addition to purely philosophical works, he is writing an autobiography which will be an examination of his own life from the personal and historical point of view, which is ultimately a work quite distant from his politically engaged preoccupations of the times. As for so-called existentialism's public, this public seems to address its attention today at least partially to Heidegger's thought, for example, and consequently to a thought quite different from Sartre's own. In any case, it is different insofar as Heidegger was never in favor of engagement, which is to say, it is not a thought directly in contact with everyday events.

It may seem therefore that there are very few aspects of this heroic epoch of existentialism whose passing I regret. Far from it: it must be said that I owe a great deal to it, and in truth it can't quite be said—either in the matter of philosophy or in the matter of thought—that such an experience can be surpassed or that nothing remains of it. For philosophy and thought do not consist so much in reaching a certain place, goal, point, or conclusion, but rather in approaching this goal in a rigorous, fruitful manner. Consequently, if thought and philosophy are just that, it must be said that this experience must be attempted and that it continues to remain relevant. Especially when, as is the case with Sartre—while all the time changing, and producing a certain number of texts that may indeed refer to the events of the times—these works, like all great and good books, nevertheless offer readers a nearly perennial value.

Consequently, let us not speak too quickly of all this, of all that has passed. Sartre, in this endeavor, wrote prodigiously, and each of us gained much from this task. What was written in that period, all the same, represents a school of thought, even though we now consider the formal conclusions which were achieved at that time no longer our own.

—Trans. by Allen S. Weiss.

15

◆

Five Notes on Claude Simon (1960)

[The following contribution was first published in the journal *Méditations* (1961–62). It was then reprinted in the 1972 publication of *Entretiens*.¹ The editor's comments from the *Entretiens* publication are repeated here—Trans.]

These notes were included in the first issue of *Méditations* in the winter of 1961–62. We are grateful to M. Jean-Louis Ferrier, editor of the journal, and to the benevolent understanding of Madame Merleau-Ponty herself, who have permitted the republication of these pages in *Entretiens*. The following comments preceded the publication of these notes at the time of their first publication:

> Those who have attended Merleau-Ponty's lectures at the Collège de France are well aware that, for several years, he illustrated his courses with literary examples. The works of Proust, Stendhal, and more recently, *La Route des Flandres* by Claude Simon, were specifically commented upon. None of these lectures were written out. All that exist are a hundred or so diverse reflections, noted down—probably intended for some future use—on dated pieces of paper. Among them, these five notes on Claude Simon—from which the lively expression of his thought circulates and serves as witness to his keen interest in the work of this writer.

NOTE #1

October 21, 1960
Vision

. . . . to see is to be granted the permission to not think the thing, *since it is already seen.*

All vision, no matter what color it may be, is a kind of thought-screen (which allows for the overflowing [*foisonnement*] of other thoughts)—*Vorhabe* and sedimentation.

. . . . sensorial vision is the vision of a visionary.

Consider, for instance, the interview with Claude Simon in *Les Lettres françaises*:

"I still see before me, still before my eyes are trees as if they had been drawn from behind, with others appearing, replacing the first set. It is like a moving countryside and then there is the nearly black-green of the hay. In a fraction of a second I envisioned *La Route des Flandres*. Not the idea of the book but the book as a whole."

NOTE #2

October 1960
The Language of Claude Simon–Michel Butor

The language of Claude Simon and of Michel Butor (with the present participle, interrupted sentences, the vocative as in Butor's *Time Passing* [*La Modification*]).

. . . . signifies a certain relation to oneself.

One no longer reads "I" or "he."

It is born of intermediaries (a first-second person singular).

. . . . intermediary modes (such as the present participle, which has the value of "simultaneity")

. . . . this is not understood absolutely—either in the classical conception of the "I think" or in the conception of 'ipseity as nihilation'": for while I hold on to the circle of ipseity,[2] I trace it as well. These uses of language can be understood only if language is a being, a world—only if Speech [*la Parole*] is the circle.

NOTE #3

November 1960
Claude Simon. . . .
and "vertical" imagination

. . . . a story which he reports to Madeleine[3] in the November 19 number of *l'Express* (after having given the same account to H. Juin) concerning the conception of *La Route des Flandres*. The book was created as a *picture* which gives it—not perspectivally, as in the event of a concept,[4] but as a countryside. And the scene *"screens"* (in the Freudian sense) those elements which lie behind it and at the same time exposes them as a latent whole.

Here there is a *Vorhabe*—a sedimentation to be described in the imagination[5] no less than in Perception.

. . . . *strata*. Archaeology of thought[6] (and of the future as well). . . .

NOTE #4

December 19, 1960
Claude Simon

Claude Simon last night: I told him that his speaking and his writing are not the same. Someone who speaks is someone who has opinions, judgments, and so forth, while one who writes is one who feels and lives. He added: *and then, we have to awaken him, or shake him, or call to him* (I don't remember which word he used). Hence the one who feels and lives is not an immediate given.[7] Such a person develops by virtue of his or her work. To feel, to live, one's sensorial life is like a treasure, but a treasure which is not yet worth anything as long as there is no work to be done. Work, however, is not just "converting" the lived [*le vécu*] "into words." It is rather a matter of *making what is felt actually speak*.

NOTE #5

March 1961
"Association" as initiation

The red on the artillery soldier's uniform (cf. Claude Simon in the *Lettres françaises* text). He reports this and that—"by association," one says. It's not really that, nor is it *Verschmelzung*,[8] etc.—Rather the texture of this red has a signifying virtue, a qualitative texture above all. Then there are experiences which carry some feeling, experiences that have been lived *through him* (like things through their names). In this way—following an archaic structure—we will always be a mediator of these experiences. Because our experience is not a flat field of qualities but rather always invoked by this or that fetish, a fetish which intercedes on its own behalf.

—Trans. by Hugh J. Silverman.

Appendices

APPENDIX 1:

Merleau-Ponty's Early Project Concerning Perception

FORREST W. WILLIAMS

On April 8, 1933, Maurice Merleau-Ponty, who was then teaching at a *lycée* in Beauvais, applied to the *Caisse National des Sciences* for a subvention, which he received, to undertake a project of study on the nature of perception. In 1934, he requested a renewal, and submitted an account, which he titled "The Nature of Perception," of what he had already accomplished and of what he proposed to do next. The renewal request was not granted.

Apart from three book reviews and some remarks made at a philosophy conference, *La Structure du comportement*, which was completed in 1938 and published in 1942, is generally considered the first evidence of Merleau-Ponty's major philosophical concerns. In a sense, that is so. However, the two earlier texts translated here, relatively short and schematic though they are, may nevertheless be of interest to students of Merleau-Ponty's philosophy. As can be shown, I think, by a brief analysis of their contents, Merleau-Ponty had articulated fairly clearly, some four years before the completion of *Structure*, a number of motifs that proved to be fundamental throughout his intellectual career. Naturally, his ideas were to expand and develop from 1933 to the drafts for *Le Visible et l'invisible* on which he was working at the time of his death in 1961. Therefore, it is also interesting to notice themes of his later work that were not envisaged at the outset. Professor Susanne Langer remarked in *Feeling and Form* that thinking at its best tends to develop, not by starting with the ultimate questions ("the problem of beauty," "the problem of Being," "the problem of mind," and the like), but by attacking an issue both specific and fecund. "A single problem," she wrote, "doggedly pursued to its solution, may elicit a new logical vocabulary, i.e., a new set of ideas, reaching beyond the problem itself and forcing a more negotiable conception of the whole field."[1] A brief look at these earliest of formal philosophical statements by Merleau-Ponty, with the subsequent development of his views in mind, suggests indeed that he had taken a firm grip by 1933 on a specific set of issues in the field of psychological research that were to prove philosophically fertile and that were to lead to vaster questions.

Although the concerns expressed by Merleau-Ponty in 1933–34 clearly anticipate much of his first book (*Structure*), and some of *Phénoménologie de la perception*, their philosophical horizon was certainly far narrower than that which he ultimately offered to modern phenomenology. Thus, although Merleau-Ponty stressed the problem of "perception of one's own body," a theme which was eventually to lead to his distinctive notion of "bodily intentionality," its real importance in his thought is apparent to us only with the advantage of hindsight. There is no hint of the "bodily reversibility" which he fastened upon more and more in his later works, where the phenomenon of the touched becoming the touching is a bodily anticipation of the reflexivity of thought. Consequently, we find also no indication of the limitations

146

which he later placed upon intellectual reflexivity because of the limitations he experienced in the "touched-touching" state of affairs, namely, that the wanted coincidence is ever imminent yet never realized;[2] like Apollo in pursuit of Daphne, one might say. In the 1933 text, he was not yet speaking of Edmund Husserl and phenomenology, and in neither text is there any sign of the subsequent importance of the work of Martin Heidegger. Consequently, there is no apparent readiness to take on the epistemology and metaphysics of the "object" which later challenged him more and more (notably, of course, in the drafts and working notes for *Visible*). That the philosophical crisis posed by "le Grand Objet" was not yet evident to him was surely due in part to the more or less non-historical approach of these early statements. His eventual concern with language is not anticipated; nor can one guess the relevance to the study of perception of the arts, for example, painting. Much less could one guess that the study of the nature of perception could lead into political and social issues, especially those surrounding marxism and, finally, into nothing less than a new ontology.

Yet for all the great difference in range, in horizon, these texts of 1933–34 also reveal with what maturity of mind, even before his first book, Merleau-Ponty had already defined the direction and many of the principal motifs of the succeeding 28 years of creative work. The most striking and persistent theme of his *oeuvre* was his insistence on the *philosophical* importance of the basic concept of *Gestaltpsychologie*. We know that Merleau-Ponty had become familiar, by 1934 at least, with the thought of Aron Gurwitsch, whose 1929 article in the *Psychologische Forschung* is cited in the 1934 text. As the subtitle of the article ("Phänomenologie der Thematik und des reinen Ich: Studien über Beziehungen von Gestalttheorie und Phänomenologie") clearly showed, Gurwitsch wished to call attention to the Husserlian implications of the notion of Gestalt, terming the Gestalt psychologists' rejection of the traditional "constancy hypothesis" tantamount to a phenomenological reduction.[3] Similarly—and very likely prompted by the Gurwitsch article and Paris lectures—the 1934 statement sees profound implications in the notion of Gestalt.[4] Already he was criticizing the Gestalt psychologists for failing to live up to their own findings, a charge that he was to press vigorously a few years later in *Structure*, where he in effect accused them of running with the hares of Gestalt theory while hunting with the hounds of Cartesian dualism. Thus, what began in 1933–34 as a specific issue in experimental psychology became for him a guiding thread of all his philosophy. Much more than the concept which can be found neatly defined in any dictionary today, it became for him one of those indices that generate inquiry and questions to the end, rather than winding them down. He never pretended to have exhausted this notion which he placed at the center of his 1933 study project, as is tellingly shown in one of his last working notes, where he asked, "What is a Gestalt?"[5]

During the late 20s and early 30s, Merleau-Ponty was faced in the academies with problems posed primarily in a Kantian or neo-Kantian fashion. But unlike such influential thinkers as Léon Brunschvicg, who concentrated chiefly on what might be called "intra-philosophical" questions, Merleau-Ponty seemed to have been moved to philosophical inquiry rather more by current contradictions which were not necessarily associated already with philosophical difficulties. (In this he was more like Henri Bergson and William James, and even Edmund Husserl, who came to philosophy through the study of mathematics.) His lifelong affinity for current issues in the wide world—viz., the artistic transformations of modern painting, the political disappointments of both East and West, the vexing "Freudian unconscious," the child psychology of Piaget and others, the American and French investigations in cultural anthropology—was already evident in 1933–34, in his ambition to liberate empirical psychology from the grip of Critical philosophy. At that time—and indeed, to this day among those who are not strict behaviorists banning any reference to "mind" at all—most psychologists assumed a Kantian or neo-Kantian epistemology, according to which perceiving consists in applying intellectual interpretations to "sensations" or "sensory signs." He saw the entire "intellectualist" tradition from Descartes to Kant, however great their other differences, to be alike in misconstruing the nature of perceptual experience. Moreover, in the 1934 statement Merleau-Ponty was already hinting at the notion, fully developed in *Phénoménologie*, that the other favorite of many experimental psychologists, the philosophy of empiricism, was in no better a position: indeed, might even betray the very same misconception in a different form. He objects in the same sentence to psychologies which would make of normal perception either a "brute given" or a "construction." Later, it became clear that he believed both empiricism and Critical philosophy invented "facts" out of supposed elements and inferences for whose occurrence in perception there is no evidence. Yet another anticipation of his later writings may be found in the expressed desire to include the topics of psychopathology and developmental psychology in his study of perception. The discussion of Gelb and Goldstein's brain-injured soldier in *Phénoménologie* comes immediately to mind, as does the 1950–51 course at the Sorbonne on the child's relations with others.[6]

Some other motifs worth noting do not all survive intact. Certainly the notions of perceptual distance and perceptual depth as something other than the Cartesian "width seen sideways" were to remain and become crucially important; for example, in *Phénoménologie*, in the discussion of Descartes' *Dioptrique* in *L'Oeil et l'esprit*, and most powerfully in *Visible*, where these motifs enabled Merleau-Ponty to disclose a commingling of the visible and the invisible in a philosophy quite different from the more traditional equating of the visible with the sensory given and the invisible with the intellectually conceived. The rather definite line imagined between the phenomenological and the psychological, however, did not withstand the test of time; nor did the line between essence and fact, eidetic and inductive. In his reference in the 1934 statement to binocular vision and the disparity of retinal images, he spoke of the latter as a "condition" of vision; later, he was to question the notion of "conditions and conditioned" in terms of a "circular causality." In *Visible*, he was to return to this issue to say that these "conditions" are "not really conditions, since the images are defined as disparate only by relation to a perceptual apparatus that seeks its equilibrium in the fusion of analogous images, and hence here the 'conditioned' conditions the condition."[7]

But this step could not be taken, it seems, until the specific problem of perception addressed in 1933–34 had turned into a clue—the richest and most suggestive clue—to nothing less than a new ontology, a theory of Being. The objections in these early texts to Critical philosophy and to empiricism as employed by psychologists had to grow into a massive confrontation with the entire tradition of absolutized "objectivity," "Being-as-object," and its inevitable counterpart, "subjectivity." Such a confrontation also had to wait upon, and in a sense was equivalent to, a rejection of the vocabulary of "consciousness" in which Merleau-Ponty was still involved in 1933–34, and from which he was trying to liberate himself in *Phénoménologie*.[8] What Merleau-Ponty clearly saw in 1933, these early statements reveal, was a crisis in psychology that was conspicuously evident in what was being said about perception. The sense of philosophy as we have understood it in the West, and therefore of

Western culture itself, as in crisis, was still some years off. Even allowing for differences in tone due to differences in context (a formal application for a grant, a note to oneself), some measure of the trajectory from Merleau-Ponty's study project published here to the project on which he was working when he died may be gained by juxtaposing the first lines of each:

It has seemed to me that in the present state of neurology, experimental psychology (particularly psychopathology), and philosophy, it would be useful to take up again the problem of perception, and particularly perception of one's own body.

Our state of non-philosophy—The crisis has never been so radical.[9]

APPENDIX 2:

Merleau-Ponty and the Husserl Archives at Louvain

H. L. Van Breda

Attentive readers of Maurice Merleau-Ponty know that during the preparation of his *Phenomenology of Perception* he was able to study firsthand many of Husserl's still unpublished manuscripts housed at Louvain.[1] Indeed, in the *Phenomenology* he often uses terms and expressions borrowed from the manuscripts and draws upon their resources to explore certain Husserlian doctrines.

In at least two places he makes explicit reference to the Louvain manuscripts. First, after citing an expression from the *Ideen II* manuscript,[2] we read in a note on page 108: "We are indebted to Mgr. Noel and the Institut Supérieur de Philosophie of Louvain, trustees of the collected *Nachlass*, and particularly to the kindness of the Reverend Father Van Breda, for having been able to consult a certain amount of unpublished material."[3] Then, in the bibliography, he specifies that, "with the kind permission of Mgr Noel and the Institut Supérieur de Philosophie of Louvain," he has made use of three manuscripts: "*Ideen zu einer reinen Phänomenologie und phänomenologischen Philosophie, II* (unpublished); *Umsturz der Kopernikanischen Lehre: die Erde als Ur-Arche bewegt sich nicht* (unpublished); *Die Krisis der Europaischen Wissenschaften und die transzendentale Phänomenologie*, II and III (unpublished).[4]

In Merleau-Ponty's work published since 1945, there are few clear traces of his consultations of the manuscripts. Nonetheless, these traces do exist, most notably in an article written near the end of his life to commemorate the centennial of Husserl's birth, where he makes explicit reference to them.[5]

My intention in the following notes is not to uncover in Merleau-Ponty's work the possible sediments deposited by Husserl's unpublished manuscripts. My purpose is rather to furnish future historians of French philosophy with some precise facts, preserved in our notes and correspondence, that will indicate *which manuscripts Merleau-Ponty in fact consulted* (or at least which ones he may have consulted) and *when these consultations took place.*

Elsewhere[6] I have told how, in the fall of 1938, I succeeded in transporting from Fribourg-en-Brisgau [Freiburg-im-Breisgau] to Louvain the some forty thousand pages of unpublished shorthand manuscripts left by Husserl after his death earlier that same year. In the same article, I explained that Mrs. Husserl also entrusted me with some ten thousand pages of longhand transcriptions of these shorthand texts, elaborated by Husserl's assistants while he was still alive. Before the end of 1938, all of these documents were once again assembled at the archival center of what was then part of the Institut Supérieur de Philosophie of the University of Louvain. Shortly thereafter, during the spring of 1939, the systematic elaboration of the documents was begun under the direction of Ludwig Landgrebe and Eugen Fink,

Husserl's last two assistants. By June of 1939, we were able to integrate Husserl's important library into the collection of documents we had already come to call the Husserl Archives at Louvain.

It was in March of 1939 that Merleau-Ponty first contacted me to inquire into Husserl's philosophical legacy and to ask whether he could consult the manuscripts at Louvain. A few days after his letter, I had the pleasure of receiving him at Louvain, and of offering him a certain number of manuscripts to study. Before entering into the details of his visit, I should note that Merleau-Ponty was the first researcher from outside of Louvain to consult the archives.

Eugen Fink had arrived in Louvain from Fribourg-en-Brisgau [Freiburg-im-Breisgau] on March 16, 1939. Soon thereafter he started work on the transcription of the group C manuscripts—on time and temporality—that Husserl had written between 1928 and 1930. Less than a week later, I received a letter from Merleau-Ponty, from which I will cite the important passages:

Monday, March 20 (1939)

Sir,

On the advice of Mr. Jean Hering,[7] I am taking the liberty to request some information about the *Nachlass* of Husserl. Excuse me for forcing upon you the inconvenience of a response.

I am currently pursuing a study of the *Phenomenology of Perception* for which it would be extremely useful for me to acquaint myself with volume II of the *Ideen*. There was, I believe, a typed copy that Husserl's students used to consult. Does this copy still exist, and do you think I would be able to consult it in Louvain? If you require letters of introduction from Prof. Brunschvicg or from another professor I would be very much obliged if you would notify me.

Allow me to ask you whether Fink's work, a fragment of which just appeared in the *Revue internationale de philosophie*,[8] is to be published soon in Belgium.

Finally, I have been unable to procure a copy of Husserl's posthumous work [*Erfahrung und Urteil*] published by Landgrebe at the Academia Verlag in Prague.[9] I don't expect to receive a response directly from Prague. I wonder if it is available in Belgium? (I haven't seen it anywhere in Paris.) I would be very grateful if you could tell me if it is. I am all the more eager to read it since Prof. Koyré has entrusted me with an article for the homage to Husserl upcoming in *Recherches philosophiques*. . . .

Yours truly,

(signed) Maurice Merleau-Ponty
Charge d'enseignement,[10]
Ecole normale supérieure

I answered Merleau-Ponty's letter eight days later (on March 28). I told him, first, that we did have a longhand copy of volume II of the *Ideen*, as well as transcriptions of other texts that would probably be useful to him; also, that he would be able to consult a copy of *Erfahrung und Urteil*. All of these documents would willingly be at his disposal if he came to Louvain: it was impossible for me to forward them (the manuscripts) because it was prohibited to send them anywhere, and the book, because it was the only copy that had arrived in Belgium from Prague. I added that Louvain might not be able to grant him permission to cite the manuscripts, as the rules for use by third parties had not yet been made definite. In closing I told him that I believed Mr. Fink did not intend to publish any work in Belgium in the near future, nor had he begun the continuation of his article in the *Revue internationale de philosophie*.

On Thursday, March 30, Merleau-Ponty wrote back that he would be coming to Louvain in two days. He added: "Unfortunately, I will only be able to stay in Belgium for five or six days; I would like to take full advantage of my short stay by concentrating on the sections of the work [the *Nachlass*] of most immediate interest to me." These sections were a series of paragraphs from the *Ideen II*.

This part of the letter ends with a remark that, given the threats that were then emerging on international horizons, was probably too optimistic: "I may be able to return to Belgium later to continue my consultations."

Merleau-Ponty arrived in Louvain on the afternoon of April 1 and stayed until the evening of the 6th or the morning of the 7th. In any case, he returned to Paris before April 9, which was Easter Sunday. During his stay in Louvain, he lived and worked in the modest Saint-Augustin pension, near the library of the Institut Supérieur de Philosophie.

In the course of his visit, I had the opportunity to introduce him to Eugen Fink. Although each man encountered serious difficulties in expressing himself in the language of the other, they enjoyed a long and very interesting exchange of opinions. For the first time, I was vested with the role of translator between phenomenologists of different nationalities, a role that was to fall to me quite often in the years to come.

Merleau-Ponty was able to consult Ludwig Landgrebe's volume of *Erfahrung und Urteil*. However, he did not meet Landgrebe because he had not yet arrived from Prague. (Landgrebe came to Louvain on April 24 as a collaborator with Eugen Fink.)

I showed my visitor from Paris the collection of Husserl's original shorthand manuscripts. Unfortunately, we could only examine the title pages and could not delve into their contents, for at the time the manuscripts were still on display in the University Library. They were moved to the Institut Supérieur only in January of 1940—just four months before most of the University Library was destroyed by German bombs.

Then, Merleau-Ponty accompanied me to the Franciscan Convent, where from the fall of 1938 until the end of 1940 I kept in my cell the transcriptions made by Husserl's assistants. It was these transcriptions that he studied on his first consultation of the manuscripts; the three unpublished texts of Husserl cited at the end of the *Phenomenology of Perception* belonged to this group of transcriptions. Some details of these three dossiers should now be given.

The first dossier contained Landgrebe's typed transcription of volume II of the *Ideen*, completed between 1924 and 1925.[11] Mrs. Marly Biemel used this text as the basis[12] for the 1954 edition she published under the title *Ideen zu einer reinen Phänomenologie und phänomenologischen Philosophie, Zweites Buch, Phänomenologische Untersuchungen zur Konstitution*.[13]

The second dossier was also a transcription by Landgrebe, completed in Prague between 1936 and 1938.[14] Merleau-Ponty makes several references to it in the *Phenomenology* and he returns to it again in "The Philosopher and His Shadow."[15] It is a twenty-four-page, in-quarto transcription of a manuscript Husserl wrote between May 7 and 9, 1934, which under the classification system implemented by Husserl himself bears the signature D 17. The group D manuscripts largely concern what Husserl called "primordial constitution" [*primordial Konstitution, Urkonstitution*]. Above all, they contain elaborations of the idea of the intentional genesis of the most original layers of consciousness of things, and a doctrine of the transcendental aesthetic, understood in Husserl's own terms. On the cover of the manuscript Husserl summarizes its contents as follows: *Umsturz der Kopernikanischen Lehre in der gewohnlichen weltanschaulichen Interpretation. Die Ur-Arche Erde bewegt sich nicht.—Grundlegende Untersuchungen zur phänomenologischen Ursprung der Körperlichkeit, der Raumlichkeit der Natur im ersten naturwissenschaftlichen Sinne. Alles notwendige Anfangsuntersuchungen.*[16]

The third transcription that Merleau-Ponty consulted was made by Eugen Fink from paragraphs 28 to 73 of Husserl's last great work, *Die Krisis der Europaischen Wissenschaften und die transzendentale Phänomenologie* [*The Crisis of European Sciences and Transcendental Phenomenology*]. In the bibliography of the *Phenomenology* it is mistakenly cited as constituting parts II and III of the *Krisis*; in fact it was made from parts III A and III B. (In 1936, the first two parts of the *Krisis* had already appeared in Belgrade in the journal *Philosophia*, published by Arthur Liebert. The third part was finally published—along with the first two—in 1954, by Walter Biemel in volume VI of *Husserliana*.)[17]

In September 1939, war broke out between France and Germany, and on May 10, 1940, Belgium was invaded. Thus, the year 1939 and the ensuing war years were not, to be sure, very auspicious ones for "returning to Belgium" and "continuing consultations" of Husserl's unpublished works, as Merleau-Ponty had hopes of doing earlier that year. He returned to Belgium and to Louvain only in 1946—and this time not to consult Husserl's texts but to lecture in various Belgian cities.

Though the war prevented him from completing his intended project of study in Louvain, an initiative by a group of philosophers in Paris resulted, upon our suggestion, in the transfer of a series of manuscripts from Louvain to Paris. The texts were housed in Paris from April 1944 until 1948, and they were thus accessible to Merleau-Ponty. Before discussing the details of this initiative—the first attempt (unsuccessful, by the way) to find a suitable institution or public library in Paris to house a large portion of the Louvain manuscripts, and to make them available to qualified researchers[18]—I should briefly describe the work of transcription and other activities of the Archives during the war.

Between their arrival in the spring of 1939 and May 10, 1940, Ludwig Landgrebe and Eugen Fink transcribed and made five typed copies of a significant number of Husserl's shorthand manuscripts. Landgrebe devoted himself to the 38 dossiers, classed under the heading B 1, that bore the general title "Paths Toward the Reduction" [*Wege zur Reduktion*]; there Husserl expounds the different possibilities open to the philosopher who makes the phenomenological reduction. When on May 10, 1940, Landgrebe's work was interrupted by the war, he had already copied more than 30 of the dossiers and had completed in addition approximately 2800 pages of transcription in quarto. Fink first transcribed the 17 manuscripts of group C, written after 1928 and dealing almost exclusively with the question of the constitution of time [*Zeitkonstitution als formale Konstitution*]. Then he transcribed about 10 of the 18 manuscripts of group D that, as noted above, largely concern the question of primordial constitution. By May of 1940, Fink had completed more than 870 typed pages of transcription of the C manuscripts, and some 1550 pages of the D manuscripts.

In November of 1940, Fink and Landgrebe were forced to leave Belgium and to return to Germany. Those who remained in Belgium from 1940 to 1944 to care for the Archives were required by the German presence to exercise extreme caution, so as not to expose Husserl's legacy to the harsh fate that the Nazis had in store for literature produced by "non-Aryans." Yet never, even during the darkest years of the war, did we completely halt our work of transcription; we continued to answer inquiries about the manuscripts, and made the documents themselves available to Belgian, Dutch, and French researchers.

In the spring of 1942, we decided to do even more. We engaged several collaborators at the Archives, German and Austrian emigrés who had fled the racist laws of the Third Reich and whose erudition eminently qualified them to work with the manuscripts. What is more, we contacted—as secretively as possible—certain Dutch and French phenomenologists, in order to allow them to consult the manuscripts. To make these contacts more effectively, I undertook a trip of more than fifteen days to Holland in late April–early May 1942; and between the end of May and the beginning of August, I went to Paris twice, staying for a total of more than four weeks.

The first mission I undertook in Paris was to relay to various persons messages that had been given to me by H. J. Pos and Edith Stein in Holland.[19] I had, in fact, for a long time run into Edith Stein in Carmel D'Echt, all the while with the distressing premonition of the terrible fate she was soon to meet at the hands of the Nazis. With H. J. Pos, however, I could only exchange a few letters, for at the time he was interned at the camp in Vught, and despite my efforts, I was unable to visit him.

The real goal of our two trips to Paris was nonetheless quite different. Since my meetings with Gaston Berger in Fribourg-en-Brisgau in 1938,[20] and especially since Merleau-Ponty's visit to Louvain, I had become convinced that in Paris's many philosophical circles—particularly among a group of young philosophers at the Ecole Normale—there was a burgeoning interest in Husserl's thought. The phenomenological studies published by Gaston Berger and by J.-P. Sartre had confirmed my conviction, as did reports from various other sources.[21] I was thus certain that in Paris a significant number of philosophers would welcome any possibility of gaining access to Husserl's manuscripts and would help me—even in 1942—in my efforts to establish a center for the Husserl transcriptions there. The ultimate goal of our two trips to Paris was to lay the foundations for such a center. Of course, we were required by the Nazi presence to keep this goal a secret.

The manuscripts we hoped to bring to Paris included, above all, a complete set of Landgrebe's and Fink's transcriptions. Some other texts, of which the Archives had more than one copy, could also be added.[22] Our idea for the center was that these documents could be consulted on the spot, in one of the public libraries, and that a small group of philosophers would care for them and administer their consultation.

In Paris, our negotiations soon led to the formulation of a written contract between the Institut Supérieur de Philosophie of Louvain and a group of Parisian philosophers, specifying the terms of our loan. Though we seemed to be quite close to finishing the deal, we soon came up against very serious problems in transporting the texts from Louvain to Paris. Then, toward the summer of 1942, we encountered an even more formidable obstacle. The Parisian promoters of the project realized that if the overseeing committee was to have the desired authority, it should include one or two professors who held official chairs of philosophy. Sounded out on several occasions, these professors were rather hesitant; in the end they went so far as to refuse their collaboration.

In many ways, their refusal was understandable, due to the heavy responsibilities—moral, financial, and other—that would fall to such a committee during wartime. In any event, all further steps to constitute a Parisian committee failed, one after the other; we were forced to annul the contract and finally to abandon the project itself.

It was not until after the war, however, that official negotiations between Paris and Louvain broke down definitively. In response to a new proposal I had submitted to him, Emile Bréhier, then the director of philosophical studies at the Sorbonne, wrote to me on January 2, 1946:

> I wonder if it is really useful now for us to have a copy of all or part of Husserl's manuscripts in Paris. First, thanks to your devotion, the most interesting of them will soon be published, which is even better; furthermore, Louvain is close enough for those few interested persons in France to visit.

Let me turn now to describing in more detail the role Merleau-Ponty played in all of these transactions. In the process, I will be able to furnish more details on the very prudent attitude assumed by the professors at the Sorbonne. At the same time, I will have the occasion to recount how, in the spring of 1944, some twenty-one hundred pages of Husserl transcriptions were nonetheless transported to Paris, where Merleau-Ponty was able to consult them.

Above I mentioned a group of French philosophers who served as the "promoters" of the project in Paris, working tirelessly for its realization. All of these promoters were part of the scene at the Ecole Normale Supérieure, and the oldest of them was only thirty-nine years old. The simple enumeration of their names will suffice to show our considerable good luck in having them as partners in our discussions. Besides Merleau-Ponty, there were Jean Cavaillès (who was shot by the Nazis in Arras in 1944), Jean Hyppolite, and the Indochinese philosopher Tran Duc Thao. The representative of the Grandes Ecoles Catholiques was Father L.-B. Geiger.[23]

As the oldest and already a *chargé d'enseignement* at the Sorbonne, Jean Cavaillès was from the start more or less the leader of the group. His departure from Paris toward the beginning of August 1942, and his activities in the Resistance, however, put a tragic and premature end to his collaboration. The two other members who were by far the most active between 1942 and 1946 were Merleau-Ponty and Tran Duc Thao; I met and corresponded with them the most.

On June 1, 1942, after a first exchange of views on the proposed center, Merleau-Ponty wrote me the following observations:

> I have considered what you told me the other day, and after consulting with my friends Hyppolite and Sartre, I believe we may now have the necessary elements to form a center for Husserl studies [in Paris]. It would be easy for us to get in touch with Le Senne, Lavelle[24] or any of the professors of the past generation, if you so desire. Personally, I would have more confidence in an undertaking with people of my own age. . . .
>
> In my opinion the only chance for survival of such a center is if it is built around a specific project of translation and publication. After all, Husserl's philosophy is almost entirely contained in the unpublished manuscripts; one must admit that, until their publication, his thought will remain more a "style" (to speak in the terms of the *Krisis*) than a specific philosophy [*une philosophie précise*]. Do you think it would be possible, as you were suggesting the other day, to establish a depository here to which you would turn over, for example, copies of groups C and D? The study of these texts would allow us to recommend certain of them for publication in French. There would be no lack of publishers interested in such a collection.
>
> We would very much like to see this project through to its end; it is possible that the philosophical public itself is growing weary of the "myth" of Husserl. It is no doubt time to give them something concrete and positive.

A few days after receiving this letter, I met Merleau-Ponty one last time before returning to Belgium. At his request I gave him a typed copy of the doctoral dissertation I had defended on August 2, 1941, in Louvain, dealing with the "phenomenological reduction in Husserl's final philosophy." The main text was written in Dutch, my native tongue, and Merleau-Ponty was unable to read it. He was, however, more interested in the numerous passages of Husserl's unpublished manuscripts that I cited in the notes to the text, and particularly in a ninety-page appendix where I reproduced five of Husserl's posthumous writings.

In this appendix (which he did not return until April 1944), Merleau-Ponty found Husserl's German text, written in 1927, that had appeared in 1929 under the title "Phenomenology" in the fourteenth edition of the *Encyclopedia Britannica*.[25]

The appendix also contained a very detailed table of contents from the second part of Husserl's extensive study entitled *Studien zur Struktur des Bewusstseins*, that Landgrebe had written in 1925, drawing upon texts that Husserl had placed at his disposal. This second part was entitled *Weltkonstitution, Gemüt, Wille*.[26]

From the group of manuscripts dealing with the *Krisis*, we transcribed in this same appendix the complete list of titles of paragraphs (from paragraph 1 to paragraph 73), as well as the text of paragraphs 38 and 53.[27] Finally, there was also a copy of a letter in German that Husserl had sent to Lucien Lévy-Brühl (on March 11, 1935), thanking him for a dedicated copy of his book, *La Mythologie primitive*.[28]

Having returned to Belgium in mid-June, I sent a letter on July 14 to Cavaillès and Merleau-Ponty, informing them that the academic authorities of Louvain had agreed to our projects. I added that the text of the contract (regulating the conditions of the loan) would be completely worked out in Louvain in the very near future. Could they possibly come to Belgium, I asked, to discuss the contract and to agree upon the documents to be sent to Paris?

On July 27, the eve of his departure for the "free zone" and shortly before his first arrest by the Nazis, Jean Cavaillès responded to my letter to say that he saw few obstacles left and that we could hope to create the center soon. In September he expected that we could once again take up our discussions.

This was to be the last time I would hear from him. Jean Cavaillès finished September 1942 in a Nazi concentration camp in southern France. Toward the middle of November, I sent him another letter, but it was returned by the censor without explanation. It was only in the spring of 1943 that I learned, bit by bit, the real reason for his prolonged silence.

On October 1, Merleau-Ponty, returning from holidays, answered my letter of July 14:

> I can't tell you how satisfied I am to see that our project has been approved and now has the chance to be brought to fruition. In Marseilles I was able to consult, with G. Berger, the *Sixth Meditation*;[29] I read it in the tranquility of the small university town of Aix-en-Provence, and it increased my curiosity [for the unpublished manuscripts]. I am personally very happy about the success of your negotiations.

Doubtless totally unaware of Cavaillès' arrest and awaiting his return to Paris, Merleau-Ponty mentions that he won't be able to come to Louvain himself. He continues: "I think that Cavaillès will be very happy to accept your invitation to Louvain and to work out all the details of the matter with you."

In the winter of 1942–43, tensions and troubles intensified from week to week, as much in France as in Belgium. All unnecessary travel and any correspondence in the least bit compromising was avoided as far as possible. At the end of December 1942, Merleau-Ponty sent me a dedicated copy of *The Structure of Behavior*, which had just been published. Several weeks later I thanked him in a letter that a friend was able to deliver directly to his home in Paris. Then, for nearly eight months, no news reached me from Paris.

Things would have probably remained in this state until the liberation of France if, in the fall of 1943, Mr. Tran Duc Thao hadn't decided to resume a project he had first sought to undertake in the winter of 1942. In order to write a dissertation on Husserl's phenomenological method, and on the advice of Merleau-Ponty, he had resolved to follow his friend's example and come to Louvain to consult the unpublished manuscripts. At the start of 1942, the conditions of the war had prevented him from making the trip to Louvain. On the basis of our correspondence we were glad to accept him into the group of Parisian "promoters" as soon as we arrived in Paris. Once negotiations were underway, Mr. Thao, hopeful that we would soon be finished, no longer spoke of making a trip to Louvain. Yet, as the transportation of the manuscripts had to be continually deferred, he finally reverted to his original plans and wrote to me (on September 27, 1943) that he would like to spend several weeks in Louvain.

This time he succeeded in overcoming all obstacles, and between January 20 and April 15, 1944, he made two trips to Louvain, each of about three weeks. In addition to his consultation of the manuscripts, he was charged by his friends at the Ecole Normale—particularly Merleau-Ponty—to continue to discuss all possibilities of creating a Paris center for Husserl's posthumous works.

First, the two of us put the finishing touches on the contract that, contingent upon the success of our discussions, would be signed between Paris and Louvain. I was told he and his friends at the Sorbonne fully expected that René Le Senne would now agree to preside over the Paris committee. Also, Jean Nabert, director of the Victor-Cousin Library, had in general agreed to house the documents in his library. Thao believed we could soon bring our plans to fruition, and if we had no objections, he would volunteer to bring the first package of manuscripts with him on his return to Paris, around February 15.

Though he could not know for certain whether those in Paris would sign, Thao's account convinced us that an agreement was imminent. After a final consultation with my colleagues at Louvain and with the full consent of Mrs. Husserl herself,[30] we entrusted Mr. Thao with some three thousand pages of transcriptions to take to France at his own risk.

Once in Paris, however, Thao was forced to admit that the time was unfortunately not yet ripe for the realization of our project. On Sunday, February 18, he related our deliberations to Le Senne, and showed him the contract and the manuscripts we had given him. The next day, Le Senne informed us that, after a thorough examination of the entire situation, he found it impossible to sign the contract and thus could not accept receipt of the documents.

Although Merleau-Ponty and the other supporters of the Paris center could still understand Le Senne's reasons—debatable as they were, yet all the same based in reality—certain rumors that appeared completely groundless to them spread through philosophical circles in Paris, and they were deeply angered. When Mr. Thao returned to Louvain in early March, he reluctantly brought back the manuscripts and told us of the rumors in Paris and of how his friends intended to respond to them. It was evident, he informed us, that we could no longer count on any official support from the Sorbonne. If we still wanted to house the manuscripts in Paris, we would have to confide in a select group of philosophers of the "upcoming generation."

In a letter of March 31 that reached us while Thao was still in Louvain, Merleau-Ponty had ultimately arrived at the same conclusions as his friend. He began by suggesting that we change the wording and modify the terms of the contract; he continued:

> If you don't feel able to proceed in this direction, Thao will tell you that he and I are ready to assume responsibility for the manuscripts, making them available to other researchers as far as you see fit. In this case I would prefer that no library be solicited; it would thus be clear that we did not need the help of anyone else and, consequently, that we have the general interest in view.

Alluding more directly to certain unpleasant rumors circulating in Paris, but without naming names, he concluded: "I would be obliged to have a letter from you that we might show . . . to the others and that would put an end to either their hesitation or their calumnies.[31] This entire affair is incredible [*Cette histoire est invraisemblable*]."

When this letter reached us we had already decided to cease our effort to come to an agreement with the official representatives of the Sorbonne and, instead, to personally entrust Merleau-Ponty and Thao with a selection of manuscripts.

On March 31, we had already drawn up a document—signed by Thao—describing in detail the texts we entrusted him with that same day. It also stated the precise limits of their use, and Thao formally agreed to return the transcriptions within two months if we were to reclaim them. It was understood that Merleau-Ponty would enjoy the same privileges agreed to by his friend.

The dossiers Thao brought back to France in his luggage (around April 10) comprised more than twenty-one hundred longhand pages. The first series of dossiers contained the German text of the *Cartesian Meditations*[32] (386 pages), as well as a complete copy of the third part (560 pages) of the *Krisis*.[33] These transcriptions had just been made in 1943 by Stephan Strasser,[34] who with his wife and mother-in-law we were able to enlist as collaborators at the Archives, just as the Nazis were preparing to send them to a death camp.

To their diligence we owed yet a third transcription that Thao brought to Paris—a text of 155 pages bearing the signature F I 17. It represented the transcript of a course conceived as a general introduction to phenomenology, given in Göttingen in 1909. It bore the title *The Idea of Phenomenology and Its Method* [*Idee der Phänomenologie und ihre Methode*].[35] In addition to these three longer texts, there were 42 shorter dossiers, containing approximately 870 pages of transcriptions from group C, which deals largely with problems of temporality (*Zeitkonstitution als formale Konstitution*).

These texts stayed in Paris from April 1944 until the end of December 1946, when, with the exception of the 42 dossiers from group C, we took them back to Louvain. These latter texts Thao had asked us to leave a bit longer in Paris; they were returned toward the end of 1948. For several years, then, Merleau-Ponty had the possibility of consulting these texts. I am convinced that in the *Phenomenology of Perception* and in many studies published since, one can discern undeniable traces of these documents. Above all, I believe it would be easy to discern reflections of his reading of the C manuscripts (dealing with temporality).

Often during the ten years between 1949 and 1958, Merleau-Ponty kindly gave us his advice and support in the organization and execution of various projects at the Archives.[36] Under all circumstances we found in him a true and particularly devoted friend, although in our correspondence from the period I can find signs of only one loan of manuscripts.

In January 1950, we entrusted him with Stephan Strasser's transcription of three texts Husserl had composed for his classes, bearing the signatures F I 4, F I 17, and F I 33. He consulted these dossiers at his home in Paris, not returning them until January 1955.

As noted above, F I 17 was composed in Göttingen in 1909 and is called *The Idea of Phenomenology and Its Method*. F I 4 was also written in Göttingen, but for a course offered in 1912; this transcription of 47 pages is entitled *Introduction to Phenomenology*. Dossier F I 33 contains, in 183 pages of transcription, large segments of a course of 1926–1927, given at Fribourg-en-Brisgau; it is devoted to the problem of the possibility of an intentional psychology (*Möglichkeit einer intentionalen psychologie*). Our annotations indicate that Merleau-Ponty borrowed these three texts for specific reasons: they all deal in a detailed manner with problems related to ideation and with the relationship between phenomenology and psychology, themes that Merleau-Ponty himself dealt with on a regular basis between 1950 and 1953.[37]

From 1955 to 1958, Merleau-Ponty made no further consultations of the manuscripts. In 1959, for the first time in years, he expressed interest in seeing certain texts that he planned to use for one of his courses at the Collège de France.

Only a few months earlier, a Center for Husserl Archives had finally been created at the Sorbonne, to house a great number of transcriptions from Louvain. At the third philosophy colloquium at Royaumont in 1957, devoted to Husserl's work and thought, we had had the chance to resume our long-cherished project, with Gaston Berger and with the philosophers at the Sorbonne. This time we encountered nothing but understanding and goodwill from our interlocutors. A few months later, the University of Paris Library received over one hundred of Husserl's unpublished manuscripts.

During the negotiations (in the summer and fall of 1957) that led to the realization of the center, Merleau-Ponty gave us, his advice and help unsparingly. Without hesitation he agreed to be on the center's directorial committee. And when, in May of 1958, Mr. Georges Calmette announced that the texts were available to researchers, he took care to inform his students and auditors at the Collège de France, and soon showed his personal interest in the center.

In a long letter of June 14, 1959, he furnished me once again with clear proof of his special interest.[38] First, he informed me of a reform that the professors of the Collège soon expected to introduce into the curriculum: "The Collège de France is going to officially reinstitute a practice that has long existed in fact: that of genuine seminars, which will replace a certain number of ex cathedra courses (at most, half of a professor's course load)." This decision greatly pleased him, and of course he planned to comply with it: "I envisage for January a seminar devoted to interpretation [the French word *"explications"* is unclear in the original text] and commentary upon the texts of Husserl's late philosophy.[39] Naturally, I think the public would be particularly responsive to unpublished manuscripts (I would, moreover, have recourse to the *Krisis*, of which I have translated and interpreted several fragments this year)." For this purpose, he continued, "I would like to be able to reflect upon your texts. I believe my project will be agreeable to you; tell me what you think of it at your convenience."

Meanwhile, he had gone to consult the Husserl manuscripts in Paris but found that many of the texts he would have liked to read—though listed in the complete card index of transcriptions—were not in the Paris center.[40] "Would it be possible," he continued, "for me to consult copies of them in Paris, or if not, to be loaned a copy in person, at the end of a stay in Louvain?"

On June 25, I answered his letter and explained why a portion of the manuscripts were missing from the Paris center: either we had no available copies to lend or those we did have were defective in some way. Nonetheless, we had decided to photograph these texts on microfilm; soon, I told him, at least some of them could be placed at his disposal. In any event, I was very pleased with his idea of devoting a seminar to Husserl's late thought and I offered to help him in any way I could.

Unfortunately, the process of transferring the texts to microfilm took much longer than planned; it wasn't until toward the end of 1960 that we were able to have a full set made. Merleau-Ponty was thus unable to use them for his projected seminar. It seems that—for this reason and others—his seminar on Husserl's late philosophy never took place.[41]

The signatures of the unpublished manuscripts Merleau-Ponty had found in the index of transcriptions but was unable to consult can be reproduced here from the same letter of June 14. The first six texts belong to the group A V and deal, in general, with intentional anthropology and with the relations between the person and the environing world [intentionale Anthropologie: Person und Umwelt]. The exact references are: A V 6, A V 11, A V 12, A V 13, A V 14, and A V 15. Five other texts mentioned belong to the group A VII, which is devoted largely to the perception of the world as horizon [Weltperzeption]: A VII 1, A VII 5, A VII 7, A VII 8, A VII 31. The last manuscript noted in his letter, K III 18, is a 94-page text written in 1936 that elaborates upon certain parts of the Krisis; it is entitled, "Possibility of an Ontology of the Lifeworld; Possibility of an Ontology of Man."[42]

As for the texts available for consultation at the Paris center, it seems probable that, between June 1959 and the end of 1960, Merleau-Ponty studied a number of manuscripts written between 1928 and 1937. It is logical that he would have studied above all certain texts from group D, dealing with primordial constitution, texts from group K III [Krisis-Gruppe],[43] as well as texts from group E III, dealing with problems of transcendental anthropology that are at the heart of the problematic of intersubjectivity and of language.

Here I have arrived at the end of my account. If I have been drawn to talk at length about the Archives and not always about Merleau-Ponty, I am glad now to let him speak one last time.

By a stroke of good luck, the following letter fell into my hands. Each time I read it I am filled with emotion; each time, I hear once again the voice of an incomparable friend and colleague. Here then are the principal passages from a letter of September 18, 1949, that Merleau-Ponty addressed to the Director's office of UNESCO, expressing his appreciation for Husserl's literary legacy and for the work of the Archives at Louvain:

Having been able for more than ten years to appreciate the work undertaken by the Husserl Archives, I would like, as far as I am able, to call your attention to their exceptional interest and value.

The Husserl Archives seek both to acquaint people with Husserl's already published work as well as to bring forward his unpublished work. Now, whatever contemporary philosophers may think of this or that particular conclusion of his thought, they probably agree that Husserl's philosophical endeavor deserves by now the name of a classic: it has sought to situate in its proper place all that history, psychology, and sociology have taught us about ourselves, without allowing this multitude of external determinations to encroach upon the proper function of philosophical judgment and reason. Equally opposed to dogmatism and to irrationalism, Husserl truly confronted the crisis faced by the mathematical and physical sciences—as well as by the human sciences—as a result of their own development; he sought to lay a new foundation for reason, yet with an awareness of the teachings of experience. . . .

Husserl's own scruples dictated that he present to the public only written works of polished perfection. His philosophical influence has thus been exercised largely through his teaching, and the majority of his manuscripts were left unpublished at his death. Among his published writings one of the most accomplished works[44] was at first only a long introduction that he began to compose for reasons of circumstance. His posthumous writings thus contain—with the texts of certain of the most famous of his courses—material for works of the utmost importance, that would have been published had only Husserl been less demanding of himself. For want of general publication, the most mature developments and results of these important investigations would remain unknown without the work of the Archives; for his published writings (which, besides, have become rare) only adumbrate their content.

Since 1938,[45] when I was introduced by Mr. Jean Hering, Professor in the Department of Protestant Theology at Strasbourg, I have been allowed to consult some of Husserl's unpublished texts at the Husserl Archives in Louvain, which were first organized by Father Van Breda. I have stayed in contact with the Archives ever since.

The work of deciphering, transcribing, classifying and filing the manuscripts, in view of a complete edition, has always been conducted according to the strictest philological methods and in a spirit of absolute devotion to philosophy—at times under nearly heroic conditions. Scholars from many countries—particularly former students of Husserl—who like myself have been generously allowed to benefit from this careful labor, agree with me that we could have wished for nothing better. . . .

Yours truly,

(signed) Maurice Merleau-Ponty
Professor, University of Lyon

—Trans. by Stephen Michelman.

APPENDIX 3

Husserl's Concept of Nature (Merleau-Ponty's 1957–58 Lectures)

Xavier Tilliette

Merleau-Ponty had chosen to lecture on the philosophy of Nature during the semester of 1957.[1] He did not complete the announced program, but owing to its momentum he returned to and extended it in the following years. These two conjoint lectures are transcribed with the kind authorization of his literary inheritors and thanks to the hospitality of Jean Wahl. These lectures were delivered on March 14 and 25, implying an interruption whose reason we have forgotten. Dedicated to Husserl, the lectures were situated exactly at the turning point of the course, coming at the end of a historical survey. Before arriving at Husserl, and without having bound himself very strictly to a chronological order, Merleau-Ponty had successively examined the natural philosophies of Descartes, Kant, Schelling, Brunschvicg, Hegel, the Romantics, and Bergson. Then he grappled with the conceptions of scientists themselves and scientific philosophers such as Whitehead and Ruyer, paying particular attention to the auto-critique of contemporary science and the transformation of its ontological presuppositions. Pressed for time, he was satisfied to sketch out the problems of animate nature, and he concluded by recalling the interrelation of the natural and the cultural. Once having completed such a critical clearing away, it was necessary first to introduce a philosophy of Being in order to later open onto a philosophy of Nature. This vast project, which coincided with the work he was getting ready to lay out, was proposed by Merleau-Ponty in his customary formulations: "Nature is the being which is behind us. In front of us there is language and corporeal phenomena. But that which is beyond beings is not of another order" (May 20).[2]

The text we present seems to us to have a threefold interest. It faithfully restores an echo—alas already distant!—of Merleau-Ponty's language, reflecting as it were his half-improvised speech, sure in step and supple in form. A large part of the course consisted in historical commentary, but Merleau-Ponty was not tied down by rigorous "pre-readings." His own contribution, unobtrusive as it was, was nevertheless constant, insinuating like a reagent or a solvent, and thereby all the more effective. It was a matter of sizing up the history of philosophy, the thought of others "in the making," as an operative reflection for his own project. This intervention is even more effaced and marginal in our text, because it treats Husserl, with whom Merleau-Ponty's thought has a well-known affinity. And this is the second theme of interest which we find in these pages, the *Deckung*, the mutual "encroachment" of two philosophies. To tell the truth, Husserl was not an instructor of Merleau-Ponty as much as an initiator and revealer: in the field of his writings, Merleau-Ponty has traced out new furrows, concerned to free up the implicit Husserl who resembled him like a brother. Taking as a point of departure a paragraph of *Ideen II*, Merleau-Ponty summoned from the horizons of the whole work the expressions, allusions, and themes which a prolonged familiarity had allowed him to assimilate. This can be seen from the references which we have supplied. Finally, this extract constitutes a sort of draft of the article entitled "The Philosopher and His Shadow," published in the commemorative collection *Edmund Husserl* in 1959, and reproduced in *Signs*. The relationship is evident, the correspondence sometimes literal, and their double testimony confirms the oblique character of the relation between Husserl and Merleau-Ponty, as corroborated by a note of November 1960, the last wherein the philosopher of Freiburg is mentioned: "In *Ideen II*, Husserl, 'disentangles' 'unravels' what is entangled. The idea of chiasm and *Ineinander* is on the contrary the idea that every analysis that *disentangles* renders unintelligible—This is bound to the very meaning of *questioning* which is not to call for a response in the indicative—" (*The Visible and the Invisible*, p. 268).

Thus, a modest marker is added to the path of Merleau-Ponty's research, of which the "working notes," belatedly edited by Claude Lefort, preserves a living trace, manifesting their interrogative tone. We present these λέχτα of Merleau-Ponty in as accurate a version as possible; in any case, one which is unaltered, though we cannot claim to have no omissions. However, we thought it helpful to add some remarks and references. Merleau-Ponty already deserves to be treated as an author destined to survive. Moreover, we were spurred on by a secret vow: that this contribution incite other, more assiduous or qualified listeners to exhume and collate their notebooks, in order to hasten the at least partial reconstitution of the unforgettable lessons of which this is a sample.

XAVIER TILLIETTE

I

In *Ideen II*, Husserl envisions a sphere of pure things (*blosse Sachen*),[3] things which are nothing but things, without predicates of value or use. This is the Nature of the scientists, of Descartes, the Nature of the sciences of nature. But it has its foundation in the structure of human perception. It is not an arbitrary abstraction; the demarcation which delimits this sphere is indicated in advance within the essence of the constituting consciousness. The idea of such a Nature, *blosse Sachlichkeit* [mere thingness],[4] is circumscribed a priori when we make ourselves into pure theoretical subjects.[5] We will thus encounter purely material things, a layer of spatio-temporal materiality. Once this reduction is effected, this putting between parentheses,[6] the concept of the pure thing takes on a general significance. The indistinct given becomes the objectifiable given.

The I becomes indifferent and it has as its correlative the *blosse Sache* [mere thing].[7] This subject is not indifferent in the sense of being inactive, but its activity is turned toward the *erscheinendes Sein* [being as it appears].[8] The real, the true, the in-itself is the correlative of a pure spectator, an I which has decided to know the world. This conception extends by itself, without limits, applying itself to the *Weltall* [world in its totality].[9] In this sense it is everything. When a philosopher journeys he carries these notions with him![10] Everything is *Natur*, resting on itself, brought back to itself.

Now, all that science can tell us is *vorgezeichnet* [predelineated][11] within the perception of a sensible object (on the condition that there is another natural attitude which one could call personalist, for example, when I converse with someone).[12] It is a matter of understanding this attitude, justifying it, founding it, and going beyond it.

This universe of theories refers back to another universe, preceding it, primordial. It is a matter of unearthing a more original world *vor aller Thesis* [before any thesis].[13] This operation is a *Rückdeutung* [interpreting back].[14] The life of consciousness presupposes the *vorgebende Erlebnisse* [pregiving experiences],[15] a *vortheoretische Konstituierung* [pretheoretical constitution].[16] The originary constitutive objects are given to us *leibhaft* [bodily].[17] That is to say, consciousness has a very strong intuition of the insurmountable character of the perceived. It is stuck, bogged down in the perceived thing, even though the *blosse Sachen* form a thin universe. This pre-thetic universe is inscribed in the sense of the *blosse Sachen*, sedimented in them. The entire history of consciousness is found sedimented in Descartes. Pure things are idealizations, ensembles constructed upon what is solid. One must dig beneath them.

It is necessary to know what the movement is in order to relativize it. Otherwise, there will never be an indisputable movement. The scientific universe does not rest on itself. It presupposes a sphere of experience which is the level upon which the other, the scientific universe, can draw. What is found in this sphere? A first intentional reference concerns the incarnate subject, the *Subjektleib* [subject-body],[18] organ of the I can (*Ich kann*).[19] The motor possibilities of my own body, for example, its perceptual deformations, are inscribed in primordial experience, before all science. To read psychological manuals one would often believe that perception is a knowledge, an analysis, a filtering. . . . In reality, the movements of my body are subtracted from the appearance of certain givens. (Thus, in walking, the gaze spontaneously re-establishes the fixed line of the horizon and it is only when one pays attention to one's perception that one sees the landscape jump.)[20] Perceptual consciousness is not a mental alchemy, it is global, total. The *ich kann* is the power of organizing at each step certain unfoldings of perceptual appearances. Husserl advances the idea of a transitional synthesis (*Ubergangssynthesis*).[21] We effect the transition with our body; this is the *ich kann*. Each perception is a moment in the carnal unity of my body; the thing is a type of carnal unity which fits within the total functioning of my body, bringing about certain movements and kinesthesias.[22] My relation to the body is not that of a pure I to an object. My body is not an object but a means, an organization.[23] With my body I organize in perception an association with the world. With my body and through my body I inhabit the world.[24] The body is the field in which perceptions are localized. "Let us imagine consciousness in relation to a locomotive," says Husserl rather bizarrely:[25] in this imaginary experiment, in this extreme hypothesis, the impossibility of perception is evident, because the locomotive is a purely physical body. In me, sensing is localized in my body as its field. It is my body which *senses*.

Husserl evokes the experience of touching.[26] If my right hand is touching (as Malebranche said),[27] my left hand, the hand touched, plays the role of a thing. But let us suppose that my left hand begins to feel. The contribution of the left hand is suddenly distinct; in a snap the relations are reversed. There is therefore an overlapping, *Deckung*,[28] of the two relations; I can reverse them. As a physical thing, the hand remains unchanged. But "I touch myself touching." Thus my body realizes *eine Art von Reflexion* [a kind of reflection],[29] a grasp of itself by itself, a sort of *Cogito* or act of the subject. But it is not an intangible subject; this subject is like a collapsing of space, a large piece of extension intimate with itself[30]—as if space began to know itself. One can call this a relationship of compresence.[31] Husserl emphasized the enigmatic character of this *reizbarempfindendes Ding* [thing giving rise to sensations][32]—this *subjektives Objekt* [subjective object][33] which mimics the intimacy of the mind with itself. How can we reconcile these two aspects, the objective and the subjective, and, in the final account, the scientific and the primordial?

My body is a thing-origin, a standard, the zero of orientation.[34] It always furnishes me with a sort of measure. My body is always here: all places originate from it, from its location. It is the standard of spatiality. In general, the body is always given as the level for all positions. There is a strange teleology of the body,[35] seized by the "optimal forms,"[36] clear and rich, without distinction. The body furnishes the canon, the norm for perception. It is the *Rechtsgrund* [basis of justification].[37] But I can take back, correct my norms. We find an absolute foundation in the relative. It is this which founds science.

That is what is buried in perception, its front and back. The body is *Selbstverges-senheit* [self-forgetfulness],[38] precisely because it functions. . . . But is the body the only thing presupposed by perception? There is another content. The thing, correlative to the activity of the body, is indeed taken into the interior of my body's activity as into a cocoon; it is a solipsistic thing. . . .[39] So we must have access to a second fundamental ground upon which the *blosse Sache* is constructed. In fact, a more complete inspection, an objectification of my body, in order to make it into a completed object without lacunae, is lacking. It is necessary to bring the other [*autrui*] into play. To tell the truth, the term solipsism[40] is not entirely accurate: a true solipsism (if it were possible) would not know that it is isolated, would be unaware that it is alone, would presuppose the absolute inexistence of others. Here is rather an absolute point of reference, an egocentrism. Let us say that the thing is taken up into a sort of individual haze.[41]

The *Einfühlung* [empathy],[42] the intervention of other perceiving subjects, is a decisive experience, bringing determinations which will confer upon the thing its truth. For Husserl, the perception of the other is the pure and simple replica of the consciousness that I have of my body. I discover myself as bound singularly to a body. Husserl develops the idea of "introjection."[43] This operation does not consist in transferring onto the other what I know of myself through projection or transference.[44] Rather, it is a *corporeal* operation and is not directed toward a consciousness transcendent to this body. When I clasp the hand of another, the experience is entirely on the model of that discussed earlier.[45] He is also the one who clasps my hand. There is, first of all, the position of a sensing and perceiving subject, an esthesiological position.[46] The first ground of the *Einfühlung* is furnished by the body's *Empfindsamkeit* [capability of sensing]. I grasp a body's immediate, sensory, carnal connection[47] with the landscape, with objects. Only secondarily do I perceive the other as soul, then as mind. This comes about as a sort of allurement. The *Cogito* of another is a *Naturfactum* [fact of nature]. At the level of the body, originarily, I see a body that perceives. *Ein ich denke taucht auf* [an I think occurs].[48] The incentive to perceive the other is found in our adherence to the same world. In the *Einfühlung*, I experience a subject who is me and who is not me.[49]

This is indispensable for generating the pure thing. From pre-man I become man. That is to say, a localized being, enclosed in my body as in a sack, reduced to an object, without lacunae.[50] Perceptions become events, temporalized, localized, whereas previously they were coextensive with time and space. I seek to verify them. I will become a thing myself. The *Raumding* [spatial thing][51] completes its self-constitution. The universe of the *blosse Sachen* again closes up around me; it is fastened shut. Before, my perception was a laceration. . . . The universe becomes a universe for X, for all subjects.[52] The true thing, in short, is not that which is true for

God, the thing in itself for an infinite knower. We can not achieve His condition, Husserl remarks. It would be necessary that He figure in our perception, in other words, that He be human. Intersubjectivity is intercorporeity.[53] God as an instance of truth would become caught up in the tissue of these carnal men. . . .[54] Thus the pure thing appears, at the terminus of Western philosophy and adult thought.

In his more recent texts, Husserl could be seen as having subjectivized, psychologized the perceived world. In reality, it is not necessary to present things this way. Husserl, in fact, introduces a whole system of experience, including quasi-objects. The *Umwelt* [surrounding world][55] is different from the world of constituted science, the world of pure things. It is a lived world which cannot be derived from the *blosse Sachen*. Husserl deals with beings which are not yet objects. He describes what he calls the universe of the earth, of primordial contact, the ground [*sol*] of experience.[56] Not the earth as a *Körper* [physical body], but the earth before the work of homogenization. The earth has since been converted into a thing and an object. In pre-Copernican experience, it is the stock from which objects are engendered. In prescientific experience there is by no means any "earth," or earth in movement. Its immobility is manifest. But neither is it resting. The originary earth is neither at rest nor in movement, it is on this side of rest and movement, according to a type of being which includes all further possibilities of experience. It is something initial, a possibility of reality,[57] the earth as a pure fact, the cradle, the basis and the ground of all experience.[58] Knowledge has effaced all this, it has forgotten this ontological relief, the open horizons of the *Offenheit* [openness].[59] Science has initiated a sort of conversion, in reality infinite. From which comes the sciences of the infinite, with their infinitely large or small realities. It is a forming, through a generalized and reiterated usage, of possibilities at work in the primordial world. We have spread the initial power of the *Boden* [ground] over the whole universe. And we have posited an objective and homogeneous world. Husserl wonders if there is the possibility of a double *Boden* for a miraculous traveller, aviator or bird, who could cross the space from one planet to another. No, he answers: there are indeed two residences, but only one trajectory, only one flight, only one ground. Or must one alternately relativize two *Boden*? No, because wherever I go, everywhere I settle, I make it a *Boden*, I link the new to the old. I cannot think two earths: they are two pieces of the same earth, one single humanity, grasped in communicative experience. For humankind, there is nothing except humankind. If I enter into communication with another planet, it is a double, a variant of the earth; its inhabitants, if we recognize them, are variants of humanity. Animals also have a share in this common inherence. The most singular, the most carnal, is the most universal. It is ineradicable; one cannot be rid of it. If I live on a slow spacecraft, I consider it to be my native country; if it lands, my ground of experience enlarges, but never completely splits in two.

II

We have, with Husserl,[60] inquired into the intentional implications of consciousness, its "archeology."[61] As the foundation of the *blosse Sachen*, we have discovered the consciousness of my body and of other bodies. This conditions the presentation of the perceived-being—my body and other bodies communicating with mine, because my individual perspective must, so to speak, get in line with others. The other's perception of me is correlative with my perception of the other.[62] Therefore, one must posit a *Subjektleib*[63] over against the perceived being, and posit a cosubjectivity for the *Kulturwelt* [cultural world]. But isn't that a psychological rendering of ontological notions? The being which is truly true is the being for everyone, and thus one would head toward the presupposed subjective base. . . . Does Husserl deserve this reproach? The existence of states of consciousness, of psychological states, is the psychologistic postulate. In fact, the *Rückdeutung*, the retro-reference, is completely different from the psychologistic mania. Husserl intends to introduce a new ground of being. He aims at noematic terms, a noematic ground deeper than the *blosse Sachen*. In *Ideen II* one might have the impression of psychologism. But what is underneath is not a psychological bric-a-brac but a mode of original being, being in the wild state,[64] the "logos of the esthetic world"[65]—because the articulated logos[66] derives from a sense immanent in the perception of the primordial world, the *Erfahrungsboden* [ground of experience].[67] We are indeed in an ontological regime. For example, we have said that the earth is a pre-object possessing a mode of being prior to idealization; it is the ground, the first level, which afterwards is converted into an object. An alteration in this ground—for example, inhabiting in thought another planet—is an act of idealization and objectification. In this new perspective, the earth is a homogeneous being, having no privilege at all, a *Körper*. But the umbilical relation is not annulled: it is simply sublimated, transferred, generalized, multiplied. The earth is always at the margin of my perception like a frame or a level. It is the weighty mass, on the other side of which opens my structure of the *Umwelt*. On the contrary, the scientific world is an infinite world which flies above everything and is not planted here. This is the difference between *Unendlichkeit* [infinity] and *Offenheit* [openness].[68] But this objectification uses, rather than ruptures, the original tie to the earth. In this way we can understand the imagined reciprocity to which we previously referred. The two planets are but one *Boden* divided in two parts. Two earths still make a single earth. There is but one humanity and there is never anything but a single *Boden*.[69]

The order of objective thought is therefore not exhaustive. The earth is not, as it were, pinned down;[70] it is not a place in the sense that objects in the world have a place. The earth is our stock, our *Urheimat* [primal home]. It is the root of our spatiality, our shared native land, the seat of an *Urhistorie* [primal history],[71] an originary insertion. Husserl called this the originary *arche*.[72] This means that it founds a pre-existence or a primordial existence. In this way, Husserl's philosophy is close to that of Heidegger.[73]

Husserl addresses himself to some objections. For example, life could disappear from the earth! All incarnate life has disappeared; there are no longer intentional references. . . .[74] But *nothing* can diminish the manifestness of these intentional references, nothing can prevail against the indisputable *fact*.[75] Physics rests on the carnal; the paradox rests on a certain philosophy of subjectivity and of the transcendental (cf. Kant). Husserl himself takes another route. I cannot engender my relation to my body. The world with its lower depths serves as an intransigent level for it. Thus, I cannot believe in the antipodes opposite to me in the same way that I believe in things nearby. There is, in fact, a chain of motivations, of horizons. The antipodes are simultaneous only through a sort of temporal cloth or fog. It is a question of comprehending their existential basis, which rests on the possible transition from here to there, and which is like the reduplication of my other for myself; cf. a text by Bergson in *Durée et simultanéité*.[76] Husserl sought an "esthetic" foundation and rehabilitated a philosophy of Nature, a framework of the perceived world. There is never a nature-cause of which we would be the effects. But one divines something outside of the moves made by subjects. Subjects are not the initiators, pure interiorities over against things. Nature is this chance offered to corporeality and intersubjectivity.

Thus we have to deal with a new and very different conception of Nature which comprises a relation of an original, primordial or carnal, character and the sphere of the *Urpräsentierbar* [primally presentable].[77] The latter is the unsurpassable plenitude of what is perceived in the flesh and blood by me, and more so by others. This arises from an *Urerkenntnis* [primal knowledge], identically the same for all other subjects. Its foundation is a being which is not an object but is sensed being, that with which I maintain a communication I can never leave behind, the first universal of sensation. *Animalia* are objectivities of a very special type; they presuppose the *Urpräzensen* [primal presences].[78] The domain of what all others perceive exerts a pull on my subjectivity. Nature and the body (or the soul) are in *Wechselbezogenheit, in Eins mit einander* [reciprocal relationship, in unity with one another].[79]

Such ideas were difficult for Husserl, being himself very reflective in temperament. To constitute (the task of philosophy!) is traditionally to retrace the product to the thought which produced it. Now, this reciprocity is no longer a linear relation. How can we reconcile the two aspects? It is necessary to understand the problem of constitution very broadly.[80] There are several constitutions: one of expressly intellectual activity and another, deeper one of time.[81] Fink speaks of another intentionality which is latent or operative.[82] This domain could be constituted by a relation to an even deeper ground. There would be a philosophy of a thoroughly constituting consciousness and, at the same time, another level of constitution. The *blosse Sachen* proceed from a first reflection, from the natural attitude. The analysis carried out above[83] would be of a preparatory and provisional nature, destined for a second draft. Phenomenology proper, after the reduction, would concern itself with the pure I and its intentional correlates, the pure I as the final subject of all subordinate constitutions. All would be constituted and produced by the acts of this final phenomenological consciousness, which is responsible for the acts of the natural attitude. This seems in contradiction with the previous account. If everything correlates with the act of an I, we return to transcendental idealism.[84]

One in fact must guard against the danger of a restoration of a naturalist philosophy. This is why Husserl seemed to turn back and say that the underlying sphere of primordial intentionalities was engendered by the act of an I. But in reality, one must first give credit to a world of *doxa*,[85] to its more or less clear solicitations. The task of reflective philosophy is impossible, because it brings with it all that is unreflected.[86] The natural attitude is not false, and through it philosophy begins.[87] Husserl's hesitations only underline the necessity and difficulty a philosophy of nature presents for the school of transcendental idealism; cf. *Ideas I*, p. 298.[88]

—Trans. by Drew Leder.

Notes

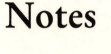

["Trans." signifies a note provided by the translator. "Eds." designates a note of clarification included by the editors of this volume.]

INTRODUCTION: Philosopher at Work!

1. Subsequently published as *The Visible and the Invisible*, trans. Alphonso Lingis (Evanston: Northwestern University Press, 1968).
2. Maurice Merleau-Ponty, "Eye and Mind," trans. Carleton Dallery in *The Primacy of Perception and Other Essays*, ed. James M. Edie (Evanston: Northwestern University Press, 1964), pp. 159–90. The essay was first published in *Art de France* in January of 1961 and reissued as a separate book by Gallimard in 1964.
3. See "Philosophy and Non-Philosophy since Hegel" in *Philosophy and Non-Philosophy since Merleau-Ponty* (Continental Philosophy–I), edited by Hugh J. Silverman (London and New York: Routledge, 1988), pp. 9–83.
4. See Martin Heidegger, *Hegel's Concept of Experience*, trans. anon (New York: Harper and Row, 1970), which was included in *Holzwege* as "Hegel's Begriff der Erfahrung" (1950). And see Hugh J. Silverman, "Merleau-Ponty and Heidegger: Interpreting Hegel," in *Inscriptions: Between Phenomenology and Structuralism* (London and New York: Routledge, 1987), pp. 108–22.
5. Forrest Williams chronicles the context and development of Merleau-Ponty's early philosophical career in Appendix I to this volume.
6. For a full account of his Lyon lectures in 1946–48, and a summary of their content, see "Merleau-Ponty on Language and Communication" in Silverman, *Inscriptions*, pp. 95–107.
7. Translations of some of the lectures Merleau-Ponty gave at the Sorbonne have appeared. See *Consciousness and the Acquisition of Language*, trans. Hugh J. Silverman (Evanston: Northwestern University Press, 1973). Also, see "Phenomenology and the Sciences of Man" and "The Child's Relations with Others" in *The Primacy of Perception and Other Essays*, ed. James M. Edie (Evanston: Northwestern University Press, 1964), and "The Experience of Others: A Lecture Course by Merleau-Ponty," trans. Fred Evans and Hugh J. Silverman, in *Review of Existential Psychology and Psychiatry*, XVIII, Nos. 1, 2, 3 (1982–83), pp. 33–66. We will be bringing out in the next few years a two-volume compilation and translation of the lecture courses from these three years (also with Humanities Press).

8. Maurice Merleau-Ponty, *Signs*, trans. Richard McCleary (Evanston: Northwestern University Press, 1964).
9. Maurice Merleau-Ponty, *Themes from the Lectures*, trans. John O'Neill (Evanston: Northwestern University Press, 1970).
10. See p. 174 of the *Phenomenology of Perception*, where Merleau-Ponty "inverts" Marcel's distinction.

PART I: *Interviews and Dialogues*

CHAPTER 1: Merleau-Ponty in Person (1960)

1. [Jean-François Revel, *Pourquoi des philosophes?* (Paris: Jean-Jacques Pauvert, 1957)—Trans.]
2. [The reference is to *La Nouvelle Revue française*, which was revived in 1953 and became one of the major outlets of intellectual expression in France in the 50s and 60s. Merleau-Ponty is apparently referring to Heidegger's piece, translated into French as "The Path" ["*Le Sentier*"] by Jacques Gérard, which appeared in the *N.R.F.* in early 1954. It is a translation of Heidegger's "*Der Feldweg*," which is included in *Aus Der Erfahrung des Denkens*, Vol. 13 of Heidegger's *Gesamtausgabe* (Frankfurt: Klostermann, 1983). See *La Nouvelle Revue française*, No. 3 (Jan.–June 1954), pp. 41–45—Trans.]
3. [Merleau-Ponty was actively involved in this meeting of such noteworthy philosophers as Ryle, Quine, Ayer, Wahl, and Van Breda. See "Phenomenology and Analytic Philosophy" in this volume—Eds.]
4. [This meeting was similar to the one in which Merleau-Ponty participated in Venice in 1956, apparently with the same general contentiousness between Eastern Bloc and Western philosophers. See "East-West Encounter" in this volume—Eds.]
5. [Merleau-Ponty deals with precisely this critical problem in his last lecture course, "Philosophy and Non-Philosophy since Hegel." See "Philosophy and Non-Philosophy since Hegel" in *Philosophy and Non-Philosophy since Merleau-Ponty* (Continental Philosophy–I), edited by Hugh J. Silverman (London and New York: Routledge, 1988), pp. 9–83—Trans.]
6. [The political movement "Poujadisme" maintains that nothing is more important politically than the immediate desires of "the people." Named after Pierre Poujade, Merleau-Ponty's contemporary, who founded *l'Union de défense des commerçants et des artisans*. He was a self-proclaimed "man of the people" and an outspoken opponent of government controls, taxation, etc. He tended to blame intellectuals for many of France's problems. See Merleau-Ponty's column, "Le Forum," in March 19, 1955, issue of *L'Express*, "*M. Poujade, a-t-il un petit cerveau?*"—Trans.]

CHAPTER 2: Crisis in European Consciousness (1946)

1. [This piece is selected from a long conference in which Merleau-Ponty participated in 1946. We have included only Merleau-Ponty's comments—Eds.]
2. [We abridge the comments by Jaspers, Lukács, et al., which intervene here. Merleau-Ponty's subsequent responses in the afternoon session make the nature of these comments clear—Eds.]
3. These questions remain unanswered. (Ed., *La Nef*) [The editor of the journal in which this transcript first appeared is referring to the fact that Lukács does not

respond to Merleau-Ponty's earnest and prolonged question. It is worth noting that Merleau-Ponty's concerns here are reflected in numerous essays of the period, most notably those found in *Sense and Non-Sense* (Evanston: Northwestern University Press, 1964). During the five years after the war, Merleau-Ponty read Marxist writings sympathetically and supported the efforts to establish a bonafide "social democracy" which were apparently underway in the Soviet Union. However, Merleau-Ponty, along with most French intellectuals, was deeply affected by the increasingly verified allegations of Stalinist atrocities. The shift in his philosophical attitude toward marxism and communism can be seen in a comparison of *Humanism and Terror* (Boston: Beacon Press, 1969) and *Adventures of the Dialectic* (Evanston: Northwestern University Press, 1973), the two texts having appeared originally in 1947 and 1955, respectively. Also see the conference *East-West Encounter*, included in this volume—Eds.]

CHAPTER 3: *L'Express* "Forum" (1954–55)

1. [These short pieces are representative of the issues Merleau-Ponty dealt with in his 1954–55 column in *L'Express*. We have selected only those which seemed to extend beyond the immediate context of France in the mid-50s—Eds.]

CHAPTER 4: East-West Encounter (1956)

1. [This dialogue first appeared as "Discordia Concours, Rencontre Est-Ouest à Venise" in *Comprendre, Revue de politique de la culture* (published by the *Société Européenne de Culture*, Venice, 1956). In 1956, March 25–31, Merleau-Ponty participated in a meeting of the *Société Européenne de Culture* in Venice. This particular meeting, which was to capitalize on the recent "thawing-out" of Cold War relations between the Soviet Union and the West, was publicized as an "East-West Encounter," its stated purpose being "to engender cultural relations more vigorous than those of past years," and more particularly "to permit the opening of a dialogue wherein divergences of opinion on political matters would be examined, in order to understand and transcend them." To this end, artists, writers, and intellectuals from both Eastern and Western European countries were invited—Merleau-Ponty and Sartre among them—to participate in discussions on topics ranging from the general relationship between culture and politics to the specific question of the meaning and substance of the individual cultured person's political engagement. The following text is a transcript of the meeting's second session. It has been chosen for inclusion in this volume because it is the one in which Merleau-Ponty figures most prominently. He had been invited to open this session with a statement of his views on culture, politics, and engagement. His statement provides both the point of departure and the broader conceptual context for the ensuing discussion, in which he also took part.

It is worth noting that, apropos of the alleged "thawing out" of the official Soviet stance on cultural/political matters during Khrushchev's administration, somewhat similar developments have taken place in the late 1980s in the context of Gorbachev and "Glasnost." Thus the kinds of questions raised here by Merleau-Ponty and others concerning the real meaning of the "thaw" and its possible consequences for cultural and intellectual life both in Eastern Europe and in the West are once again relevant, more than three decades later—Trans.]

2. [Ignazio Silone (born Secondo Tranquilli, 1900–78), Italian novelist, essayist, and playwright. Best known for the novels *Fontamara* (1930) and *Bread and Wine*

(1935), and the essay "Uscita di sicurezza" in *The God That Failed: Six Studies in Communism* (New York: Harper, 1950; a volume to which Stephen Spender, another participant in this East-West dialogue, also contributed). Silone helped establish the Italian Communist Party in the early 20s, but left the party in 1941, citing "disillusionment." He then came to consider himself an "independent socialist" or, as he says during this conference, a "democratic socialist." All his writings are decidedly political, evincing his faith in the "masses" and stressing the need for action or engagement—Trans.]

3. [Umberto Campagnolo, Italian political theorist, author of a number of books on politics and law, including *Nations et droit, le développement du droit international entendu comme développement de l'état* (Paris: F. Alcan, 1938) and *Repubblica federale europea: unificazione giuridica dell'Europa* (Milano: L'Europa Unità, 1945); Secretary General for the *Société Européenne de Culture* in 1953—Trans.]

4. [Giovanni Ponti, Italian writer and art critic. Author of *Le arti in Italia* (Milano: Domus, 1939), *Milan Today* (Milan: Milano Moderna, 1958), and *Enamels* (Milan: D. Guarnati, 1958)—Trans.]

5. [*Homme de culture* has been variously translated throughout this piece as "cultured man," "man of culture," and "cultured human being." Those who use the term here—and it is used often—seem to take it to mean any serious and proficient member of the intellectual or artistic community, regardless of social or political background. The term and its translated forms are obviously not meant to exclude *female* intellectuals or artists, although it is worth noting that no women were invited to participate in this particular discussion—Trans.]

6. [Stephen Spender (1909—); English poet, essayist, and literary critic. Contributor, along with Silone and others, to *The God that Failed: Six Essays in Communism* (New York: Harper, 1950). Author of many books of poetry, including *The Edge of Being* (New York: Random House, 1949) and *Collected Poems, 1928–1953* (New York: Random House, 1955). He also translated, along with J. B. Leishman, Rainer Maria Rilke's *Duino Elegies* (New York: Norton, 1939), and wrote a series of essays called *The Year of the Young Rebels* (New York: Random House, 1969) having to do with the student uprisings throughout America and Europe in 1968. Spender joined the British Communist Party in 1936, only to withdraw after a few weeks, citing (like his colleague Silone) disillusionment. Yet he continued his political engagement through his works, and expressed—with reservations—a certain sympathy and enthusiasm for the "young rebels" of 1968—Trans.]

7. [Pious XII was Pope from 1939 to 1958—Trans.]

8. [Sartre is doubtless referring to Pierre Hervé and his *La Révolution et les fétiches* (Paris: Table Ronde, 1956)—Trans.]

9. [Guiseppe Ungaretti; Italian poet, essayist, literary critic, and translator. Nominated for the Nobel Prize in Literature, 1969. Wrote numerous volumes of poetry, including *La Guerre* (in French) (Paris: Etablissements de LUX, 1919) and *Life of a Man* (New York: New Directions, 1958). Translated Shakespeare, Blake, and Mallarmé (among others) into Italian—Trans.]

10. [Konstantin Fedin (1892–1977); Soviet writer. Described as "one of the founders and creators" of Soviet literature, Fedin turned from his early experimental techniques to the officially approved school of Soviet realism. His major novels include *Rape of Europe*, *Brothers*, *An Unusual Summer*, and *First Joys*. Fedin served as head of the Soviet Writers Union—Trans.]

11. [Boris Polevoi, a.k.a. Boris Nicolayevich (1908–81); Soviet journalist and novelist. Polevoi served as a war correspondent for Pravda, 1941–45, and as a board member for the Soviet Writers Union from 1948 until his death. He is best known for the novel *The Story of a Real Man* (Moscow: Foreign Language Publishing House, 1949)—Trans.]

12. [Carlo Levi (1902–75), Italian doctor, painter, sculptor, journalist, writer, and politician. Levi founded the Italian Action Party, an anti-fascist movement, in 1930, as well as numerous left-wing journals. He served two terms as an independent senator in the Italian Senate (1963–72) but is best remembered as the author of *Christ Stopped at Eboli: The Story of a Year* (New York: Farrar, Strauss, 1947), a book recounting his year spent as a visiting doctor among the peasants in Gagliano, a small town in Italy's poorest region—Trans.]

13. [Guido Piovene (1907–74), Italian journalist and novelist, author of *Confessions of a Novice* (London: W. Kimber, 1950) and *In Search of Europe: Portraits of the Non-Communist West* (New York: St. Martin's, 1975). Piovene was director of the Arts and Sciences Division of UNESCO, 1949–50, and a member of the Executive Council of the Congress for Cultural Freedom—Trans.]

14. [Jaroslaw Iwaszkiewicz (1894–1980), Polish poet, novelist, playwright, essayist, and translator. A prolific writer for some sixty years, Iwaszkiewicz was chairman of the Polish Writers Union and author of many novels. He translated numerous works into Polish from Russian, French, Spanish, English, Danish, and Italian; he also wrote biographies of Chopin and Bach. A film adapted from his short story, "The Maidens of Wilko," was a candidate for a 1980 Academy Award. Iwaszkiewicz was a deputy in the Polish Parliament at the time of his death—Trans.]

15. [J. D. Bernal (1901–71), English physicist and writer; member of the Royal Society; winner of the Lenin Peace Prize in 1953. Known simply as "the Sage" in scientific circles of his time, due to his encyclopaedic knowledge and commitment to world peace, Bernal (despite his pronounced leftist tendencies) was recruited by the Allies in World War II to be one of the major engineers of the D-Day landing operation. His major works include *The Social Function of Science* (New York: Macmillan, 1939), *World without War* (New York: Monthly Review Press, 1958), and *Science in History* (Cambridge: MIT Press, 1971)—Trans.]

16. [Jean-Marcel Bruller, a.k.a. Vercors (1902–); French novelist, essayist, and artist; co-founder in 1941 of Editions de Minuit. Major writings include *The Silence of the Sea* (New York: Macmillan, 1944) and *Cent ans d'histoire de France*, 2 volumes (Paris: Plon, 1981–82)—Trans.]

17. [Alan Pryce-Jones (1908–); British essayist, editor, and poet; edited *The London Mercury*, 1928–32, and *The Times Literary Supplement*, 1948–59. Major writings include *The Spring Journey* (1931) and *27 Poems* (1935)—Trans.]

18. [Marko Ristic, Yugoslavian writer. None of his works have yet been translated into English—Trans.]

CHAPTER 5: Phenomenology and Analytic Philosophy (1960)

1. [This transcript of the 1960 conference at Royaumont appeared in a volume edited by Jean Wahl, *La Philosophie analytique* (Paris: Éditions de Minuit, 1962). The piece was originally entitled "La Phénoménologie contre *The Concept of Mind*," but we have taken the liberty of giving it a less combative title. We have also taken the liberty of truncating the last few pages of the piece—Eds.]

2. [The transcript continues for a few pages more, yet without any further contributions by Merleau-Ponty to the discussion—Eds.]

PART II: *Texts*

CHAPTER 6: The Nature of Perception: Two Proposals (1933)

1. [For an account of the philosophical background of these proposals, see the report by Forrest Williams, "Merleau-Ponty's Early Research Projects," included in this volume as Appendix I—Eds.]

CHAPTER 7: Christianity and *Ressentiment* (1935)

1. [We have taken the liberty of modifying Gerald Wening's notes by deleting all references to French or German editions of texts which are now available in English translation. Beyond this minor modification, the notes are the same as those offered by Wening—Eds.] Max Scheler, *Ressentiment*, trans. William W. Holdheim (New York: Schocken Books, 1961).
2. Scheler cites the case of a sick person "incapable, because of repressed hatred, of reading any books whatsoever" (*Ressentiment*, p. 70).
3. Ibid., p. 72.
4. Ibid., p. 76.
5. Ibid., p. 78.
6. Friedrich Nietzsche, *Genealogy of Morals*, trans. Walter Kaufmann (New York: Random House, 1967), p. 36. Cited by Scheler, *Ressentiment*, p. 44.
7. *Genealogy of Morals*, p. 34. Cited by Scheler, pp. 43–44.
8. *Ressentiment*, p. 88.
9. Ibid., p. 135.
10. Ibid., p. 134.
11. Ibid., p. 105.
12. Luke XII: 24, 27; cited by Scheler, *Ressentiment*, pp. 89–90.
13. Scheler, *Ressentiment*, p. 91.
14. Ibid., pp. 98–99.
15. Ibid., pp. 99–100.
16. Ibid., p. 89, note 12.
17. Ibid., p. 89.
18. Cf. Edmund Husserl, *Ideas pertaining to a Pure Phenomenology and to a Phenomenological Philosophy* (Volume One), trans. Fred Kersten (Boston: Martinus Nijhoff, 1982), para. 19.
19. One exception is: *Nature et formes de la sympathie*, trans. M. Lefebvre (Paris: Payot, 1928). The phenomenological attitude of Scheler is not explicitly defined in this place, although it is continually supposed and mentioned (cf. pp. 7, 265, 267). In *Ressentiment*, Scheler returns to his great works (p. 87, note 7, and p. 102). One wonders when they will appear in French; Scheler's original German essay on *Ressentiment* appeared for the first time in 1912.
20. Scheler does not intend to say that it is the essence of love, for example, to pursue *another* to be human; it can be seen that there is an intentional love of the self, but in this latter case the love is not a state but a *turning toward* some terminus.
21. Cf. Husserl, *Ideas*, para. 19.
22. On all these points, cf. G. Gurvitch, *Les Tendances actuelles de la philosophie allemande* (Paris: J. Vrin, 1930), pp. 95–100.

23. On this point, as well as the distinction between *sittliches Erfassen* and *Streben*, cf. Gurvitch, Ibid., pp. 86ff.
24. Scheler, *Ressentiment*, p. 58.
25. Such an identification is far removed from his regular attitude (does he always identify himself with one of these pretences which his sincerity uses in turns?): "A strong and well-constituted man digests his experiences (deeds and misdeeds all included) just as he digests his meats, even when he has some tough morsels to swallow. . . . You can adopt such a theory, and yet *entre nous* be nevertheless the strongest opponent of all materialism." *Genealogy of Morals*, para. 16, cited by Léon Brunschvicg, *Les Progrès de la conscience dans la philosophie occidentale* (Paris: F. Alcan, 1927), p. 417 [Merleau-Ponty's italics].
26. Scheler, *Ressentiment*, p. 71.
27. Ibid., p. 117.
28. Ibid., p. 117.
29. Ibid., p. 117.
30. Ibid., p. 67.
31. Scheler, as cited and translated through Gurvitch, Ibid.
32. Scheler, *Ressentiment*, p. 82.
33. Ibid., p. 109, note 35.
34. Ibid., pp. 109–10.
35. Ibid., p. 108, also p. 133.
36. Scheler's reader might find, perhaps, that the presentation of his thought is an awkward approach. The following reason is provided: Scheler wants to show that "it is impossible to make Christianity militant in any sense"—either against war, pain of death, aristocratic organization (pp. 119, 120, note 11), or against class struggle (p. 108). We have the perfect right to say that Christianity, for Scheler, is independent of all politics and every preservative attitude. It need only be remarked that insufficient care has been given to explicit explanations.
37. Ibid., p. 97.
38. Ibid., pp. 132–33.
39. One sees the extent to which Scheler merits the nickname given by Troeltsch: "the Catholic Nietzsche."
40. Scheler, *Ressentiment*, p. 114.
41. Ibid., p. 72.
42. Ibid., pp. 149–52.
43. Ibid., p. 156.
44. Ernest Bertram, *Nietzsche, Essai de mythologie*, trans. R. Pitrou (The Hague: Reidel, 1932).
45. Ibid., p. 77.
46. Letter to E. Rohde, cited by Bertram. Ibid., p. 65.
47. Ibid., p. 86.
48. Scheler, *Ressentiment*, p. 120.
49. *Nouvelle Revue française*, July 1932, pp. 103, 109.
50. Jean Wahl, *Vers le Concret* (Paris: J. Vrin, 1932), Preface.

CHAPTER 8: Being and Having (1936)

1. Gabriel Marcel, *Être et Avoir*, Volume I (Paris: Éditions Montaigne, 1935). [Translated as *Being and Having: An Existential Diary*, trans. Katherine Farrer (Gloucester, Mass.: Peter Smith, 1976). Henceforth references are given to the English translation—Trans.]

2. Descartes, *Oeuvres philosophiques*, Tome II (1638–42), ed. F. Alquié (Paris: Garnier, 1967), pp. 426–27.
3. Scheler. [The metaphor here is clearly meant to suggest a pessimistic, minimal, or "conservative" interpretation—Trans.]
4. *Being and Having*, p. 17.
5. Ibid., pp. 11–12.
6. See the article "Existence et Objectivité," reprinted at the end of the *Journal métaphysique*. ["Existence and Objectivity," in *Metaphysical Journal*, trans. Bernard Wall (Chicago: Henry Regnery, 1950)—Trans.]
7. *Being and Having*, p. 108.
8. Ibid., p. 158.
9. Ibid., p. 25.
10. Ibid., p. 25. It is true that the forms that are within matter can become corrupted. But in that case they move from being to non-being, and it is not, strictly speaking, form itself that becomes corrupted: it is not form that is the subject of that corruption. On the other hand, it is precisely that soul itself that becomes lost. The problem is one of those that theology addressed quite deliberately, in its effort to rationalize the revelation using concepts elaborated by Greek philosophy.
11. *Being and Having*, p. 121.
12. Ibid., p. 98.
13. [My italics—Trans.]
14. Ibid., p. 122.
15. Ibid., p. 211.
16. Ibid., p. 122. [Translated there as "active intuition"—Trans.]
17. Ibid., p. 99.
18. Ibid., p. 24.
19. Our review stresses the paradoxical and indefensible element in these views.
20. *Being and Having*, p. 50.
21. Ibid., p. 50.
22. See in particular the analyses of hope.
23. *Being and Having*, p. 122.
24. *Positions et approches concrètes des mystères ontologiques* (Paris: J. Vrin, 1949), p. 298. ["On the Ontological Mystery," in *The Philosophy of Existence*, trans. Manya Harari (New York: Citadel Press, 1964), p. 44—Trans.]
25. *Being and Having*, p. 142.

CHAPTER 9:   On Sartre's *Imagination* (1936)

1. [*L'Imagination* (Paris: Alcan, 1936; 2nd ed., Presses Universitaires de France, 1948); translated by Forrest W. Williams as *Imagination* (Ann Arbor: University of Michigan Press, 1962)—Trans.]
2. [Referenced pages of first French, then English editions of Sartre's work are inserted in brackets in the text. Quotes from Sartre are my translations—Trans.]
3. [Sartre's second book referred to here is *L'Imaginaire: Psychologie phénoménologique de l'imagination*, translated by Bernard Frechtman as *Psychology of the Imagination* (New York: Philosophical Library, 1948)—Trans.]

CHAPTER 10:   On Sartre's *The Flies* (1943)

1. [Sartre's play was initially published in 1943 by Gallimard. It first appeared on stage on June 3 of that same year with Charles Dullin as producer and actor. The

Vichy press quickly forced the closing of the play, but it was revived later that same year (September 1943)—Eds.]

CHAPTER 11: Apology for International Conferences (1947)

1. [In English in the original—Trans.]
2. It was not known at the time that he was a former diplomat. They would have just as willingly given the floor to a Kolkhoz worker if there had been one in Geneva.
3. ["It's not a question of socialism." That is, the Soviet policy of good relations with the West entailed renouncing any attempt to convert democracies to socialism—Trans.]

CHAPTER 12: The Founders of Philosophy (1956)

1. [Cf. Romans 10:12—Trans.]

CHAPTER 13: The Discovery of History (1956)

1. [Here Merleau-Ponty is using *"conditionné"* ("conditioned") in the sense in which it is used by psychology. Our institutions are conditioned to history in the same way in which reflexes may become conditioned by repeated exposure to a specific set of stimuli—Trans.]

CHAPTER 14: The Philosophy of Existence (1959)

1. [This piece was first presented on November 17, 1959, as a segment of a Canadian radio program, "Conference." A transcript (from which this translation is taken) was published subsequently in the December 1966 issue of *Dialogue* (V, No. 3)—Eds.]

CHAPTER 15: Five Notes on Claude Simon (1960)

1. [This number of *Entretiens* (published in the second trimester of 1972) was devoted entirely to the work of Claude Simon. It included comments and a text by Claude Simon himself, as well as essays by figures such as Tom Bishop, Serge Doubrovsky, Ludovic Janvier, Jean Ricardou, Raymond Jean, Richard Howard, John Fletcher, and others. Each of the five notes was published on a separate page—Trans.]
2. [See Sartre's *Being and Nothingness* for the background to the "circle of ipseity" idea—Trans.]
3. [Madeleine Chapsal?—to whom Merleau-Ponty himself gave an interview in 1960—Trans.]
4. [*l'avènement du concepte. Avènement* is the term selected by the French translators of Heidegger's term *Ereignis*, namely: event, appropriation, happening, occurrence. Merleau-Ponty is indicating that this is different from the kind of envisioning that the novelist relies upon—Trans.]
5. [*l'imaginaire*—Trans.]
6. [It should be noted that Foucault did not publish his *Archaeology of Knowledge* until 1968, following upon the 1966 publication of *The Order of Things*. The role of Merleau-Ponty in the background of Foucault's thought is often underplayed—Trans.]
7. [The "immediate givens of consciousness" was Bergson's expression, which served as the title for his book, *Essai sur les données immédiates de la conscience* (Paris: F. Alcan, 1924). The English translation had a slightly different title: *Time*

and Free Will: An Essay on the Immediate Data of Consciousness (New York: Harper, 1960)—Trans.]
8. ["Intermingling or intertwining." See *The Visible and the Invisible* and Merleau-Ponty's account of the "chiasm" or the "intertwining"—Trans.]

Appendices

APPENDIX 1:   Merleau-Ponty's Early Project Concerning Perception

1. Susanne K. Langer, *Feeling and Form* (New York: Charles Scribner's Sons, 1953), p. 9.
2. Cf. Maurice Merleau-Ponty, *The Visible and the Invisible* (Evanston, Ill.: Northwestern University Press, 1968) ed. Claude Lefort, trans. Alphonso Lingis, p. 9. Henceforth cited as *Visible*.
3. Cf. Aron Gurwitsch, "Phenomenology of Thematics and of the Pure Ego: Studies of the Relation between Gestalt Theory and Phenomenology," in *Studies in Phenomenology and Psychology* (Evanston, Ill.: Northwestern University Press), esp. pp. 192ff.
4. Aron Gurwitsch gave a series of lectures entitled "The Historical Development of Gestalt Psychology" at the Institut d'Histoire des Sciences in Paris in 1933–34. Merleau-Ponty probably attended those lectures, as his assistance in preparing them for publication was acknowledged. (See Gurwitsch, "Phenomenology of Thematics," p. 3, n. 1. See also Theodore F. Geraets, *Vers une nouvelle philosophie transcendantale* [The Hague: Martinus Nijhoff, 1971], p. 13).
5. Merleau-Ponty, *Visible*, p. 204 (working note dated September 1959).
6. Merleau-Ponty, *The Primacy of Perception* (Evanston, Ill.: Northwestern University Press, 1964), "The Child's Relations with Others," pp. 96–155. (These lectures, as well as "Phenomenology and the Sciences of Man" in the same volume, are attributed to the year 1960. I take this opportunity to correct the date. Both series of lectures were courses given by Merleau-Ponty at the Sorbonne in 1950–51).
7. Merleau-Ponty, *Visible*, p. 22.
8. See Merleau-Ponty's comment in *Visible*, p. 183 (working note dated February 1959).
9. Ibid., p. 165 (working note dated January 1959).

APPENDIX 2:   Merleau-Ponty and the Husserl Archives at Louvain

1. On the creation of the Archives, see H. L. Van Breda, "Le Sauvetage de héritage husserlien et la fondation des Archives Husserl," in *Husserl et la pensée moderne, Phaenomenologica 2* (The Hague: M. Nijhoff, 1959).
2. Marly Biemel edited this text in *Husserliana*, IV (1952), *Gessamelte Werke; auf Grund des Nachlasses veroffentlicht von Husserl-Archiv*, under the direction of H. L. Van Breda (The Hague: M. Nijhoff, 1950—).
3. Maurice Merleau-Ponty, *Phenomenology of Perception*, trans. Colin Smith (London: Routledge & Kegan Paul, 1962), p. 92; in French, *Phénoménologie de la perception* (Paris: Gallimard, 1945), p. 108. [Henceforth cited as *PP*—Trans.]
4. *PP*, p. 459; p. 523 in the French. [Certain of the works of Husserl cited by Merleau-Ponty as unpublished have since been published and translated into English, for example, *The Crisis of European Sciences and Transcendental*

Phenomenology, trans. David Carr (Evanston: Northwestern University Press, 1970) and *Ideas II*, trans. as *Studies in the Phenomenology of Constitution* by Richard Rojcewicz and Andre Schuwer (Dordrecht: Kluwer, 1989)].

5. In "Le Philosophe et son ombre" ["The Philosopher and His Shadow"], *Edmund Husserl, 1859–1959: Recueil commémoratif publié a l'occasion du centenaire de la naissance du philosophe*, ed. H. L. Van Breda and J. Taminiaux, *Phaenomenologica 4* (The Hague: M. Nijhoff, 1959), pp. 195–220. Reprinted in Maurice Merleau-Ponty, *Signes* (Paris: Gallimard, 1960), pp. 210–29; in English see *Signs*, trans. Richard McCleary (Evanston: Northwestern University Press, 1964), pp. 159–81.

6. See H. L. Van Breda, "Le Sauvetage de l'héritage," cited above, note 1.

7. Jean Hering was a disciple and friend of Husserl who was one of the first to attract the attention of French philosophers to Husserlian phenomenology. He held a chair in Protestant theology at Strasbourg.

8. Eugen Fink, "Das Problem der Phänomenologie Edmund Husserls," *Revue Internationale de Philosophie*, 2 (1939), pp. 226–70.

9. Merleau-Ponty is referring to the first edition of Husserl's *Erfahrung und Urteil: Untersuchungen zur Genealogie der Logik*, rev. and ed. Ludwig Landgrebe (Prague: Academia, 1939). [In English see *Experience and Judgment: Investigations in the Genealogy of Logic*, rev. and ed. Ludwig Landgrebe, trans. James S. Churchhill and Karl Ameriks (Evanston: Northwestern University Press, 1973).] Immediately after the invasion of Czechoslovakia in the spring of 1939, the Nazis destroyed all of the copies of this edition that they found at the publisher. In March I had received a copy from Mr. Landgrebe and in May one hundred other copies arrived, sent by the publisher only a few days before the invasion.

10. [A *Chargé d'enseignement* is roughly equivalent to a university lecturer or assistant professor in the American university system. In fact from 1935 to 1939 Merleau-Ponty was an *agrégé-répétiteur* at the Ecole normale supérieur, which means he helped students prepare material assigned by a professor. This slight modification of his title was perhaps intended to make his request more convincing—Trans.]

11. See Marly Biemel's introduction in *Husserliana*, IV, p. xviii.

12. Ibid., pp. xviii–xx.

13. See note 2 above.

14. Concerning Landgrebe's work in Prague, see H. L. Van Breda, "Le Sauvetage de l'héritage," pp. 15–16 and 35–36.

15. See note 3 above.

16. [Fred Kersten's translation reads: "Overthrow of the Copernican theory in the usual interpretation of a world view. The original *arche*, Earth, does not move. Foundational investigations of the phenomenological origin of corporeality, of the spatiality pertaining to Nature in the first sense of the natural sciences. Of necessity all are initial investigations." In *Husserl: Shorter Works*, ed. Peter McCormick and Frederick Elliston (Notre Dame: University of Notre Dame Press, 1981), p. 231—Trans.]

17. *Husserliana*, IV, pp. 105–276.

18. Such a center was finally created in 1958 at the Sorbonne in the University of Paris Library.

19. [Edith Stein (1891–1942), a German Jewish philosopher, was Husserl's assistant from 1916 to 1918. In 1922 she converted to Catholicism and began to seek a

philosophical synthesis of Husserlian phenomenology and Christian theology, especially the thought of Thomas Aquinas. She was killed by the Nazis in 1942. For a sample of her work in English, see *Writings*, selected and trans. Hilda Graef (Westminster, Maryland: Newman Press, 1956).

H. J. Pos, a Dutch philosopher and follower of Husserl, died in 1955. He is cited and commented on by Merleau-Ponty in *Primacy of Perception* [ed. James Edie (Evanston: Northwestern University Press, 1964), pp. 80–81] as the author of an article on phenomenology and linguistics, published in the *Revue Internationale de Philosophie*, 2 (January 1939), pp. 354–65. None of his writings are currently available in English—Trans.]

20. Concerning these meetings, see H. L. Van Breda, "Le Sauvetage de l'héritage," pp. 14–15.

21. One of these sources was Mrs. Husserl's correspondence with Jean Hering and many other French philosophers between 1939 and 1940. (Mrs. Husserl lived as a boarder in a convent near Louvain from 1939 to 1946.)

22. From the summer of 1942, new transcriptions were made by Mr. and Mrs. Stephan Strasser and Mrs. Ida Theumann, Mrs. Strasser's mother.

23. [Jean Cavaillès was a French philosopher who worked largely in the field of philosophy of mathematics, apprenticing under Léon Brunschvicg. He has the rare distinction of also being a founding member of the French Resistance. For a detailed and moving account of his life, see *Jean Cavaillès: Philosophe et combattant*, by his sister, Gabrielle Ferrières (Paris: Presses Universitaires de France, 1951). For a sample of his work, see *Méthode axiomatique et formalisme* (Paris: Hermann, 1938; 1981).

Jean Hyppolite (1907–68) became the director of the Ecole Normale Supérieure after the Second World War, and then a professor at the Collège de France. His translation of Hegel's *Phenomenology of Spirit* in two volumes (Paris: Aubier, 1939–41) and his great interpretive essay, *Genèse et structure de la Phénoménologie de l'Esprit de Hegel* (Paris: Aubier, 1947), played a major role in the introduction of Hegel's thought into contemporary French philosophy. For a sample of his work in English, see *Genesis and Structure of Hegel's Phenomenology of Spirit*, trans. Samuel Cherniak and John Hackman (Evanston: Northwestern University Press, 1974).

Tran Duc Thao (1917–) was born in Vietnam. By 1943 he had passed the highly selective *agrégation* exam in philosophy in Paris. Two of his most important works, influential among students of phenomenology in France for years, have recently been translated into English: *Phenomenology and Dialectical Materialism*, trans. D. J. Herman and D. J. Morano (Boston: Reidel, 1985); and *Investigations into the Origin of Language and Consciousness*, trans. D. J. Herman and R. L. Armstrong (Boston: Reidel, 1983).

For a sample of the work of Father L.-B. Geiger, see *La Participation dans la philosophie de Saint Thomas d'Aquin* (Paris: J. Vrin, 1942)—Trans.]

24. [René Le Senne (1882–1954), French psychologist and moral philosopher, taught at the Ecole Normale Supérieure, and then in 1942 moved on to a professorship at the Sorbonne. With Louis Lavalle he founded the *Philosophie de l'esprit* series (published by Aubier). His works include *Traité de morale générale* (Paris, 1942) and *Introduction à la philosophie* (Paris, 1939).

Louis Lavelle (1883–1951) was Professor of Philosophy at the Sorbonne from 1932 to 1934, and then at the Collège de France. His works include *La présence totale* (Paris: Aubier, 1934), and *La conscience de soi* (Paris: Grasset, 1939)—Trans.]

25. [Edmund Husserl, "Phenomenology," in the *Encyclopaedia Britannica* (London, 1929), trans. C. V. Salmon—Trans.]
26. [Husserl's *Studien zur Struktur des Bewusstseins* was possibly later incorporated by Landgrebe into the *Crisis* or into *Experience and Judgment*—Trans.]
27. See *Husserliana*, VI, pp. 146–51 and 182–85.
28. [Lucien Lévy-Brühl, *La Mythologie primitive* (Paris: Alcan, 1935). Husserl's letter to Lévy-Brühl has recently been published in French in *Gradhiva*, 4 (1988), pp. 63–72. Merleau-Ponty discusses and quotes passages from this letter in *The Primacy of Perception*, pp. 90–91—Trans.]
29. *The Sixth Meditation* is a text by Eugen Fink conceived as a continuation of Husserl's five *Cartesian Meditations*. Fink discussed the work in detail with Husserl, yet it still contains, in the form of a "phenomenology of phenomenology," a very probing critique of Husserlian thought. Gaston Berger owned a copy of Fink's text which was read by a fair number of young French phenomenologists; some of them even mistook it for an expression of Husserl's own thought. [For a sample of Gaston Berger's work in English, see *The Cogito in Husserl*, trans. Kathleen McLaughlin (Evanston: Northwestern University Press, 1972)—Trans.]
30. Though forced into hiding, Mrs. Husserl was still living in Louvain. Notwithstanding her advanced age, she closely followed all matters concerning her husband's manuscripts.
31. Merleau-Ponty had first written the word *méfiances* (distrust, suspicions) and then erased it and replaced it with the word *calumnies*. [Although Van Breda never specifies just what these "calumnies" or "unpleasant rumors" intimated, we can infer from Merleau-Ponty's remarks in his letter of March 31 that they included the accusation that he and his colleagues were not acting in the "general interest" but rather in the special interests of the Victor Cousin Library—and perhaps, correlatively, in their own special interests to have the manuscripts all to themselves(!)—in their first attempt to establish a center for Husserl's unpublished manuscripts in Paris—Trans.]
32. A French translation of *Cartesian Meditations* had appeared in 1931 [*Méditations cartésiennes*, trans. Gabrielle Pfeiffer and Emmanuel Levinas (Paris: Armand Colin, 1931)]. It was only in 1950, in the first volume of *Husserliana*, that Stephan Strasser published a critical edition in the original German.
33. Published in 1954 by Walter Biemel in volume IV of *Husserliana*, pp. 105–276.
34. [Stephan Strasser's works available in English include: *Phenomenology and the Human Sciences* (Pittsburgh: Duquesne University Press, 1963); *The Idea of Dialogical Phenomenology* (Pittsburgh: Duquesne University Press, 1969); and *Phenomenology of Feeling*, trans. Rober E. Wood (Pittsburgh: Duquesne University Press, 1977)—Trans.]
35. [Edmund Husserl, *Die Idee der Phänomenologie: fünf Vorlesunngen*, ed. Paul Janssen (Hamburg: Meiner, 1986); *The Idea of Phenomenology*, trans. William P. Alston and George Nakhnikian (The Hague: Martinus Nijhoff, 1964)—Trans.]
36. Merleau-Ponty was particularly active in the International Philosophy Colloquium organized by the Archives in Brussels in April of 1951. He not only presented a paper—"On the Phenomenology of Language"—but also participated in the discussions at most of the other papers. His paper was published with others from the colloquium in a volume entitled *Problèmes actuels de la phénoménologie* (Paris, 1952). The paper can also be found in *Signs*, pp. 84–97.
    In April of 1957, Merleau-Ponty also attended one session of the Third

Colloquium of Philosophy at Royaumont, organized with the help of the Archives and centered on Husserl's work and thought.

37. [The relationship between phenomenology and psychology was indeed of central interest to Merleau-Ponty between 1949 and 1952, when he occupied the Chair of Child Psychology and Pedagogy at the Sorbonne. In the résumés of his courses from these years (available now in a complete French edition, *Merleau-Ponty à la Sorbonne: résumé de cours, 1949–1952* (Paris: Cynara, 1988), references to Husserl are ample and include references to Husserl's later work, and even to his unpublished manuscripts. Indeed, Merleau-Ponty devoted an entire course to precisely the question of the relationship between phenomenology and psychology as conceived by Husserl. A complete translation of these lectures is now in preparation by Hugh J. Silverman, Stephen H. Watson, and James Barry Jr., for publication by Humanities Press International. Also, see "Phenomenology and the Sciences of Man," trans. John Wild, in *The Primacy of Perception*, ed. James Edie (Evanston: Northwestern University Press, 1964), pp. 43–95. On page 46, note 3, and again on page 82, note 21, Merleau-Ponty recognizes the work of Van Breda and the Archives at Louvain—Trans.]

38. After completing the present article, I found another letter from Merleau-Ponty in our files, addressed February 15, 1959, as well as my response to his letter, sent on March 6. In this letter he asks: "I would like to know whether, in the unpublished *Forschungsmanuskripte*, there are other texts on the *Lebenswelt* as the basis [*soutien*] of historicity; on the *Lebenswelt* insofar as it receives the *Gebilde* of culture and even of philosophy, as soon as they become 'sedimented'; and on language?"

I responded: "The most important texts that deal with the themes you mentioned in your letter belong to groups A V, A VII, E III, and K III." I pointed out that the complete file of theses transcriptions could be found at the Paris center. What stands out in his letter, I might note, is his desire to resume his study of the manuscripts; it is possible he had already begun to consider using them in a seminar at the Collège de France.

39. Merleau-Ponty's letter of February 15 (see note 38 above) suggests that the intended themes of the seminar were the *Lebenswelt* and—or—language. Manuscripts A V, A VII, and K III all deal with the *Lebenswelt*.

40. For each dossier, this card-index provides—beyond the signature and number of pages—the official title of the manuscript, its date of composition, and a list of [relevant] subtitles in the same transcription.

41. [Merleau-Ponty did in fact devote an entire course at the Collège, in the first half of the academic year 1959–60, to Husserl's later thought, centered on the translation and commentary of two texts: *Die Frage nach dem Ursprung der Geometrie als intentional-historisches Problem* (see "The Origin of Geometry" in *The Crisis of European Sciences and Transcendental Phenomenology*, trans. David Carr, published by Northwestern University Press, 1970, pp. 353–78), and *Umsturz der kopernikanischen Lehre* (see "Foundational Investigations of the Phenomenological Origin of the Spatiality of Nature" in *Husserl: Shorter Works*, ed. Peter McCormick and Frederic Elliston, published by University of Notre Dame Press, 1981, pp. 222–33). Also, see "Husserl at the Limits of Phenomenology" in Merleau-Ponty, *Themes from the Lectures*, trans. John O'Neill (Evanston: Northwestern University Press, 1970), pp. 113–23—Trans.]

42. As all the texts Merleau-Ponty desired to study deal with the *Lebenswelt*, the

constitution of the world in general, and consciousness of the world as horizon, it seems beyond doubt that he intended to speak of the *Lebenswelt* in his seminar.

43. In 1940, the numerous manuscripts Husserl was working on during the last years of his life, while in the process of writing the *Crisis*, were compiled under the signature K III.

44. Merleau-Ponty is referring to Husserl's work of 1929, *Formale und transzendentale Logik: Versuch einer Kritik der logischen Vernunft*, ed. Paul Janssen (The Hague: M. Nijhoff, 1969). [In English, *Formal and Transcendental Logic*, trans. Dorion Cairns (The Hague: M. Nijhoff, 1977)—Trans.]

45. Merleau-Ponty's visit to Louvain took place in 1939, not in 1938.

APPENDIX 3: Husserl's Concept of Nature (Merleau-Ponty's 1957–58 Lectures)

1. [Translator's Note: Xavier Tilliette's article appeared in the *Revue de métaphysique et de morale* in 1965. The introduction and notes (except where indicated otherwise) were supplied by Professor Tilliette. I would like to thank James Barry Jr. for his painstaking assistance in correlating the original footnotes with their English translations, and Edward Casey for his helpful comments on the main text. In addition, I would like to thank Richard A. Cohen, whose meticulous reading has contributed greatly to this translation.

   Works cited in Tilliette's notes will be indicated according to the following key:

TEXTS BY EDMUND HUSSERL

Crisis   *The Crisis of European Sciences and Transcendental Phenomenology.* Trans. David Carr. Evanston, Illinois: Northwestern University Press, 1970.

CM   *Cartesian Meditations.* Trans. Dorian Cairns. The Hague: Martinus Nijhoff, 1982.

EJ   *Experience and Judgment.* Trans. James S. Churchill and Karl Ameriks. Evanston, Illinois: Northwestern University Press, 1973.

FTL   *Formal and Transcendental Logic.* Trans. Dorian Cairns. The Hague: Martinus Nijhoff, 1969.

Ideas   *Ideas pertaining to a Pure Phenomenology and to a Phenomenological Philosophy (First Book).* Trans. Fred Kersten. Boston: Martinus Nijhoff, 1982.

Id. II   *Ideen Zu Einer Reinen Phänomenologie und Phänomenologischen Philosophie II* (Husserliana IV). Ed. Marly Biemel. The Hague: Martinus Nijhoff, 1952.

Id. III   *Ideen Zu Einer Reinen Phänomenologie und Phänomenologischen Philosophie III* (Husserliana V). Ed. Marly Biemel. The Hague: Martinus Nijhoff, 1952.

LI   *Logical Investigations.* Trans. J. N. Findlay. London: Routledge and Kegan Paul, 1970.

Time   *The Phenomenology of Internal Time-Consciousness.* Trans. James S. Churchill. Bloomington, Indiana: Indiana University Press, 1973.

Texts by Maurice Merleau-Ponty

Ph. P   *Phenomenology of Perception.* Trans. Colin Smith. New York: Humanities Press, 1962.

PP   *Primacy of Perception and Other Essays.* Ed. James Edie. Evanston, Illinois: Northwestern University Press, 1973.

Signs   *Signs.* Trans. Richard C. McCleary. Evanston, Illinois: Northwestern University Press, 1964.

VI   *The Visible and the Invisible.* Trans. Alphonso Lingis. Evanston, Illinois: Northwestern University Press, 1968.

HT   *Humanism and Terror.* Trans. John O'Neill. Boston: Beacon Press, 1968.]

2. [The source of this quotation is unclear.]
3. *Id. II,* 24–27. Cf. *Signs,* pp. 162–63.
4. *Id. II,* 25.
5. *CM,* pp. 35, 37.
6. *Id. II,* 25, 27.
7. *Id. II,* 26.
8. *Id. II,* 26.
9. *Id. II,* 1, 27. Cf. *Ideas,* p. 163.
10. Here, through the fault of the scribe, the development appears to be truncated. The missing link is that "everything is directed toward a spatio-temporal world" (*Id. II,* 28). Merleau-Ponty means that thought and the theoretical subject are not abstracted from the corporeal subject, and that the universal observer accompanies the inhabitant of the world under the presupposition of a Nature coextensive with the totality of beings. This was inspired directly by Husserl: "Men, and not only human bodies, go for a drive . . ." (*Id. II,* 32). Cf. 203: "They go for a walk, make a visit . . . while their minds travel along with their bodies in the space of a single objective *Umwelt.*" And *Id. II,* 167–68.
11. *Id. II,* 25, 35, 253; *EJ,* p. 13.
12. *Id. II,* 139, 173, 180, 183 (the personalistic attitude). Concerning the natural attitude, cf. *Id. II,* 64, 161, 174, 180, 182, 208; *Ideas,* pp. 62, 141; *Id. III,* 145, 149; *CM,* p. 82; *FTL,* p. 213; *Ph. P,* p. 61.
13. *Id. II,* 22.
14. *Id. II,* 17. Cf. *zurückgedeutet, Id. II,* 214; *Id. III,* 81. See *Signs,* pp. 165, 177–78.
15. *Id. II,* 4, 6–7, 22–23. Cf. *Signs,* p. 165.
16. *Id. II,* 5 (and *Vorkonstituierung* [Pre-constitution]); cf. *Id. II,* 9, 11, 19, 385; *EJ,* pp. 62, 187.
17. "In person, in the flesh and blood." A Husserlian word par excellence (*leibhaft, leibhaftig*), characteristic especially of *Ideas.* Cf. *Ph. P,* pp. 319–20.
18. *Id. II,* 55, 158; cf. 150.
19. *Id. II,* 11–12, 152, 253, 257, 261, 329–30. Cf. *CM,* p. 97; *FTL,* p. 165; *EJ,* p. 38; *Ph. P,* pp. 137, 314; *Signs,* pp. 88, 94, 166; *VI,* pp. 38, 255; *PP,* p. 162.
20. "When I walk in the street with eyes fixed on the horizon of the houses, the whole of the setting near at hand quivers with each footfall on the asphalt, then settles down in its place" (*VI,* p. 7).
21. *EJ,* pp. 224, 230, 280. The expression which is cited several times in *Ph. P,* pp. 30, 265, 419, is not found in *Id. II,* where it is nonetheless the question of *Übergang* [transition] (*Id. II,* 14) and *Übergangserlebnisse* [the experience of transition]

(*Id. II*, 38). It is frequently implied in *EJ* (for example, pp. 114, 131, 206–207, 208–209, 217, 230, 240, 323 (p. 206: the synthesis of transitions) and in *Time*, cf. pp. 103, 158–59, 186. *EJ* also employs the term *synthetische Übergange* [synthetic transition], cf. pp. 154–55, 207, 325. Cf. *CM*, pp. 61–62; *FTL*, pp. 163–64, 315; *VI*, p. 230.

22. *EJ*, p. 84; *CM*, pp. 97, 116.
23. *Id. II*, 56, 96; cf. 167, 204, 236, 244–46, 282, 288, 391.
24. Cf. *Ph. P*, pp. 139, 331–33, 429–30; *Signs*, p. 166; *PP*, pp. 159, 166. This theme is the leitmotive of a dissertation by Willi Maier, *Das Problem der Leiblichkeit bei Jean-Paul Sartre und Maurice Merleau-Ponty* (Tübingen: Niemeyer, 1964).
25. *Id. III*, 117. "Suppose, Husserl says, that a consciousness were to experience satiety whenever a locomotive's boiler was full, and warmth each time its fire was lit; the locomotive would still not be its body" (*Signs*, p. 166).
26. *Id. III*, 123; *Id. II*, 145, 150, 166; *Signs*, p. 166.
27. This expression does not seem to occur in Malebranche. Perhaps it is a mistaken recollection.
28. *Id. III*, 123. This term of mathematical origin, which already appeared in the *Logical Investigations* (pp. 286, 451, 695, 790–91), appears more often in *Time*, *Ideas*, *Id. II*, *CM* and *FTL*, and is found even more frequently in *EJ*. Merleau-Ponty sometimes translated it as *empiètement* [encroachment] (*VI*, p. 135; *PP*, pp. 162, 173). In his last book he defined *Deckung* as follows: "A coincidence always past or always future . . . [which] therefore is not a coincidence, a real fusion, as of two positive terms or two elements of an alloyage, but an overlaying, as of a hollow and a relief which remain distinct" (*VI*, pp. 122–23).
29. "*Une espèce de 'réflexion*'," *Meditations cartésiennes* (Paris: Colin, 1931)], p. 81 (cf. *Ph. P*, p. 93). This expression was expunged from the German text and, curiously enough, is not found in the critical apparatus. [Translator's note: Cairn's English version uses the phrase "reflexively related to itself" (*CM*, p. 97)]. A note in *EJ* (p. 55) may justify this suppression by underlining the radical difference between such a "reflection" and reflection in the usual sense. See however *Id. II*, 5 and 185n. (*Reflexion in der Einfühlung*). Whatever it means, Merleau-Ponty was struck by this expression—he takes it up in *Ph. P*, pp. 351–52; *Signs*, pp. 166, 168; *VI*, pp. 193, 256—as he was also familiar with the example of the "hands which touch," attesting to the "reflexivity of the sensible," the "reflexivity of the body," the experience of the corporeal "quasi-reflection": *Ph. P*, p. 93; *Signs*, pp. 166, 168; *VI*, pp. 133–34, 141, 146, 148, 202–203, 246, 249, 253, 260; *PP*, p. 163 ("a sort of double crossing happens between one hand and the other").
30. Cf. *Signs*, p. 235.
31. *Kompräsenz*: *Id. II*, 161, 165, and later in *Signs*, pp. 167, 174.
32. *Reizbar*: *Id. III*, 118; cf. 123; *empfindendes Ding*, *Id. III*, 119. Cf. *Signs*, pp. 166, 168.
33. *Id. III*, 124; cf. *Id. II*, 195, 199 (*Subjekt-Objekt*); *Signs*, p. 166.
34. *Nullpunkt der Orienterung*: *Id. II*, 56, 158. Cf. *CM*, p. 123 ("*Nullkorper im absoluten Hier*"); *EJ*, p. 106; *Ph. P*, p. 299 ["constantly given reference"]; *VI*, pp. 248–49.
35. *Ideas*, pp. 116, 134; *Id. III*, 129. Cf. *Ph. P*, pp. 395–96, 398.
36. Cf. *Id. II*, 67, 69.
37. *Id. III*, 153; *Id. II*, 76. Cf. *Ideas*, pp. 328, 338; *Id. II*, 334, 366; *FTL*, p. 235, *Rechtsfrage* ["question about legitimacy"]; *Signs*, p. 167.

38. *Id. II*, 55, 81, 183–84, 373. Cf. 253, *Ichversunkenheit* [self-preoccupation]; *Ph. P*, p. 58; *Signs*, p. 173.

39. *Id. II*, 88–89; *Signs*, pp. 168, 173; *Id. III*, 130; *Ph. P*, pp. 319–20, 325.

40. On the solipsist hypothesis and the problem of a "transcendental solipsism," see *Id. II*, 81 (the text that Merleau-Ponty is referring to here). Cf. *Id. II*, 70, 73, 77, 87, 144, 161, 164–65; *CM*, p. 89; *FTL*, pp. 241–42, 270; *Ph. P*, pp. 358, 360; *Signs*, pp. 173–75 (a commentary on *Id. II*, p. 81); *VI*, pp. 10, 58–59, 71, 143.

41. "The solitude from which we emerge to intersubjective life is not that of the monad. It is only the haze of an anonymous life that separates us from being; and the barrier between us and others is impalpable" (*Signs*, p. 174). Cf. *Signs*, pp. 165–66.

42. *Id. II*, 95, 166–68, 198, 200, 244, 347; *Ideas*, pp. 101, 363; *CM*, pp. 92ff. and 146ff.; *EJ*, p. 165; *Signs*, pp. 168, 170, 175. See the note on the problem of the other in *VI*, p. 81.

43. *Id. II*, 176 ("expression prone to misunderstanding"), 161, 166, 167, 169, 175, 181, cf. 190).

44. The text seems to us to conform faithfully to the corresponding passage of *Id. II* (165–68). In the parallel development in *Signs* (pp. 166–70), Merleau-Ponty likens introspection to projection and takes Husserl in a direction opposed to transcendental idealism. The *ohne Introjektion* of *Id. II* (166) is not applied to corporeal phenomena, and "the extension of compresence" is in reality "transfer of compresence" (*Übertragene Kompräsenz*), appresentation, introjection—in truth, like a beginning and "commencement." In reality, an ambiguity hangs over Husserlian introjection, between introjection as given and introjection as operation, and, more generally, concerning the constitution of the other. Others are certainly not "duplicates of myself" but they are my "analogues." Cf. *CM*, pp. 116, 120, 124, 128, and the discussion in *Signs*, pp. 93–95. For Husserl, introjection is the "encrusted" (*eingelegt*) soul or mind in a body, grafted (*aufgepfropft*) to a body (*Id. II*, 181, 190; *FTL*, pp. 239–41), in a relation of belonging; this begins to happen in the esthesiological phase. The term, of course, comes from Avenarius (1843–96).

45. *Id. II*, 164, 166; *Signs*, p. 169. Cf. *CM*, pp. 118–20, and *Id. II*, 144–45.

46. *Id. II*, 154–55, 175–76, 211, 284–85 ("the esthesiological and psychical is the 'annex' of the physical body"); *Signs*, pp. 169–71.

47. *Eingegliedert* (*Id. II*, 159), *Glied* (*der*) "*objectiven Natur*" (*Id. II*, 171). Cf. *Id. II*, 169, 241; *Signs*, pp. 166, 171.

48. "Dass ein ich denke auftaucht, ist ein Naturfaktum." *Id. II*, 181; *Signs*, pp. 168–69. Cf. *Ph. P*, pp. 353–54.

49. *Id. II*, 168–69 and, regarding the personalist attitude, 183, 235, 240, 242.

50. *Id. II*, 180; *Signs*, pp. 164–65.

51. *Id. II*, 161, 368–69; *Ideas*, p. 89. Cf. *VI*, p. 137; *PP*, p. 163.

52. Cf. *Ideas*, p. 119.

53. *Signs*, pp. 168–69. Husserl speaks of the "intersubjective body" (*Id. II*, 295). See *Ph. P*, pp. 349, 354ff.

54. *Id. II*, 85, and *Signs*, pp. 170–71, where Merleau-Ponty comments on these "extraordinary pages." Cf. *Ideas*, pp. 149–51, 365; *FTL*, pp. 251, 283–84; *Ph. P*, pp. 358, 398. ("If I try to imagine Martians or angels or a divine thought whose logic is not mine, this Martian, angelic or divine thought must figure in my universe and would not explode it.")

55. *Id. II*, 181–82, 185, 195; *Ph. P*, pp. 86–87, 327.

56. In this paragraph Merleau-Ponty is drawing almost exclusively from the long-unpublished "Umsturz der Kopernikanischen Lehre in der gëwohnlichen weltanschaulichen Interpretation. Die Erde als Ur-Arche bewegt sich nicht," which he had already used in his thesis (*Ph. P*, pp. 71, 429). [Translator's note: an English translation of this fragmentary essay can be found in *Husserl: Shorter Works*, ed. P. McCormick and F. Elliston (South Bend: Notre Dame University Press, 1982), pp. 222–33.] Cf. *Signs*, pp. 177, 180; *VI*, p. 259.

57. *Möglichkeit an Wirklichkeit. Signs*, p. 180; *VI*, pp. 228–29.

58. Cf. *EJ*, pp. 163 (*unsere Erde*), 260 (*die Welt*); *Crisis*, pp. 131 (*Weltboden*), 354, 373 (*Urboden*); *CM*, pp. 142–43. For the characteristic terms, "ground" (*sol*), "stock" (*souche*), "cradle" (*berceau*), "native land" (*patrie*), see, for example, *Ph. P*, pp. 52–53, 323, 429–32; *Signs*, p. 180.

59. *Offenheit, offener Horizont: Id. II*, 298–99, 372; 196, 199, 380, 383; *EJ*, pp. 328, 339; *CM*, pp. 23–25; *FTL*, pp. 199–200.

60. At the beginning of this lecture, Merleau-Ponty sums up the preceding course.

61. "Husserl always regretted that the expression which truly captures the essence of philosophy had already been taken over by a positive science, that is, the expression "archeology" (Eugen Fink, *Das Problem der Phänomenologie Edmund Husserls*, Revue internationale de philosophie, I, no. 2, p. 240). Cf. *Signs*, pp. 164–65.

62. Cf. *Ph. P*, p. 349ff.; *Signs*, pp. 94–95.

63. *Id. II*, 55, 158; Cf. *Id. II*, 150 and *VI*, passim, e.g., pp. 197, 204.

64. Cf. *Signs*, pp. 170, 172, 180. "Outline of ontology projected as an ontology of brute Being—and of logos. Draw up the picture of wild Being, prolonging my article on Husserl" (*VI*, p. 165). Cf. *VI*, pp. 166–67, 183, 202 ("vertical or savage Being"), 204, 208.

65. *FTL*, pp. 292–93. Cf. *CM*, pp. 146–47; *Ph. P*, pp. 50, 429 (art hidden in the depths of Nature, operative intentionality); *Signs*, pp. 105, 173. "It is a question of that logos that pronounces itself silently in each sensible thing, inasmuch as it varies around a certain type of message, which we can have an idea of only through our carnal participation in its sense, only by espousing by our body its manner of 'signifying'. . . ." (*VI*, p. 208). Cf. *VI*, pp. 215–16.

66. The analytic logos of Husserl (*FTL*, pp. 292–93), the *logos prophorikos* of the "Working Notes" (*VI*, p. 170), "that λόγοσ uttered the internal structure sublimates our carnal relation with the world" (*VI*, p. 208 [translation altered]); *EJ*, pp. 275, 343.

67. *CM*, p. 32. Cf. *CM*, pp. 19–21; *FTL*, p. 218; *Ideas*, pp. 338–39; *Id. II*, 279; *Id. III*, 160. "The ideas are the texture of experience, its style, first mute, then uttered" (*VI*, p. 119).

68. *Id. II*, 299, 372; *EJ*, p. 137. Cf. *Ph. P*, pp. 141, 305; *HT*, p. 103, and the "Working Notes," passim.

69. *Crisis*, pp. 131, 354, 373; *EJ*, p. 30; *VI*, p. 228.

70. Cf. *Signs*, p. 180.

71. *VI*, pp. 167, 259.

72. *VI*, p. 259; *Ph. P*, pp. 71, 429. Jean Wahl prefers to translate it as *arché* (ἀρχή).

73. Cf. *VI*, pp. 185, 196, 228, 265; despite the famous *Nachwort* which reproaches Heidegger (*Id. III*, 140). See *Being and Time* (New York: Harper and Row, 1962), pp. 58–63, recalling that it was dedicated to Husserl.

74. A fiction which is a variant of the hypothesis of the *Nichtsein* or *Nichtexistenz der Welt* ["exclusion of Being" or "exclusion of the world"] (*Id. III*, 153; *Ideas*,

pp. 132–33; *CM*, pp. 17–18), of the *Weltvernichtung* (*Ideas*, p. 138). Merleau-Ponty criticizes this fiction in *VI* (pp. 171–72, 179, 196).

75. "The world is continually there for us" (*FTL*, p. 242). Cf. *CM*, p. 106.
76. Apparently the text cited in the lecture "Einstein and the Crisis of Reason" (*Signs*, p. 196).
77. Cf. *Id. II*, 163, 198; *Signs*, pp. 172, 176; *VI*, pp. 168, 180, 217, 218–19, 233, 238–39, 254.
78. *Id. II*, 162–63, 198; *Ideas*, p. 158; *Signs*, pp. 172, 176. Cf. *Ph. P*, p. 363.
79. *Id. III*, 124; *Signs*, p. 177.
80. Cf. *Signs*, p. 72; *VI*, p. 33 n.
81. *Id. II*, 24.
82. "Latent bleibende, fungierende Intentionalität" (see article cited in note 61). Cf. *Signs*, p. 165, and *Time*, pp. 158–59; *FTL*, pp. 235–36; *Ph. P*, pp. xviii, 418.
83. That is to say, Merleau-Ponty's commentary on Husserl.
84. "The most important lesson which the reduction teaches us is the impossibility of a complete reduction" (*Ph. P*, p. xiv). Since the beginning, Merleau-Ponty indicated his misgivings over the "transcendental idealism" of Husserl, a direction of Husserl's phenomenology which persisted through his later writings (*Ideas*, pp. 234–35; *Id. II*, 297; *CM*, pp. 83–84; *Id. III*, 75, 139: "The wonder of wonders is the pure Ego and pure consciousness.") Merleau-Ponty maintained and accentuated these misgivings after the *Phenomenology*. Cf. the discussions in *Signs*, pp. 109–13, 165, 179–81, and the few references made in the appendix of *VI*, pp. 172, 179, 235, 238, 243.
85. *Id. II*, 16, 276 (*verborgene Vernunft, doxa der Wahrnehmung*), 334; *FTL*, p. 302; *Crisis*, pp. 155–56; *EJ*, p. 46; *Ph. P*, pp. 39, 343, 355, 365; *VI*, pp. 3ff., 28.
86. *Id. II*, 248; *Ph. P*, pp. xvi, 60–63, 241, 359–60.
87. Cf. *Id. III*, 145 and *Signs*, p. 164.
88. *Ideas*, p. 298: "A distinct understanding of word and sentence (or a distinct, articulated effectuation of the act of stating) is compatible with the *confusion belonging to the substrata*. This confusion does not signify mere unclarity, although it can *also* signify that. The substratum can be a confused unitary something (and often is) that does not actually include in itself its articulation; but it owes [its articulation] to mere adaptation to the stratum of the logical expression actually articulated and effected in original actuality. . . . But now the analogue is also to be produced in the grounding *substratum*, everywhere unliving is to be converted into the living, all confusion into distinctness, but also all non-intuitiveness into intuitiveness." This was already the program signalled in the article "Philosophy as Rigorous Science" (in *Phenomenology and the Crisis of Philosophy*, trans. Quentin Lauer [New York: Harper and Row, 1965], pp. 99–100): "The question as to how natural, 'confused' experience can become scientific experience, as to how one can arrive at the determination of objectively valid empirical judgements, is the cardinal methodological question of every empirical science."

Bibliography

◆

MERLEAU-PONTY'S WRITINGS IN FRENCH AND ENGLISH

1942

The Structure of Behavior. Trans. Alden L. Fischer. Boston: Beacon Press, 1963; London: Methuen, 1965.
La Structure du comportement. Paris: Presses Universitaires de France, 1942.

1945

Phenomenology of Perception. Trans. Colin Smith. New York: Humanities Press, 1962; London: Routledge & Kegan Paul, 1962.
Phénoménologie de la perception. Paris: Gallimard, 1945.

1947

Humanism and Terror: An Essay on the Communist Problem. Trans. John O'Neill. Boston: Beacon Press, 1969.
Humanisme et terreur, essai sur le problème communiste. Paris: Gallimard, 1947.

1948

Sense and Non-Sense. Trans. Herbert L. Dreyfus and Patricia Allen Dreyfus. Evanston: Northwestern University Press, 1964.
Sens et non-sens. Paris: Nagel, 1948.

1953

In Praise of Philosophy. Trans. John Wild and James M. Edie. Evanston: Northwestern University Press, 1963.
Éloge de la Philosophie, Leçon inaugurale faite au Collège de France, le jeudi 15 janvier 1953. Paris: Gallimard, 1953.
Éloge de la Philosophie et autres essais. Paris: Gallimard, 1960.

1955

Adventures of the Dialectic. Trans. Joseph Bien. Evanston: Northwestern University Press, 1973; London: Heinemann, 1974.
Les Aventures de la dialectique. Paris: Gallimard, 1955.

1956

Les Philosophes célèbres. Paris: Mazenod, 1956.

189

1960

Signs. Trans. Richard C. McCleary. Evanston: Northwestern University Press, 1964.
Signes. Paris: Gallimard, 1960.
The Primacy of Perception and Other Essays on Phenomenological Psychology, the Philosophy of Art, History, and Politics. Edited by James M. Edie. Evanston: Northwestern University Press, 1964.
Les Sciences de l'homme et la phénoménologie. Paris: Centre de Documentation Universitaire, 1958.
L'Oeil et l'esprit. Paris: Gallimard, 1964.

1964

The Visible and the Invisible; Followed by Working Notes. Trans. Alphonso Lingis. Evanston: Northwestern University Press, 1968.
Le Visible et l'invisible; suivi de notes de travail. Paris: Gallimard, 1964.

1968

Themes from Lectures at the Collège de France, 1952–1960. Trans. John O'Neill. Evanston: Northwestern University Press, 1970.
Résumés de cours, Collège de France, 1952–1960. Paris: Gallimard, 1968.
L'Union de l'âme et du corps chez Malebranche, Biran et Bergson, Notes prises au cours de Maurice Merleau-Ponty. Paris: J. Vrin, 1968.

1969

The Prose of the World. Trans. John O'Neill. Evanston: Northwestern University Press, 1973.
La Prose du monde. Paris: Gallimard, 1969.
The Essential Writings of Merleau-Ponty. Edited by Alden L. Fisher. New York: Harcourt, Brace & World, 1969.

1971

Existence et dialectique. Paris: Presses Universitaires de France, 1971.

1973

Consciousness and the Acquisition of Language. Trans. Hugh J. Silverman. Evanston: Northwestern University Press, 1973.

1974

Phenomenology, Language and Sociology: Selected Essays of Merleau-Ponty. London: Heinemann, 1974.

1981

Approches phénoménologiques. Paris: Hachette, 1981.

1983

"The Experience of Others." Trans. Fred Evans and Hugh J. Silverman. In *Review of Existential Psychology and Psychiatry*, XVIII (1982–83).

1988

"Philosophy and Non-Philosophy since Hegel." Trans. Hugh J. Silverman. In *Philosophy and Non-Philosophy since Merleau-Ponty.* London: Routledge, 1988.
Merleau-Ponty à la Sorbonne: résumés de cours, 1949–1952. Paris: Cynara, 1988.

1991

Texts and Dialogues. Edited by Hugh J. Silverman and James Barry Jr. Atlantic Highlands, NJ: Humanities Press, 1991.

BOOKS, CHAPTERS, AND ARTICLES IN ENGLISH ON MERLEAU-PONTY

BOOKS

Bannan, John F. *The Philosophy of Merleau-Ponty*. New York: Harcourt, Brace & World, 1967.

Barral, Mary Rose. *Merleau-Ponty: The Role of the Body-Subject in Interpersonal Relations*. Pittsburgh: Duquesne University Press, 1965.

Bayer, Raymond. *Merleau-Ponty's Existentialism*. Buffalo: University of Buffalo, 1951.

Bologh, Roslyn Wallach. *Dialectical Phenomenology: Marx's Method*. Boston: Routledge & Kegan Paul, 1980.

Bruzina, Ronald, and Bruce Wilshire, eds. *Phenomenology: Dialogues and Bridges*. Albany: SUNY Press, 1982.

Chiari, Joseph. *Twentieth-Century French Thought: From Bergson to Lévi-Strauss*. New York: Gordian Press, 1975.

Cumming, Robert Denoon. *Starting Point: An Introduction to the Dialectic of Existence*. Chicago: University of Chicago Press, 1979.

Dallmayr, Fred R. *Twilight of Subjectivity*. Amherst: University of Massachusetts Press, 1981.

Dean, Thomas. *Post-Theistic Thinking: The Marxist-Christian Dialogue in Radical Perspective*. Philadelphia: Temple University Press, 1975.

Dillon, M. C. *Merleau-Ponty's Ontology*. Bloomington: Indiana University Press, 1988.

Ellis, Ralph. *An Ontology of Consciousness*. Dordrecht: Nijhoff, 1986.

Fairchild, David. *Prolegomena to a Methodology: Reflections on Merleau-Ponty and Austin*. Washington, DC: University Press of America, 1978.

Froman, Wayne Jeffrey. *Merleau-Ponty: Language and the Act of Speech*. Lewisburg, PA: Bucknell University Press, 1982.

Gier, Nicholas F. *Wittgenstein and Phenomenology: A Comparative Study of the Later Wittgenstein, Husserl, Heidegger, and Merleau-Ponty*. Albany: SUNY Press, 1981.

Gillan, Garth, ed. *The Horizons of the Flesh: Critical Perspectives on the Thought of Merleau-Ponty*. Carbondale: Southern Illinois University Press, 1973.

Hadreas, Peter J. *In Place of the Flawed Diamond: An Investigation of Merleau-Ponty's Philosophy*. New York: Peter Lang, 1986.

Jenner, F. A., and A. J. J. De Koning, eds. *Phenomenology and Psychiatry*. London: Academic Press, 1982.

Johnson, Galen, and Smith, Michael B., eds. *Ontology and Alterity*. Albany: SUNY Press, forthcoming.

Kaelin, Eugene Francis. *Art and Existence: Phenomenological Aesthetics*. Lewisburg, PA: Bucknell University Press, 1970.

———. *An Existentialist Aesthetic: The Theories of Sartre and Merleau-Ponty*. Madison: University of Wisconsin Press, 1962.

Kearney, Richard. *Modern Movements in European Philosophy*. Manchester: Manchester University Press, 1986.

Kockelmans, Joseph J., ed. *Phenomenology, the Philosophy of Edmund Husserl and Its Interpretation*. Garden City, NY: Anchor Books, 1967.

Kruks, Sonia. *The Political Philosophy of Merleau-Ponty*. Atlantic Highlands, NJ: Humanities Press, 1981.

Kwant, Remy C. *From Phenomenology to Metaphysics: An Inquiry into the Last Period of Merleau-Ponty's Philosophical Life*. Pittsburgh: Duquesne University Press, 1966.

———. *The Phenomenological Philosophy of Merleau-Ponty*. Pittsburgh: Duquesne University Press, 1963.

Langan, Thomas. *Merleau-Ponty's Critique of Reason*. New Haven: Yale University Press, 1966.

Lanigan, Richard L. *Speaking and Semiology: Maurice Merleau-Ponty's Phenomenological Theory of Existential Communication*. The Hague: Mouton, 1972.

Lauer, J. Quentin. *Triumph of Subjectivity: Introduction to Transcendental Phenomenology*. New York: Fordham University Press, 1958.

Lee, E. N., and M. Mandelbaum, eds. *Phenomenology and Existentialism*. Baltimore: Johns Hopkins Press, 1967.

Low, Douglas Beck. *The Existential Dialectic of Marx and Merleau-Ponty*. New York: Peter Lang, 1987.

Luijpen, William A. *Existential Phenomenology*. Pittsburgh: Duquesne University Press, 1960.

———. *Phenomenology and Atheism*. Pittsburgh: Duquesne University Press, 1965.

Madison, Gary Brent. *The Phenomenology of Merleau-Ponty*. Athens: Ohio University Press, 1981.

Mallin, Samuel B. *Merleau-Ponty's Philosophy*. New Haven: Yale University Press, 1979.

O'Neill, John. *Perception, Expression, and History: The Social Phenomenology of Maurice Merleau-Ponty*. Evanston: Northwestern University Press, 1970.

———. *The Communicative Body: Studies in Communicative Philosophy, Politics and Sociology*. Evanston: Northwestern University Press, 1989.

Poster, Mark. *Critical Theory and Poststructuralism: In Search of a Context*. Ithaca: Cornell University Press, 1989.

Rabil, Albert, Jr. *Merleau-Ponty: Existentialist of the Social World*. New York: Columbia University Press, 1967.

Sallis, John. *Phenomenology and the Return to Beginnings*. Pittsburgh: Duquesne University Press, 1973.

Sallis, John, ed. *Merleau-Ponty: Perception, Structure, Language*. Atlantic Highlands, NJ: Humanities Press, 1981.

Schmidt, James. *Maurice Merleau-Ponty: Between Phenomenology and Structuralism*. New York: St. Martin's Press, 1985.

Schrader, George Alfred, ed. *Existential Philosophers: Kierkegaard to Merleau-Ponty*. New York: McGraw-Hill, 1967.

Shapiro, Kenneth Joel. *Bodily Reflective Modes: A Phenomenological Method for Psychology*. Durham: Duke University Press, 1985.

Sheets, Maxine. *The Phenomenology of Dance*. Madison: University of Wisconsin Press, 1966.

Silverman, Hugh J., and F.A. Elliston, eds. *Jean-Paul Sartre*. Pittsburgh: Duquesne University Press, 1980.

Silverman, Hugh J., John Sallis, and Thomas Seebohm, eds. *Continental Philosophy in America*. Pittsburgh: Duquesne University Press, 1983.

Silverman, Hugh J. *Inscriptions: Between Phenomenology and Structuralism.* New York: Routledge and Kegan Paul, 1987.

Silverman, Hugh J., et al., eds. *The Horizons of Continental Philosophy.* Dordrecht: Kluwer, 1988.

Silverman, Hugh J., ed. *Philosophy and Non-Philosophy Since Merleau-Ponty.* London: Routledge, 1988.

Smith, Colin. *Contemporary French Philosophy: A Study in Norms and Values.* New York: Barnes & Noble, 1964.

Strasser, Stephan. *Understanding and Explanation: Basic Ideas Concerning the Humanity of the Human Sciences.* Pittsburgh: Duquesne University Press, 1985.

Taminiaux, Jacques. *Dialectic and Difference.* Trans. Robert T. Decker and Robert Crease. Atlantic Highlands, NJ: Humanities Press, 1983.

Taylor, Mark C. *Altarity.* Chicago: University of Chicago Press, 1987.

Van Peursen, C. A. *Body, Soul, Spirit.* London: Oxford University Press, 1966.

Waldenfels, Bernhard, ed. *Phenomenology and Marxism.* Trans. J. Claude Evans. London: Methuen, 1985.

Warren, Scott. *The Emergence of Dialectical Theory: Philosophy and Political Inquiry.* Chicago: University of Chicago Press, 1984.

Yolton, John W. *Thinking and Perceiving: A Study in the Philosophy of Mind.* La Salle, IL: Open Court, 1961.

Zaner, R. M. *The Problem of Embodiment: Some Contributions to a Phenomenology of the Body.* The Hague: Nijhoff, 1964.

ARTICLES AND CHAPTERS IN BOOKS

Abram, David. "Merleau-Ponty and the Voices of the Earth." *Environmental Ethics,* 10: 101–20 (Summer 1988).

Allen, Jeffner. "Through the Wild Region: An Essay in Phenomenological Feminism." *Review of Existential Psychology & Psychiatry,* 18: 241–56 (1982–83).

Anderson, Stephen J., and Wain Saeger. "Behavior, Mind and Existence: Toward a Primary Triangulation of Human Action." *Behaviorism,* 7: 37–63 (Spring 1979).

Appelbaum, David. "A Note on 'Pratyaksa' in Advaita Vedanta." *Philosophy East and West,* 32: 201–205 (April 1982).

Aronson, Ronald. "Vicissitudes of the Dialectic: From Merleau-Ponty's *Les Aventures de la Dialectique* to Sartre's *Second Critique.*" *The Philosophical Forum,* 18: 358–91 (Summer 1987).

Ashbaugh, Anne Freire. "The Philosophy of Flesh and the Flesh of Philosophy." *Research in Phenomenology,* 8: 217–23 (1978).

Ballard, Edward G. "The Philosophy of Merleau-Ponty." *Tulane Studies in Philosophy,* 9: 165–87 (1960).

Bannan, John F. "Merleau-Ponty Mismanaged." *Journal of Existentialism,* 7: 459–76 (Summer 1967).

———. "The Later Thought of Merleau-Ponty." *Dialogue,* 5: 383–403 (1966).

———. "Merleau-Ponty on God." *International Philosophical Quarterly,* 6: 341–65 (September 1966).

———. "Philosophical Reflection and the Phenomenology of Merleau-Ponty." *The Review of Metaphysics,* 8: 418–42 (March 1955).

Barral, Mary Rose. "Merleau-Ponty on the Body." *The Southern Journal of Philosophy,* 7: 171–79 (Summer 1969).

———. "Thomas Aquinas and Merleau-Ponty." *Philosophy Today*, 26: 204–16 (Fall 1982).

Barry, James, Jr. "The Textual Body: Incorporating Writing and Flesh." *Philosophy Today*, 30: 16–31 (Spring 1986).

———. "The Physics of Modern Perception: Beyond Body and World." *Journal of Speculative Philosophy*, 4: 287–97 (1990).

Bate, Michele. "The Phenomenologist as Art Critic: Merleau-Ponty and Cézanne." *The British Journal of Aesthetics*, 14: 344–50 (Autumn 1974).

Baysden, Richard. "Luijpen's Existential Phenomenology: A Structural Analysis." *Dialogue*, 15: 12–17 (October 1972).

Beberman, Arleen. "Death and Life." *The Review of Metaphysics*, 17: 18–32 (September 1963).

Bertram, Maryanne. "The Different Paradigms of Merleau-Ponty and Whitehead." *Philosophy Today*, 24: 121–32 (Summer 1980).

———. "A Kuhnian Approach to Merleau-Ponty's Thought." *Philosophy Research Archives*, 13: 275–83 (1987–88).

Bien, Joseph. "Man and the Economic: Merleau-Ponty's Interpretation of Historical Materialism." *Southwestern Journal of Philosophy*, 3: 121–27 (Spring 1972).

———. "Existential Phenomenology and Marxism: An Encounter." *Journal of Social Philosophy*, 13: 1–11 (May 1982).

———. "Two Approaches to History: Phenomenology and Marxism." *Journal of Thought*, 13: 315–19 (November 1978).

Blinder, David. "The Controversy over Conventionalism." *The Journal of Aesthetics and Art Criticism*, 41: 253–64 (Spring 1983).

Bourgeois, Patrick L. "The Epistemic Dimensions of Existential Phenomenology." *Philosophy Today*, 30: 43–47 (Spring 1986).

———. "The Integration of Merleau-Ponty's Philosophy." *Southwest Philosophical Review*, 5: 37–50 (July 1989).

Busch, Thomas. "Merleau-Ponty and the Problem of Origins." *Philosophy Today*, 2: 124–30 (Summer 1967).

Camele, Anthony M. "Time in Merleau-Ponty and Heidegger." *Philosophy Today*, 19: 256–68 (Fall 1975).

Carr, David. "Husserl's Problematic Concept of the Life-World." *American Philosophical Quarterly*, 7: 331–39 (1970).

Carruba, Gerald J. "The Phenomenological Foundation of Marxism in the Early Works of Maurice Merleau-Ponty." *Dianoia*, 1: 37–55 (Spring 1974).

Casalis, Matthieu. "Merleau-Ponty's Philosophical Itinerary: From Phenomenology to Onto-Semiology." *Southwestern Journal of Philosophy*, 6: 63–69 (Winter 1975).

Casey, Edward S. "Habitual Body and Memory in Merleau-Ponty." *Man and World*, 1: 279–98 (1984).

Cayard, W. Wallace. "Bertrand Russell and Existential Phenomenologists on Foundations of Knowledge." *Journal of the West Virginia Philosophical Society*, 1: 7–22 (Fall 1976).

Charlesworth, James H. "Reflections on Merleau-Ponty's Phenomenological Description of 'Word'." *Philosophy and Phenomenological Research*, 3: 609–613 (June 1970).

Coenen, Herman. "Types, Corporeality and the Immediacy of Interaction." *Man and World*, 1: 339–59 (1979).

Cohen, Richard. "Merleau-Ponty, the Flesh, and Foucault." *Philosophy Today*, 2: 329–38 (Winter 1984).

Compton, John. "Sartre, Merleau-Ponty, and Human Freedom." *The Journal of Philosophy*, 7: 577–88 (October 1982).

Cook, Deborah. "Writing Philosophy and Literature: Apology for Narcissism in Merleau-Ponty." *Eidos*, 4: 1–9 (June 1985).

Coole, Diana. "The Aesthetic Realm and the Lifeworld: Kant and Merleau-Ponty." *History of Political Thought*, 5: 503–26 (Winter 1984).

Cooper, Barry. "Hegelian Elements in Merleau-Ponty's *La Structure du Comportement*. *International Philosophical Quarterly*, 15: 411–423 (December 1975).

Coyne, Margaret Urban. "Merleau-Ponty on Language." *International Philosophical Quarterly*, 20: 307–26 (September 1980).

Crosson, Frederick J. "Phenomenology and Realism." *International Philosophical Quarterly* 6: 455–46 (September 1966).

Crowther, Paul. "Merleau-Ponty: Perception Into Art." *The British Journal of Aesthetics*, 22: 138–49 (Spring 1982).

———. "Experience of Art: Some Problems and Possibilities of Hermeneutical Analysis." *Philosophy and Phenomenological Research*, 43: 347–62 (March 1983).

———. "Merleau-Ponty: Vision and Painting." *Dialectics and Humanism*, 15: 107–18 (Winter-Spring 1988).

Culler, Jonathan. "Phenomenology and Structuralism." *The Human Context*, 5: 35–41 (Spring 1973).

Dallmayr, Fred R. "Marxism and Truth." *Telos*, 29: 130–59 (Fall 1976).

Daly, James. "Merleau-Ponty's Concept of Phenomenology." *Philosophical Studies* (Ireland), 16: 137–164 (1967).

———. "Merleau-Ponty: A Bridge between Phenomenology and Structuralism." *The Journal of the British Society for Phenomenology*, 2: 53–58 (October 1971).

Dauenhauer, Bernard P. "Renovating the Problem of Politics." *The Review of Metaphysics*, 29: 626–41 (June 1976).

———. "One Central Link between Merleau-Ponty's Philosophy of Language and His Political Thought." *Tulane Studies in Philosophy*, 29: 57–80 (December 1980).

Deutscher, Max. "Some Recollections of Ryle and Remarks on His Notion of Negative Action." *Australasian Journal of Philosophy*, 60: 254–264 (September 1982).

Devettere, Raymond J. "Merleau-Ponty and the Husserlian Reductions." *Philosophy Today*, 17: 297–308 (Winter 1973).

———. "The Human Body as Philosophical Paradigm in Whitehead and Merleau-Ponty." *Philosophy Today*, 20, 317–26 (Winter 1976).

De Waelhens, Alphonse. "The Philosophical Position of Merleau-Ponty." *Philosophy Today*, 7: 134–49 (Summer 1963).

Dillon, M. C. "Gestalt Theory and Merleau-Ponty's Concept of Intentionality." *Man and World*, 4: 436–59 (November 1971).

———. "Sartre on the Phenomenal Body and Merleau-Ponty's Critique." *The Journal of the British Society for Phenomenology*, 5: 144–58 (May 1974).

———. "Sartre's Inferno." *Thought*, 52: 134–50 (June 1977).

———. "Eye and Mind: The Intertwining of Vision and Thought." *Man and World*, 13: 155–72 (1980).

———. "Merleau-Ponty and the Transcendence of Immanence: Overcoming the Ontology of Consciousness." *Man and World*, 19: 395–412 (1986).

———. "Apriority in Kant and Merleau-Ponty." *Kantstudien*, 78: 403–23 (1987).

Dolgov, K. M. "The Philosophy and Aesthetics of Maurice Merleau-Ponty." *Soviet Studies in Philosophy*, 14: 67–92 (Winter 1975–76).

Doud, Robert. "Whitehead and Merleau-Ponty." *Process Studies*, 7: 145–60 (Fall 1977).

———. "Sensibility in Rahner and Merleau-Ponty." *The Thomist*, 44: 372–89 (July 1980).

———. "Wholeness as Phenomenon in Teilhard de Chardin and Merleau-Ponty." *Philosophy Today*, 24: 90–103 (Summer 1980).

Dreyfus, H. L., and Todes, S. J. "The Three Worlds of Merleau-Ponty." *Philosophy and Phenomenological Research*, 22: 559–65 (June 1962).

Duhan, Laura. "Ambiguity of Time, Self, and Philosophical Explanation in Merleau-Ponty, Husserl, and Hume." *Auslegung*, 13: 126–38 (Summer 1987).

Edie, James M. "The Significance of Merleau-Ponty's Philosophy of Language." *Journal of the History of Philosophy*, 13: 385–98 (July 1975).

———. "Merleau-Ponty: the Triumph of Dialectics Over Structuralism." *Man and World*, 17: 299–312 (1984).

Ellis, Ralph D. "Prereflective Consciousness and the Process of Symbolization." *Man and World*, 13: 173–92 (1980).

Embree, Lester. "Gurwitsch's Critique of Merleau-Ponty." *The Journal of the British Society for Phenomenology*, 12: 151–63 (May 1981).

Epstein, Fanny L. "The Metaphysics of Mind-Body Identity Theories." *American Philosophical Quarterly*, 10: 111–21 (April 1973).

Epstein, Michele F. "The Common Ground of Merleau-Ponty's and Wittgenstein's Philosophy of Man." *Journal of the History of Philosophy*, 13: 221–34 (April 1975).

Evans, C. Stephen. "Behaviorism as Existentialism: Ryle and Merleau-Ponty on the Mind." *The Journal of the British Society for Phenomenology*, 14: 65–78 (January 1983).

Fandozzi, Phillip R. "Art in a Technological Society" in *Research in Philosophy & Technology, Vol II*. Paul T. Durbin, ed. pp. 111–18. Greenwich: Jai Press, 1979.

Fóti, Véronique M. "Painting and the Re-Orientation of Philosophical Thought in Merleau-Ponty." *Philosophy Today*, 24: 114–20 (Summer 1980).

———. "Heidegger's and Merleau-Ponty's Turn from Technicity to Art." *Philosophy Today*, 30: 306–16 (Winter 1986).

Fotinis, Athanasios P. "Perception and the External World: A Historical and Critical Account." *Philosophia* (Athens), 4: 433–48 (1974).

Frantz, John J. "Merleau-Ponty's Notion of 'Flesh': A Look at the Development of a New Philosophical Insight." *Dialogue (PST)*, 14: 46–51 (January 1972).

Friedman, Robert M. "Merleau-Ponty's Theory of Intersubjectivity." *Philosophy Today*, 19: 228–42 (Fall 1975).

———. "The Formation of Merleau-Ponty's Philosophy." *Philosophy Today*, 17: 272–78 (Winter 1973).

Froman, Wayne. "Merleau-Ponty on Beginning: An Interrogation of Acting." *Agora*, 4: 58–77 (1979–80).

Gallagher, Shaun. "Lived Body and Environment." *Research in Phenomenology*, 16: 139–70 (1986).

———. "Hyletic Experience and the Lived Body." *Husserl Studies*, 3: 131–66 (1986).

Gans, Steven. "Schematism and Embodiment." *The Journal of the British Society for Phenomenology*, 13: 237–45 (October 1982).

Garcia, Reyes. "A Short Critique of the Role of the Sign in Eco's *A Theory of*

Semiotics." *Auslegung*, 7: 163–83 (Spring 1980).

Gay, William C. "Phenomenology and Structuralism." *Man and World*, 12: 322–38 (1979).

Gehl, Paul F. "An Answering Silence: Claims for the Unity of Truth Beyond Language." *Philosophy Today*, 30: 224–33 (Fall 1986).

Gerber, Rudolph J. "Merleau-Ponty: The Dialectic of Consciousness and World." *Man and World*, 2: 83–107 (February 1969).

———. "Causality and Atheism." *Proceedings of the American Catholic Philosophical Association*, 44: 232–40 (1970).

Gier, Nicholas F. "Intentionality and Prehension." *Process Studies*, 6: 197–213 (Fall 1976).

———. "Wittgenstein, Intentionality and Behaviorism." *Metaphilosophy*, 13: 46–64 (January 1982).

Gill, Jerry H. "Post-Critical Philosophy of Religion." *International Philosophical Quarterly*, 22: 75–86 (March 1982).

Glenn, John D. "The Behaviorism of a Phenomenologist: The Structure of Behavior and the Concept of Mind." *Philosophical Topics*, 13: 247–56 (Spring 1985).

———. "Merleau-Ponty and the Cogito." *Philosophy Today*, 23: 310–20 (Winter 1979).

———. "Merleau-Ponty's Existential Dialectic." *Tulane Studies in Philosophy*, 29: 81–94 (December 1980).

Grene, Marjorie. "The Aesthetic Dialogue of Sartre and Merleau-Ponty." *The Journal of the British Society for Phenomenology*, 1: 59–72 (May 1970).

———. "Merleau-Ponty and the Renewal of Ontology." *The Review of Metaphysics*, 29: 605–25 (June 1976).

Haight, David. "The Source of Linguistic Meaning." *Philosophy and Phenomenological Research*, 37: 239–47 (December 1976).

Hall, Harrison. "The Continuity of Merleau-Ponty's Philosophy of Perception." *Man and World*, 10: 435–47 (1977).

———. "The A Priori and the Empirical in Merleau-Ponty's Phenomenology of Perception." *Philosophy Today*, 23: 304–09 (Winter 1979).

———. "Painting and Perceiving." *The Journal of Aesthetics and Art Criticism*, 39: 291–95 (Spring 1981).

Hall, Ronald L. "Freedom: Merleau-Ponty's Critique of Sartre." *Philosophy Research Archives*, 6: no. 1391 (1980).

———. "The Origin of Alienation: Some Kierkegaardian Reflections on Merleau-Ponty's Phenomenology of the Body." *International Journal for Philosophy of Religion*, 12: 111–22 (1981).

Hamrick, William S. "Language and Abnormal Behavior: Merleau-Ponty, Hart, and Laing." *Review of Existential Psychology & Psychiatry*, 18: 181–203 (1982–83).

———. "Fascination, Fear and Pornography: A Phenomenological Typology." *Man and World*, 7: 52–66 (February 1974).

———. "Whitehead and Merleau-Ponty: Some Moral Implications." *Process Studies*, 4: 235–51 (Winter 1974).

———. "Ingarden and Artistic Creativity." *Dialectics and Humanism*, 2: 39–49 (Autumn 1975).

———. "Towards a Phenomenology of Legal Rules." *The Journal of the British Society for Phenomenology*, 10: 9–22 (January 1979).

Heinzig, Dennis. "M. Merleau-Ponty and Ludwig Wittgenstein: A Synthesis." *Auslegung*, 14: 19–36 (Winter 1987).

Hohler, Thomas P. "The Limits of Language and the Threshold of Speech." *Philosophy Today*, 26: 287–300 (Winter 1982).

Holland, Nancy J. "Merleau-Ponty on Presence: A Derridean Reading." *Research in Phenomenology*, 16: 111–20 (1986).

Howard, Dick. "A Marxist Ontology: On Sartre's Critique of Dialectical Reason." *Cultural Hermeneutics*, 1: 251–80 (November 1973).

———. "Introduction to Lefort." *Telos*, 2–30 (Winter 1974–75).

Hurst, William J. "Merleau-Ponty's Concept of the Self." *International Philosophical Quarterly*, 22: 227–40 (December 1982).

Jacobson, Paul K. "Language, Thought, and Truth in the Works of Merleau-Ponty: 1949–1953." *Research in Phenomenology*, 9: 144–67 (1979).

———. "The Return of Alcibiades: An Approach to the Meaning of Human Sexuality through the Works of Freud and Merleau-Ponty." *Philosophy Today*, 22: 89–98 (Spring 1978).

Jager, Bernd. "Exploration." *Humanitas*, 12: 311–31 (November 1976).

Jolivet, Regis. "The Problem of God in the Philosophy of Merleau-Ponty." *Philosophy Today*, 7: 150–64 (Summer 1963).

Joos, Ernest. "Remarks on Bertoldi's 'Time in the Phenomenology of Perception'." *Dialogue: Canadian Philosophical Review—Revue Canadienne de Philosophie*, 15: 113–17 (March 1976).

Jung, Hwa Yol. "The Concept of the Dialectic in Hegel, Marx and Merleau-Ponty." *The Journal of the British Society for Phenomenology*, 8: 56–58 (January 1977).

Kaelin, E. F. "Merleau-Ponty, Fundamental Ontologist." *Man and World*, 3: 102–15 (February 1970).

Kearney, Richard. "Modern Movements in European Philosophy: Some Introductory Remarks." *Eidos*, 4: 51–61 (June 1985).

Kessler, Gary E. "Pragmatic Bodies versus Transcendental Egos." *Transactions of the Charles S. Peirce Society*, 14: 101–19 (Spring 1978).

Kockelmans, Joseph J. "Merleau-Ponty on Sexuality." *Journal of Existentialism*, 6: 9–30 (Fall 1965).

———. "The Function of Psychology in Merleau-Ponty's Early Works." *Review of Existential Psychology & Psychiatry*, 18: 119–42 (1982–83).

Kovacs, George. "The Personalistic Understanding of the Body and Sexuality in Merleau-Ponty." *Review of Existential Psychology & Psychiatry*, 18: 207–17 (1982–83).

Kovaly, Pavel. "Maurice Merleau-Ponty and the Problem of Self-Accusations." *Studies in Soviet Thought*, 17: 225–41 (October 1977).

Krell, David Farrell. "M. Merleau-Ponty on 'Eros' and 'Logos'." *Man and World*, 7: 37–51 (February 1974).

———. "Phenomenology of Memory from Husserl to Merleau-Ponty." *Philosophy and Phenomenological Research*, 42: 492–505 (June 1982).

Kruks, Sonia. "Merleau-Ponty, Hegel and the Dialectic." *The Journal of the British Society for Phenomenology*, 7: 96–110 (May 1976).

———. "Merleau-Ponty: A Phenomenological Critique of Liberalism." *Philosophy and Phenomenological Research*, 37: 394–407 (March 1977).

———. "Marcel and Merleau-Ponty: Incarnation, Situation and the Problem of History." *Human Studies*, 10: 225–45 (1987).

Lanigan, Richard L. "Rhetorical Criticism: An Interpretation of Maurice Merleau-Ponty." *Philosophy and Rhetoric*, 2: 61–71 (Spring 1969).

———. "Maurice Merleau-Ponty Bibliography." *Man and World*, 3: 289–319 (November 1970).

———. "Merleau-Ponty's Phenomenology of Communication." *Philosophy Today*, 14: 79–88 (Summer 1970).

Lapointe, Francois H. "The Significance of Time in Merleau-Ponty's Phenomenology of the Body and the World." *The Modern Schoolman*, 49: 356–66 (May 1972).

———. "The Phenomenological Psychology of Sartre and Merleau-Ponty: A Bibliographical Essay." *Dialogos*, 8: 161–82 (November 1972).

———. "The Body-Soul Problem in Merleau-Ponty's *The Structure of Behavior*." *The Modern Schoolman*, 50: 281–91 (March 1973).

———. "The Evolution of Merleau-Ponty's Concept of the Body." *Dialogos*, 139–51 (April 1974).

Leder, Drew. "Merleau-Ponty and the Critique of Kant." *Graduate Faculty Philosophy Journal*, 9: 61–75 (Fall 1983).

Ledermann, E. K. "Conscience and Bodily Awareness: Disagreements with Merleau-Ponty." *The Journal of the British Society for Phenomenology*, 13: 286–95 (October 1982).

Lefort, Claude. "Presenting Merleau-Ponty." Trans. Hugh J. Silverman. *Telos*, 29: 39–42 (Fall 1976).

Lessing, Abba. "Spinoza and Merleau-Ponty on Human Existence." *Proceedings of the New Mexico-West Texas Philosophical Society*: 20–24 (April 1972).

Lévi-Strauss, Claude. "On Merleau-Ponty." Trans. by Christine Gross. *Graduate Faculty Philosophy Journal*, 7: 179–88 (Winter 1978).

Levin, David Michael. "The Spacing of Comedy and Tragedy: A Phenomenological Study of Perception." *The Journal of the British Society for Phenomenology*, 11: 16–36 (January 1980).

———. "Eros and Psyche: A Reading of Merleau-Ponty." *Review of Existential Psychology & Psychiatry*, 18: 219–39 (1982–83).

———. "Sanity and Myth in Affective Space: A Discussion of Merleau-Ponty." *Philosophical Forum*, 14: 157–89 (Winter 1982/83).

———. "The Body Politic: Political Economy and the Human Body." *Human Studies*, 8: 235–78 (1985).

Levine, Stephen K. "Merleau-Ponty's Philosophy of Art." *Man and World*, 2: 438–52 (August 1969).

Levinson, Daniel. "Logic in Contingency: The Origin of Truth in Merleau-Ponty with Constant Reference to Nietzsche." *Graduate Faculty Philosophy Journal*, 5: 132–41 (Fall 1975).

Lingis, Alphonso. "The Difficulties of a Phenomenological Investigation of Language." *The Modern Schoolman*, 57: 56–64 (November 1979).

———. "Intentionality and Corporeity," in *Analecta Husserliana, Vol I.*, pp. 75–90. Dordrecht: Reidel, 1971.

———. "Sensations." *Philosophy and Phenomenological Research*, 42: 160–70 (December 1981).

Low, Douglas. "The Existential Dialectic of Marx and Merleau-Ponty." *Philosophy Research Archives*, 11: 491–511 (1985).

Lowry, Atherton C. "Merleau-Ponty and Fundamental Ontology." *International Philosophical Quarterly*, 15: 397–409 (December 1975).

———. "Merleau-Ponty and the Absence of God." *Philosophy Today*, 22: 119–26 (Summer 1978).

———. "Merleau-Ponty and the Absence of God." *Proceedings of the American Catholic Philosophical Association*, 52: 150–58 (1978).

———. "The Invisible World of Merleau-Ponty." *Philosophy Today*, 23: 294–303 (Winter 1979).

McLure, Roger. "Sartre and Merleau-Ponty," in *European Philosophy and the Human and Social Sciences*, Glynn, Simon, ed., pp. 170–211. Hampshire: Gower, 1986.

McMillan, Elizabeth. "Female Difference in the Texts of Merleau-Ponty." *Philosophy Today*, 31: 359–66 (Winter 1987).

Madison, G. B. "The Ambiguous Philosophy of Merleau-Ponty." *Philosophical Studies* (Ireland), 22: 63–77 (1974).

Marsh, James L. "The Triumph of Ambiguity: Merleau-Ponty and Wittgenstein." *Philosophy Today*, 19: 243–55 (Fall 1975).

Martin, F. David. "Sculpture and 'Truth to Things'." *Journal of Aesthetic Education*, 13: 11–32 (April 1979).

Mays, Wolfe. "Whitehead and the Philosophy of Time." *Studium Generale*, 23: 509–24 (1970).

Mazis, Glen A. "Touch and Vision: Rethinking with Merleau-Ponty, Sartre on the Caress." *Philosophy Today*, 23: 321–28 (Winter 1979).

———. "La Chair and L'Imaginaire: The Developing Role of Imagination in Merleau-Ponty's Philosophy." *Philosophy Today*, 32: 30–42 (Spring 1988).

Meier, Klaus V. "Cartesian and Phenomenological Anthropology: The Radical Shift and Its Meaning for Sport." *Journal of the Philosophy of Sport*, 11: 51–73 (September 1975).

Mickunas, Algis. "Perception in Husserl and Merleau-Ponty." *Philosophical Inquiry*, 2: 484–95 (Spring–Summer 1980).

Miller, James. "Merleau-Ponty's Marxism: Between Phenomenology and the Hegelian Absolute." *History and Theory*, 15: 109–32 (1976).

Moran, Dermot. "Heidegger's Phenomenology and the Destruction of Reason." *Irish Philosophical Journal*, 2: 15–35 (Spring 1985).

Moreland, John M. "For-Itself and In-Itself in Sartre and Merleau-Ponty." *Philosophy Today*, 17: 311–18 (Winter 1973).

Morriston, Wesley. "Perceptual Synthesis in the Philosophy of Merleau-Ponty." *Philosophy Research Archives*, no. 1129 (1977).

———. "Experience and Causality in the Philosophy of Merleau-Ponty." *Philosophy and Phenomenological Research*, 39: 561–74 (June 1979).

Murungi, John. "Merleau-Ponty's Perspective on Politics." *Man and World*, 14: 141–52 (1981).

Murphy, John W. "Merleau-Ponty as Sociologist." *Philosophy Today*, 24: 104–13 (Summer 1980).

Murphy, Richard T. "A Metaphysical Critique of Method: Husserl and Merleau-Ponty." *Boston College Studies in Philosophy*, 1: 175–207 (1966).

Nelson, Jenny L. "Television and Its Audiences as Dimensions of Being: Critical Theory and Phenomenology." *Human Studies*, 9: 55–69 (1986).

O'Connor, Tony. "Behaviour and Perception: A Discussion of Merleau-Ponty's Problem of Operative Intentionality." *The Human Context*, 7: 39–48 (Spring 1975).

———. "Ambiguity and the Search for Origins." *The Journal of the British Society for Phenomenology*, 9: 102–10 (May 1978).

———. "Categorizing the Body." *The Journal of the British Society for Phenomenology*, 13: 226–36 (October 1982).

O'Neill, John. "Can Phenomenology Be Critical?" *Philosophy of the Social Sciences*, 2: 1–13 (March 1972).

———. "The Mother-Tongue: The Infant Search for Meaning." *Revue de l'Université d'Ottawa*, 55: 59–71 (December 1985).

———. "The Specular Body: Merleau-Ponty and Lacan on Infant Self and Other." *Synthese*, 66: 201–17 (February 1986).

Olafson, Frederick A. "Merleau-Ponty's 'Ontology of the Visible': Some Exegetical and Critical Comments." *Pacific Philosophical Quarterly*, 61: 167–76 (January–April 1980).

Olkowski, Dorothea. "Merleau-Ponty's Freudianism: From the Body of Consciousness to the Body of Flesh." *Review of Existential Psychology & Psychiatry*, 18: 97–116 (1982–83).

Olkowski–Laetz, Dorothea, "Merleau-Ponty: The Demand for Mystery in Language." *Philosophy Today*, 31: 352–58 (Winter 1987).

Olson, Carl. "The Human Body as a Boundary Symbol: A Comparison of Merleau-Ponty and Dogen." *Philosophy East and West*, 36: 107–20 (April 1986).

Onyewuenyi, Innocent C. "The Concept of God in Maurice Merleau-Ponty's Philosophy." *Second Order*, 5: 66–75 (July 1976).

Ostrow, James. "One Central Link between Merleau-Ponty's Philosophy of Language and His Political Thought." *Tulane Studies in Philosophy*, 29: 57–80 (December 1980).

———. "Habit and Inhabitance: An Analysis of Experience in the Classroom." *Human Studies*, 10: 213–24 (1987).

Palermo, James. "Merleau-Ponty and Dewey on the 'Mind-Body' Question." *Philosophy of Education: Proceedings*, 34: 462–69 (1978).

Palmer, Michael D. "On Language and Intersubjectivity." *Dialogue (PST)*, 24: 47–55 (April 1982).

Pax, Clyde. "Merleau-Ponty and the Truth of History." *Man and World*, 6: 270–79 (September 1973).

Peperzak, Adrian. "Pointers toward a Dialogic?" *Man and World*, 9, 372–92 (December 1976).

Place, James Gordon. "Merleau-Ponty and the Spirit of Painting." *Philosophy Today*, 17: 280–90 (Winter 1973).

———. "The Painting and the Natural Thing in the Philosophy of Merleau-Ponty." *Cultural Hermeneutics*, 4: 75–92 (November 1976).

Pontalis, J. B. "The Problem of the Unconscious in Merleau-Ponty's Thought." Trans. Wilfred Ver Eecke and Michael Greer. *Review of Existential Psychology & Psychiatry*, 18: 83–96 (1982–83).

Primozic, Daniel T. "Merleau-Ponty's Ontology of the Lebenswelt." *Southwest Philosophical Studies*, 4: 47–50 (April 1979).

Rauch, Leo. "Sartre, Merleau-Ponty and the Hole in Being." *Philosophical Studies* (Ireland), 18: 119–32 (1969).

Reineke, Martha J. "Lacan, Merleau-Ponty, and Irigaray: Reflections on a Specular Drama." *Auslegung*, 14: 67–85 (Winter 1987).

Rosenthal, Abigail L. "Getting Past Marx and Freud." *Clio*, 15: 61–82 (Fall 1985).

Rosenthal, Sandra B., and Patrick L. Bourgeois. "Mead, Merleau-Ponty and the Lived Perceptual World." *Philosophy Today*, 21: 56–61 (Spring 1977).

———. "Pragmatism and Phenomenology." *The Southern Journal of Philosophy*, 18: 481–87 (Winter 1980).

Proceedings of the American Catholic Philosophical Association, 59: 299–307 (1985).

Ross, Howard. "Merleau-Ponty and Jean-Paul Sartre on the Nature of Consciousness." *Cogito*, 3: 115–21 (December 1985).

Rouse, Joseph. "Merleau-Ponty and the Existential Conception of Science." *Synthese*, 66: 249–72 (February 1986).

Sapontzis, S. F. "A Note on Merleau-Ponty's 'Ambiguity'." *Philosophy and Phenomenological Research*, 38: 538–43 (June 1978).

————. "Merleau-Ponty, Myth-Maker or Philosopher." *Philosophical Studies* (Ireland), 26: 41–55 (1979).

Scharfstein, Ben-Ami. "Bergson and Merleau-Ponty: A Preliminary Comparison." *The Journal of Philosophy*, 52: 380–85 (July 1955).

Schenck, David. "Merleau-Ponty on Perspectivism, with References to Nietzsche." *Philosophy and Phenomenological Research*, 46: 307–14 (December 1985).

Schmidt, James. "Lordship and Bondage in Merleau-Ponty and Sartre." *Political Theory*, 7: 201–27 (May 1979).

Schmitt, Richard. "Maurice Merleau-Ponty, I." *The Review of Metaphysics*, 19: 493–516 (March 1966).

————. "Maurice Merleau-Ponty, II." *The Review of Metaphysics*, 19: 728–41 (June 1966).

Schrag, Calvin O. "The Phenomenon of Embodied Speech." *The Philosophical Forum* (Dekalb), 7: 3–27 (June 1969).

Seckinger, Donald S. "Philosophers of Dialogue." *Journal of Thought*, 14: 305–309 (November 1979).

Shapiro, Eleanor M. "Perception and Dialectic." *Human Studies*, 1: 245–67 (July 1978).

Sheets-Johnstone, Maxine. "Existential Fit and Evolutionary Continuities." *Synthese*, 66: 219–48 (February 1986).

Sherburne, Donald W. "Whitehead's Psychological Physiology." *The Southern Journal of Philosophy*, 7: 401–407 (Winter 1969–70).

Sheridan, James F. "On Ontology and Politics, a Polemic." *Dialogue*, 7: 449–60 (December 1968).

Silverman, Hugh J. "Re-Reading Merleau-Ponty." *Telos*, 29: 106–29 (Fall 1976).

————. "Heidegger and Merleau-Ponty: Interpreting Hegel." *Research in Phenomenology*, 7: 209–24 (1977).

————. "Imagining, Perceiving, and Remembering." *Humanitas*, 14: 197–207 (May 1978).

————. "Merleau-Ponty on Language and Communication (1947–1948)." *Research in Phenomenology*, 9: 168–81 (1979).

————. "Merleau-Ponty's New Beginning: Preface to the Experience of Others." *Review of Existential Psychology & Psychiatry*, 18: 25–31 (1982–83).

Sinari, Ramakant. "The Phenomenology of Maurice Merleau-Ponty." *The Philosophical Quarterly*, 39: 129–40 (July 1966).

Singer, Linda. "Merleau-Ponty on the Concept of Style." *Man and World*, 14: 153–63 (1981).

Slaughter, Thomas F., Jr. "Some Remarks on Merleau-Ponty's Essay 'Cezanne's Doubt'." *Man and World*, 12: 61–69 (1979).

Smith, Colin. "The Notion of Object in the Phenomenology of Merleau-Ponty." *Philosophy*, 39: 110–19 (April 1964).

———. "Sartre and Merleau-Ponty: The Case for a Modified Essentialism." *The Journal of the British Society for Phenomenology*, 1: 73–79 (May 1970).

———. "Merleau-Ponty and Structuralism." *The Journal of the British Society for Phenomenology*, 2: 46–52 (October 1971).

Smith, Dale E. "Language and the Genesis of Meaning in Merleau-Ponty." *Kinesis*, 8: 44–58 (Fall 1977).

Spicker, Stuart F. "Inner Time and Lived-Through Time: Husserl and Merleau-Ponty." *The Journal of the British Society for Phenomenology*, 4: 235–47 (October 1973).

Stack, George J. "Sexuality and Bodily Subjectivity." *Dialogos*, 15: 139–53 (April 1980).

Stapp, Henry Pierce. "Quantum Mechanics, Local Causality, and Process Philosophy." *Process Studies*, 7: 173–82 (Fall 1977).

Steinbock, Anthony J. "Merleau-Ponty's Concept of Death." *Philosophy Today*, 31: 336–51 (Winter 1987).

Strong, Tracy B. "History and Choices: The Foundations of the Political Thought of Raymond Aron." *History and Theory*, 11: 179–92 (1972).

Taylor, Charles. "The Validity of Transcendental Arguments." *Proceedings of the Aristotelian Society*, 79: 151–65 (1978).

Theobald, D. W. "Philosophy and Fiction: The Novel as Eloquent Philosophy." *The British Journal of Aesthetics*, 14: 17–25 (Winter 1974).

Tibbetts, Paul. "The 'Levels of Experience' Doctrine in Modern Philosophy of Mind." *Studi Internazionali di Filosofia*, 3: 15–32 (Autumn 71).

———. "John Dewey and Contemporary Phenomenology on Experience and the Subject-Object Relation." *Philosophy Today*, 15: 250–75 (Winter 1971).

———. "Mead, Phenomenalism and Phenomenology." *Philosophy Today*, 17: 329–36 (Winter 1973).

Tiemersma, Douwe. "'Body-Image' and 'Body-Schema' in the Existential Phenomenology of Merleau-Ponty." *The Journal of the British Society for Phenomenology*, 13: 246–55 (October 1982).

———. "Merleau-Ponty's Philosophy as a Field Theory: Its Origin, Categories and Relevance." *Man and World*, 20: 419–36 (October 1987).

Townsley, A. L. "Rosmini and Merleau-Ponty: Being, Perception and the World." *Rivista di Filosofia Neo-Scolastica*, 68: 75–84 (January–March 1976).

Tuedio, James Alan. "Merleau-Ponty's Rejection of the Husserlian Ideal of a Rigorous Science." *Philosophy Today*, 25: 204–209 (Fall 1981).

———. "Merleau-Ponty's Refinement of Husserl." *Philosophy Today*, 29: 99–109 (Summer 1985).

Van Peursen, C. A. "Present-day Philosophies." *Methodology and Science*, 10: 240–57 (1977).

Van Hooft, Stan. "Merleau-Ponty and the Problem of Intentional Explanation." *Philosophy and Phenomenological Research*, 40: 33–52 (September 1979).

Vandenbussche, Frans. "The Idea of God in Merleau-Ponty." *International Philosophical Quarterly*, 7: 45–67 (March 1967).

Ver Eecke, Wilfred. "Interpretation and Perception." *International Philosophical Quarterly*, 11: 372–84 (September 1971).

Virasoro, Manuel. "Merleau-Ponty and the World of Perception." *Philosophy Today*, 3: 66–72 (Spring 1959).

Waddell, James. "Phenomenology, the Agitator and Revolution." *Journal of Social Philosophy*, 4: 8–10 (April 1973).

————. "Merleau-Ponty, Lewis and Ontological Presence." *Philosophical Topics*, 13: 239–46 (Spring 1985).

————. "Peirce and Merleau-Ponty: Beyond the Noumenal-Phenomenal Break."

Waldenfels, Bernhard. "Towards an Open Dialectic." *Dialetics and Humanism*, 3: 91–101 (Winter 1976).

Walsh, Robert D. "An Organism of Words: Ruminations on the Philosophical-Poetics of Merleau-Ponty." *Kinesis*, 14: 13–41 (Fall 1984).

Watson, Stephen. "Language, Perception and the Cogito in Merleau-Ponty's Thought," in *Merleau-Ponty: Perception, Structure, Language*, John C. Sallis, ed., pp. 142–66. Atlantic Highlands: Humanities Press, 1981.

Welch, Cyril. "Commentary on *Ontologie de la signification*." *Man and World*, 4: 258–61 (August 1971).

————. "A Preface to Reading." *Philosophy and Rhetoric*, 14: 31–50 (Winter 1981).

Wertz, Frederick J. "Merleau-Ponty and the Cognitive Psychology of Perception," in *Critical and Dialectical Phenomenology*. Donn Welton and Hugh J. Silverman, eds., pp. 265–84. Albany: SUNY Press, 1987.

Whiteside, Kerry H. "Perspectivism and Historical Objectivity: Maurice Merleau-Ponty's Covert Debate with Raymond Aron." *History and Theory*, 25: 132–51 (May 1986).

Wiggins, Osborne P., Jr. "Merleau-Ponty and Piaget: An Essay in Philosophical Psychology." *Man and World*, 12: 21–34 (1979).

————. "Political Responsibility in Merleau-Ponty's *Humanism and Terror*." *Man and World*, 19: 275–91 (1986).

————. "Merleau-Ponty's Phenomenological Ethics." *Graduate Faculty Philosophy Journal*, 10: 43–56 (Winter 1985).

Wilshire, Bruce. "The Phenomenology of Language." *The Journal of the British Society for Phenomenology*, 9: 130–33 (May 1978).

Wirt, Cliff Engle. "The Concept of Ecstasis." *The Journal of the British Society for Phenomenology*, 14: 79–90 (January 1983).

Wolin, Richard. "Merleau-Ponty and the Birth of Weberian Marxism." *Praxis International*, 5: 115–30 (July 1985).

Wyschogrod, Edith. "Exemplary Individuals: Towards a Phenomenological Ethics." *Philosophy and Theology*, 1: 9–31 (Fall 1986).

Yolton, John W. "Agent Causality." *American Philosophical Quarterly*, 3: 14–26 (January 1966).

Young, Iris Marion. "Throwing Like a Girl: A Phenomenology of Feminine Body Comportment, Motility and Spatiality." *Human Studies*, 3: 137–56 (April 1980).

Zaner, Richard M. "Merleau-Ponty's Theory of the Body-Proper as *Être-au-Monde*." *Journal of Existentialism*, 6: 31–40 (Fall 1965).

Zenzen, Michael J. "The Suggestive Power of Color." *The Journal of Aesthetics and Art Criticism*, 36: 185–90 (Winter 1977).

— Compiled by Elizabeth L. MacNabb.

Index

◆